THE EVOLVING CITIZEN

RHETORIC AND DEMOCRATIC DELIBERATION
VOLUME 4

EDITED BY CHERYL GLENN AND J. MICHAEL HOGAN
THE PENNSYLVANIA STATE UNIVERSITY

Rhetoric and Democratic Deliberation is a series of
groundbreaking monographs and edited volumes focusing
on the character and quality of public discourse in American
politics and culture. It is sponsored by the Center for Democratic
Deliberation, an interdisciplinary center for research, teaching,
and outreach on issues of rhetoric, civic engagement,
and public deliberation.

Other books in the series:

Karen Tracy, *Challenges of Ordinary Democracy:*
A Case Study in Deliberation and Dissent / VOLUME I

Samuel McCormick, *Letters to Power:*
Public Advocacy Without Public Intellectuals / VOLUME 2

Christian Kock and Lisa S. Villadsen, *Rhetorical Citizenship*
and Public Deliberation / VOLUME 3

THE EVOLVING CITIZEN

AMERICAN YOUTH AND THE CHANGING NORMS OF
DEMOCRATIC ENGAGEMENT

JAY P. CHILDERS

The Pennsylvania State University Press | University Park, Pennsylvania

Library of Congress Cataloging-in-Publication Data

Childers, Jay P., 1974–
    The evolving citizen : American youth and the changing
    norms of democratic engagement / Jay P. Childers.
        p.   cm. — (Rhetoric and democratic
        deliberation)
Includes bibliographical references and index.
Summary: "Examines, through an analysis of seven high
school newspapers, the evolution of civic and political
participation among young people in the United States
since 1965"—Provided by publisher.
ISBN 978-0-271-05411-7 (cloth : alk. paper)
1. Youth—Political activity—United States.
2. Political participation—United States.
I. Title.

HQ799.2.P6C485 2012
306.208350973—dc23
2012003116

The Pennsylvania State University Press is a member
of the Association of American University Presses.

It is the policy of The Pennsylvania State University
Press to use acid-free paper. Publications on uncoated
stock satisfy the minimum requirements of American
National Standard for Information Sciences—
Permanence of Paper for Printed Library Material,
ANSI Z39.48–1992.

This book is printed on Nature's Natural, which contains
50% post-consumer waste.

To My Family,

For Teaching Me All the Really Important Things

CONTENTS

ACKNOWLEDGMENTS

As my research on young adults and high school newspapers began many years ago while I was a graduate student at the University of Texas at Austin, writing this book has been very much like running a marathon. As in all marathons, the runner is ultimately responsible for his race, but no runner gets to the starting line without help nor finishes without encouragement. Throughout the process of researching and writing this book, I have had a great deal of help and encouragement from a small host of coaches, fellow runners, and fans.

Quite simply, this book would never have happened without the best coach one could ever ask for—Roderick Hart. It was born out of his incessant questioning many years ago and guided by his tough love throughout. I also benefited greatly from my conditioning coach, Barry Brummett, who always helped me keep my eye on the bigger picture, and my running coach, Sharon Jarvis, who never let me forget the basic principles of running—one foot in front of the other and try not to fall on your face.

Like all races, I did not start mine alone. I was surrounded by a large group of brilliant minds in Austin, Texas, each spurring me on to my best. These people included Soo-Hye Han, Johanna Hartelius, John Lithgow, Tim Steffensmeier, Jaime Wright, and Amy Young. And although she abandoned running for the less noble sport of mixed martial arts, I would never have taken my first stride without Kathleen Weir's encouragement.

Along the course, there was no shortage of fans encouraging me onward with thoughtful words and unshakable friendship. Brent Barger was always there to keep me grounded, and Genevieve Nicholson always seemed to understand my pain. I have been blessed with the best of colleagues at the University of Kansas, most notably Mary Banwart, Beth Innocenti, Robin Rowland, and Yan Bing Zhang. In addition to being wonderful colleagues, Dave Tell was a rock of stability and Alesia Woszidlo was a sanctuary of sanity. Among the many wonderful graduate students I have worked with at KU, three were particularly helpful with this project: Sue Novak, Carl Walz, and Ben Warner. In addition, a generous grant from Research & Graduate Studies at KU helped with archival collections in the summer of 2007. And I have been fortunate to work with the best of people at Penn State University and Penn State Press—Jeremy Engels, who knew just where to put the manuscript; Mike Hogan, who was the best advocate I could have hoped for; Kendra Boileau, who was the finest editor-in-chief I may ever work with; and Julie Schoelles, a manuscript editor whom I believe is of the first order.

As anyone who has ever run a marathon knows, the final 2.2 miles are the most difficult. One's body begins to revolt and one's mind forgets how to keep the body moving in the right direction. Being tired and slightly delusional, I would never have made it to the finish line without Monica Crane. Short of running the final stretch for me, she is the reason this book got finished. I only wish she had invited me for coffee sooner. Thankfully, we have many years left to pick blueberries together out on the Dandelion Moons of Pluto.

I

The American people found themselves living in an increasingly troubled nation during the 2008 presidential election. They had to filter their electoral choices through an abundance of dire circumstances. A snapshot of the United States in September 2008, just two months before Election Day, reveals the realities facing American voters. The U.S. military had around 180,000 troops engaged in the War on Terror in Afghanistan (34,000 troops) and Iraq (146,000 troops). The U.S. government had just taken over the private mortgage companies Freddie Mac and Fannie Mae in an attempt to stop the subprime mortgage crisis and the housing bubble bust, and Congress was in the process of drafting the Emergency Economic Stabilization Act of 2008, authorizing the secretary of the treasury to spend up to $700 billion to rescue the nation's failing financial institutions. The national average for a gallon of gasoline was $3.80, just below the record high of $4.05/gallon recorded two months earlier. There were approximately 45.7 million Americans without health care, according to the U.S. Census Bureau. National unemployment was at 6.1 percent and climbing. Barely more than 25 percent of Americans had a favorable view of how outgoing president George W. Bush was handling his job. Things seemed so bad that three-quarters of Americans believed the United States was headed in the wrong direction.[1]

Within this context, the two major political parties offered the American people a historic choice in the 2008 presidential election. Having survived the often heated and intense primary campaign against former first lady Hillary Clinton, Illinois senator Barack Obama officially accepted his party's nomination at the Democratic National Convention on August 28 in Denver, Colorado. Obama's nomination marked the first time in the nation's history that a nonwhite headed a major party ticket. So historic was Obama's nomination that his acceptance speech was moved outside to the Invesco

Field football stadium, where more than eighty thousand people were in attendance. Not to be completely overshadowed, the Republican Party, whose ticket was headed by Senator John McCain, announced its vice presidential nominee on August 29. That McCain's choice was the relatively unknown Alaska governor Sarah Palin drew plenty of attention. The excitement surrounding Palin's nomination was due in part to the fact that she was only the second woman nominated to a major party's national ticket, following Geraldine Ferraro, who was nominated as Walter Mondale's running mate by the Democratic Party in 1984. Palin's nomination was so energizing that more than 40 million people watched her acceptance speech at the Republican National Convention. Regardless of whether one voted Democratic or Republican, by September 2008 everyone knew the presidential election was going to produce either the first African American president or the first female vice president. Thus, the 2008 election was arguably one of the most important and most exciting in American history.

Given the national context and the historical moment, one might have expected the American people to show up in record numbers on Election Day in November 2008. Indeed, many were predicting just that. While the numerous news reports and academic predictions of record-high voter turnout did not prove to be accurate, many analysts were still pleased. Political scientist Michael McDonald was reporting by late December 2008 that 61.6 percent of eligible voters cast ballots in 2008—an increase of 1.6 percent over the 2004 presidential election.[2] While these numbers did not reach the modern high point of 63.8 percent of eligible voters who turned out to vote in 1960, the 2008 totals did far exceed the low point of just 52.6 percent of eligible voters who showed up in 1996.[3] Although not a truly historic turnout, it was still not surprising to hear praise for the many American people who voted in 2008, some of whom reportedly stood in line for more than three hours to cast their ballots. No group of Americans received more praise, however, than young adults.

As American youth voted overwhelmingly Democratic, much of the praise regarding their turnout suggested that they were, in larger part, responsible for Obama's victory. Even Obama seemed to understand the importance of young adults. During his victory speech delivered in Chicago's Grant Park on Election Night, Obama made sure to give credit to those who helped him win the election, noting at the outset of a list of demographic groups that his campaign "grew strength from the young people who rejected the myth of their generation's apathy; who left their homes and their families for jobs that offered little pay and less sleep." Senator John Kerry, the defeated 2004

Democratic presidential nominee, agreed with Obama's assessment, voicing his belief that young adults played an "essential" role in the 2008 election.[4] The importance of the youth vote to Obama's victory was so apparent that one *New York Times* reporter labeled the eighteen- to twenty-nine-year-old "young allies" who voted for Obama an entirely new generation—"Generation O."[5] In a *Washington Post* editorial just days after the election, political scientist Tracy Fitzsimmons went so far as to call 2008 the "year of the young voter."[6] According to politicians, journalists, and academics, young people had flexed their collective electoral muscles.

While the excitement about young adult voting was palpable, the reality of the voter turnout offers a more sobering picture of what actually happened in the 2008 election. According to U.S. Census Data and the Center for Information and Research on Civic Learning and Engagement (CIRCLE), the turnout for eighteen- to twenty-four-year-olds in 2008 reached only 48.5 percent. Admittedly higher than the three preceding elections, the 2008 numbers were actually lower than those in 1992 (48.6 percent) and the modern high point of 1972 (52.1 percent). In the simplest terms, fewer than half of young adults voted in a historical presidential race at a time of great national turmoil—and this despite the many direct appeals that were made to youth and the increased access to early voting in a majority of the nation's states.

Given the historical context and the increased appeals, why is it that more than half of all eligible young adults could still not be bothered to vote in 2008? Even with increasingly easy methods of voter registration and early voting in the majority of the nation's states, what made so many of them feel that voting was not worth their effort? And why did researchers and politicians get so excited about what seem to be such meager voter turnout percentages? How, that is, did we get here?

This book is an attempt to answer that final question. In doing so, I have combined two things that the vast majority of research on young adult democratic engagement has failed to bring together. Namely, I take a historical perspective *and* pay attention to what young people have been saying for themselves and to one another. In order to be both longitudinal and in-depth, this book attempts to make sense of the democratic lives of today's young people by looking back across five decades of high school newspapers. It thereby tells the evolving story of the political and civic lives of some of America's youth in their own words.[7]

Specifically, this book offers a textual analysis of seven regionally diverse American high school newspapers produced between 1965 and 2010 in order to understand the ways in which young adults writing in these papers articulate their assumptions about and deliberate over political and civic matters. My reading of these newspapers is guided by a few important assumptions. First and most important, I assume from the start that the norms of democratic citizenship evolve over time as the social and cultural norms of a society change. Second, I believe these changing norms manifest themselves in the way people write about the political world around them. Third, adolescents who are in the process of learning democratic citizenship present a particularly salient opportunity to better understand these changing norms. Finally, I believe the seven high school newspapers studied in this book can illuminate the ways in which the evolving democratic norms in the United States are manifesting themselves in some of America's young people. The first two chapters of the book unpack these guiding assumptions, present a picture of the American high school and the students who inhabit these schools, and introduce the reader to the seven schools and their newspapers. The four subsequent chapters reveal what my analysis of the seven high school newspapers illustrates about the democratic lives of the young journalists writing in them.

The story that emerges from looking back at these American youth over the past half century is primarily one of change. The young adults in this study, that is, write more often today of national and international politics than they did a half century ago (chapter 3), and they have become far more likely to describe intervention in public matters as something done from a distance through donations and volunteering (chapter 4). In addition, they have presented a more critical attitude toward politics today as they have become more immersed in the playful world of popular culture (chapter 5). The newspapers studied here also reveal young people who are still joiners, although the groups they join today are more focused on individual interests and needs (chapter 6). In the end, I show that the democratic assumptions of young adults in this study have changed, that these changes have occurred naturally, and that the ways in which they have changed suggest that we need to rethink some of our assumptions about civic education in the United States. I tell this story both by taking a broad descriptive approach to what counts as democratic engagement and through paying close attention to changing trends in how the young people writing in the seven high school newspapers discuss political and civic life.

Throughout this book, I avoid blaming young adults for the democratic attitudes they demonstrate. While I do have normative assumptions about the types of attitudes and behaviors that democracy requires of its citizens, the primary goal of this book is to look for the ways in which young people actually say they *do* democratically engage the world around them, paying particular attention to how such engagement has changed over time. I do, moreover, offer some assessments of what the story of youth engagement ultimately tells us about which direction our modern American democracy may be headed, but I try to let the evidence take me there instead of my preconceived notions of good citizenship. The evidence I use comes, most importantly, from young people themselves. If one wants to understand how we arrived at the current state of democratic participation, one needs to take heed of what these young people have been saying for themselves. Being a young citizen in a changing world is, it turns out, a complicated matter. This opening chapter offers a picture of our nation's democratic youth and the changed world this study spans.

What We Think We Know About Youth Participation

In his 2006 Grammy Award–winning single "Waiting on the World to Change," the then twenty-eight-year-old singer/songwriter John Mayer voiced a lament for his politically disaffected generation. He writes, "Me and all my friends / We're all misunderstood / They say we stand for nothing and / There's no way we ever could." After suggesting that those who would argue his generation is civically lazy and politically apathetic are simply misinformed, Mayer offers a much different perspective. He begins this corrective vision by stating that his generation is aware of what is going on around it: "Now we see everything that's going wrong / With the world and those who lead it / We just feel like we don't have the means / To rise above and beat it." More importantly perhaps, Mayer also implies that his generation's sense of futility is the result of a corrupt political system in need of a major overhaul: "It's hard to beat the system / When we're standing at a distance / So we keep waiting / Waiting on the world to change." He then goes on to suggest that his generation lacks power and gives the warning, either to that generation or to those who are misinformed about it, "And when you trust your television / What you get is what you got / Cause when they own the information, oh / They can bend it all they want." In the end, Mayer insists, "It's not that we don't care / We just know that the fight ain't fair." So he and his friends are not unaware of the problems of the world around them; rather, they are simply waiting on that world to change before they bother to engage it. As Mayer himself explained on his blog shortly after the song's release and subsequent success, his very purpose in writing it was "to express the feelings of helplessness that come with knowing what needs to change in the world but also knowing the futility of trying."[8]

One might take issue with Mayer's song for several reasons. The most obvious problem is that he seems to believe the world simply changes on its own, something for which there appears to be little historical proof. One might also question the idea that you can really care about a problem and not want to do something about it. And one could wonder how someone with such a clear voice in the larger public sphere can still speak of feeling that he does not have the means to fight the system. While these criticisms may be valid, the song does offer the listener a fairly good catalog of what political scientists have been saying about young people for the last two decades. The young Americans portrayed in Mayer's song seem, for instance, to lack a sense of both internal and external efficacy—the belief that they can influence the public sphere and that those in power actually care about what young adults have to say. Mayer sings of his generation lacking political trust in the system and in those who are running the system. He and his politically alienated and misunderstood generation even find media, specifically television, to blame and enact much of the cynicism they may have learned from watching television. In just under three and a half minutes, Mayer encapsulates many of the popular conceptions revealed in research on young adults and their attitudes toward democratic engagement in the United States. Understanding how correctly John Mayer summed up his generation, however, requires a more careful approach to the extant research on the democratic engagement of American youth.

Before turning to the large corpus of research on youth participation, it is important to note that to talk of the various indices used to measure levels of democratic engagement is to acknowledge that democracy requires certain things from its citizens. What these things are is always uncertain and rarely agreed upon by those concerned with such matters. The ambiguity surrounding the practices of democratic engagement comes from the very fact that democracy is not a stable idea. As political philosopher Charles Taylor has argued, it would be better to think of democracies instead of democracy. While it is true democracy means rule by the people, there is no uniform understanding of how the people go about the business of ruling themselves. Democracy, according to Taylor, "has to be articulated and the articulation accepted and understood as having this meaning, which means that democracy has to be imagined; in fact, it is imagined in different ways."[9] In the United States, there have been at least two primary ways of imagining democracy throughout the nation's history—republicanism and liberalism. In addition, any number of articulated variations of democratic thought exist today. While acknowledging the myriad ways in which democracy can be imagined, this book works with the assumption that there are, however, a few core civic and political practices all forms of democracy find beneficial.

At its most basic level, a healthy democracy requires a participatory and informed egalitarian citizenry living in a robust civil society with the skills necessary to engage one another in political arguments and decision-making processes. Whether one adheres to the tenets of libertarianism, communitarianism, liberalism, or some other democratic philosophy, the skills and social networks required for democratic engagement are largely universal. That is, it seems difficult to imagine any democratic theory that prefers apathetic, ignorant citizens who do not interact with one another in nongovernmental organizations and networks. Some political leaders and corporate owners might find such a scenario beneficial, but democracy surely cannot sustain such undemocratic attitudes. I find such attempts to label all political structures democratic quite problematic. For instance, one variation offered by political theorist David Held in his *Models of Democracy*—"competitive elitist democracy"—seems markedly undemocratic given that one of its conditions is a poorly informed or emotionally irrational electorate.[10] For the people to rule, surely the people need the abilities to go about ruling. So what does it mean to suggest that democracy requires informed citizens and a robust civil society?

For many, it may seem odd to point out that democracy requires the participation of an egalitarian citizenry. However, some have suggested that the political process works best when left to elected officials. Others have even suggested that lower voter turnout does not really change the will of the people. Such arguments are difficult to accept. For instance, political scientist Martin Wattenberg has made a persuasive case that voter turnout does make a difference in election outcomes because those who do vote do not truly represent the polity writ large.[11] A similar argument can be made regarding other forms of democratic engagement since elected and appointed officials are supposed to represent the will of their constituents, sometimes on issues that did not even exist in previous elections. So if a society is going to argue that the people rule, universal suffrage and high levels of political participation are essential to ensuring the people are actually doing their own governing, whether that be through direct or representative democracy.

To suggest that democratic citizens need to be informed is to acknowledge, moreover, that an individual's knowledge of political processes, public institutions, elected officials, and current affairs helps create, in the words of Michael Delli Carpini, "'better' citizens in a number of ways."[12] Greater political knowledge, it turns out, leads to an increase in political tolerance, political efficacy, and even smarter voting, since higher levels of knowledge help citizens vote for candidates who more closely reflect their views. Taking a slightly different perspective on knowledge, Henry Milner has, in addition, argued that civic literacy—"the knowledge and skills to act as competent citizens"—is the single most important factor in political participation.[13]

Finally, a healthy democracy needs citizens to be a part of and engaged in a robust civil society. According to Peter Levine, civil society refers to "the whole set of voluntary associations (formal and informal) that are outside both the state and the market. It includes churches and other religious congregations, clubs, lobbying groups, parties, unions, nonprofit corporations, and even informal networks of friends." Such organizations benefit democratic citizens because they can help individuals learn democratic decision-making skills, create a sense of civic efficacy, build social trust and tolerance, and lead to more direct forms of political engagement. These benefits matter regardless of what political party one is a member of or what democratic philosophy one adheres to. As Levine has argued, "Both libertarians and social democrats need civil society and its associated virtues and skills. The same is true of everyone who stands between them on the political spectrum."[14]

Given the argument that democracy does need certain attitudes and behaviors from its citizenry, how have young adults in the United States been doing as democratic citizens? The picture of American youth over the past few decades that has most often been painted by political scientists and sociologists is one of young adults who have become increasingly disconnected from their communities and apathetic about politics. The general argument begins by suggesting that at some prior point in American history, most notably the 1950s and 1960s, the United States was a healthy and vibrant democratic state full of highly engaged citizens. Since then, however, the American public sphere has taken a decidedly downward turn, and the national community is now in danger of collapsing.[15] So concerning is this general decline in the democratic health of the United States that one group of nineteen leading social scientists, led by Princeton political scientist Stephen Macedo, recently declared American democracy itself at risk. The rather dramatic opening paragraph of their book,

Democracy at Risk, is worth quoting here to get a sense of just how worried some scholars have become:

> American democracy is at risk. The risk comes not from some external threat but from disturbing internal trends: an erosion of the activities and capacities of citizenship. Americans have turned away from politics and the public sphere in large numbers, leaving our civic life impoverished. Citizens participate in public affairs less frequently, with less knowledge and enthusiasm, in fewer venues, and less equally than is healthy for a vibrant democratic polity. . . . Our democracy is not all that it could be. Although some aspects of civic life remain robust and some citizens still participate frequently, Americans should be concerned about the current state of affairs. The risk is not to our national survival but to the health and legitimacy of our shared political order.[16]

Although their tone may be overly dramatic, the evidence that draws the authors to make such a declarative opening statement is nothing new. While some researchers and practitioners have recently begun arguing against these negative portrayals of declining democratic engagement, the pessimistic view of American youth encapsulated by the concerns of Macedo and his colleagues remains the dominant attitude in much of the academic literature. Unpacking these concerns helps explain why so many people were so excited about the youth voter turnout in 2008.

In order to make sense of the existing research on American youth, democratic engagement needs to be understood as comprising both political and civic participation. More than a mere semantic argument, the distinction between the political and civic reveals why some have found reason to take a more positive view of youth engagement. By political participation, most researchers mean something along the lines of political scientists Sidney Verba, Kay Schlozman, and Henry Brady's definition: "activity that has the intent or effect of influencing government action—either directly by affecting the making or implementation of public policy or indirectly by influencing the selection of people who make those policies."[17] Acts of political participation include voting, working for a campaign, persuading someone to vote for a particular candidate, and contacting an elected official. In contrast, civic engagement has been more recently defined by political scientist Cliff Zukin and his co-authors as "organized voluntary activity focused on problem solving and helping others. It includes a wide range of work undertaken alone or in concert with others to effect change."[18] Most often, civic engagement consists of activities such as volunteering for non-electoral organizations, belonging to fraternal or religious organizations, donating money or goods for relief efforts, and participating in charity races. While political participation and civic engagement overlap and influence each other, these two forms of democratic engagement are often distinguished in the research, and such distinctions offer some insights into how scholars measure citizenship and in what areas young adults have been showing signs of atrophy and possible signs of renewed strength.

It has almost become taken for granted that America's young people have fallen behind in the realm of political participation. Young adults, researchers keep showing, do not participate politically at levels close to older Americans *or* at levels comparable to earlier generations of American youth. Voting is one clear political act in which today's young people have fallen behind. The voting generation gap between young and old in most modern democracies is a common concern among researchers. In most democratic states today, young adults simply vote at lower rates than older adults. In the United States, however, the generation gap is alarmingly large.[19] Even in the much-celebrated 2008 election, 20 percent fewer young adults voted than did adults over twenty-nine years old. If this were the only indicator of low youth participation, it would be lamentable but, perhaps, acceptable. However, not only are young people far less likely to vote than older Americans, but they are also far less likely to vote than young people forty and fifty years ago. Stephen Macedo and his colleagues make this point clearly in assessing voting trends after the 2004 election: "That young people today are less likely to turn out than people their age in previous generations is an especially portentous development given that lifelong electoral engagement is rooted largely in habits developed in one's youth."[20] Taken together, that today's American youth vote at lower levels than older adults *and* earlier generations of young people is alarming. It is also concerning for the nation's future democratic health, since longitudinal studies have shown that how a person votes in her youth largely predicts how she will vote as she gets older.[21]

Equally troubling, the same trends in weakening political participation among American youth exist outside the voting booth. These declines have manifested themselves in young people's actions toward elected officials, attitudes toward government, and assumptions about democracy itself. Beyond voting, political participation can include working for a political campaign, contacting an elected official, attending a political rally or speech, serving on a local governmental committee or organization, and running for a political office. According to longitudinal data, the percentage of young people engaged in any of these actions has declined by as much as half over the past half century.[22] The same pattern holds true for young people's attitudes toward government, which can be measured by examining their sense of political efficacy and their level of political knowledge about governmental affairs. Today, young people are less likely to both believe government cares about what they think and express an interest in keeping up with current events, especially local news.[23] The final indicator of declining political participation is young adults' assumptions about what democratic citizenship requires of them. For the most part, young people have increasingly come to view democratic citizenship as having very few requirements at all. In fact, the majority of young people today, as compared to older generations, believe that citizenship requires nothing special of an individual beyond simply being a good person.[24] Being a good person is certainly a positive thing, but such an attitude toward democratic citizenship does not necessarily translate into an understanding of political participation as an obligation or expectation. Moreover, it may not translate into political participation at all.

Given the evidence presented by a number of notable social scientists and the potential effects of declining political participation in the United States, one should not be surprised by the large corpus of books and essays that have emerged over the past twenty years lamenting the political vibrancy of a bygone era and warning all who will listen of the threat to American democracy that exists today. In terms of political participation, it is difficult to find anyone who argues against these trends. The empirical evidence supporting declining levels of political participation is overwhelming. Not everyone agrees, however, that the consequences of such declines warrant so much hand-wringing about the political health of the United States. While the evidence is far more contested, many social scientists are increasingly pointing toward civic engagement for signs of democratic life among American youth.

In *Bowling Alone*, one of the most important studies on democratic engagement written in the past two decades, political scientist Robert Putnam argues that the civic health of the United States has been weakening due to Americans' declining interest in joining clubs, organizations, and associations. Although he does acknowledge that communal engagement has most likely ebbed and flowed throughout American history, Putnam suggests that his data clearly shows democratic engagement was ebbing at the end of the twentieth century. He notes the declines in political participation discussed above but also argues, more importantly, that people simply join together less often than in the past: "During the first two-thirds of the [twentieth] century Americans took a more and more active role in the social and political life of their communities—in churches and union halls, in bowling alleys and clubrooms, around committee tables and card tables and dinner tables. Year by year we gave more generously to charity, we pitched in more often on community projects, and . . . we behaved in an increasingly trustworthy way toward one another. Then, mysteriously and more or less simultaneously, we began to do all these things less often."[25] Putnam's primary evidence for this final claim is the declining membership rosters of national and local membership organizations, from the PTA to churches to bowling leagues. This evidence, later echoed by Theda Skocpol,[26] led Putnam and many others who followed to believe that more recent generations of Americans were failing to understand the importance of organizing together for their communities. Putnam concludes that this loss of civic engagement—more fundamental than declines in political participation—is the root cause of the troubling state of American democracy.

Few would disagree with Putnam and Skocpol that membership in national and local organizations has declined in recent decades. Some have suggested, however, that Putnam and Skocpol too narrowly focus their attention on membership-based organizations at the expense of other types of citizen organizing and activity, which may require no membership but are no less democratically valuable.[27] Indeed, one group of researchers has recently argued in their generational analysis that while today's youngest generations have been losing interest in traditional forms of political participation, "the youngest cohort has been holding its own in the civic world of volunteering, organizational activity, fund raising, and the like." Young adults today, that is, may not be as willing as preceding generations to join their local churches, but they are just as likely to volunteer for a nonelectoral organization.[28] They may be less likely to join a local bowling league, but they are actually more likely than older Americans to take part in a local walk for charity. Ultimately, today's American youth may prefer to avoid the demands and responsibilities of membership-based organizations, but they remain, according to some, just as civically minded as previous generations.

For some, the evidence that today's youngest generations are just as likely as older adults to be civically engaged outside of membership-based organizations suggests that young people are far more engaged than they have been portrayed. According to these defenders of youth, American democracy is not at risk; young adults have simply found newer methods of democratic engagement that are largely based on a more individualized approach to citizenship. Nowhere has the defense of the youngest generation of Americans been more pronounced than in the work of Neil Howe and William Strauss. In their book *Millennials Rising*, they celebrate the nation's newest generation, whom they call Millennials, for rejecting the politics of their parents and the cynicism of the much-maligned Generation X. Instead of being concerned about American youth, Howe and Strauss laud them as the next great generation.[29] Political scientist Russell Dalton also suggests that American youth are reshaping politics in the United States. He argues that young people today have adopted a more personalized "engaged citizenship" in preference to the "duty-based citizenship" of the past. While Dalton acknowledges some concern that the new engaged citizens do not vote as often or read the newspaper as much as duty-based citizens did, he finds much to be happy about in today's young adults. He argues, in fact, that "engaged citizenship prompts individuals to be involved in a wider repertoire of activities that give them a direct voice in the decisions affecting their lives."[30] He also finds that young people today are far more tolerant of others, a positive attribute echoed in several studies.[31] With their emphasis on individualized citizenship, the new engaged citizens exercise a great deal more tolerance than young people just two decades earlier, particularly on issues of race and homosexuality.[32]

Taken as a whole, the research reveals a picture of the democratic engagement of America's young adults that is a lot like the well-known optical illusion showing a young girl or old woman, depending on how one perceives it. Depending on one's interpretation of one set of data or the other, either America's youth have begun to squander the democracy they have inherited or they have emerged as a new type of citizen set to reinvent the nation. Like most things, the truth about today's young adults is neither so bleak nor so positive. What we seem to know about young people's democratic engagement today is that it is different. Recent generations of young adults have not participated in traditional forms of political and civic engagement at rates rivaling earlier generations of young Americans, but they may be finding new ways to engage their communities and governments. Whether such new forms of political and civic engagement can sustain a democratic public sphere remains to be seen.

So we have a *what*. We have, that is, a fairly decent picture of what young people seem to be doing in the democratic public sphere. What we lack is a *how*. How did young people get to a point where voting is less important than choosing where to shop? How did they come to be more tolerant of others despite an unwillingness to join together with others? How did it happen that young adults became more willing to walk to cure breast cancer with others in their community while they cannot be bothered with the local news? How did they come to view democratic citizenship as a choice to be taken up when it is convenient or absolutely necessary, rather than as a responsibility shared by all? We know, in short, that young people have changed, but how did this change come about? More important, is this change really all that bad? Listening to what young people have had to say for themselves about citizenship over the past five decades can give us the how. But can we really trust young people to tell us their story? Indeed, we must.

Why We Need to Listen to Youth

Since the founding of the United States, observers of the democratic experiment have been concerned with the American people's level of political involvement. For Alexis de Tocqueville, this issue was best understood by looking to the nation's youth:

> A man comes to be born. . . . He grows up; manhood begins; the doors of the world finally open to receive him; he enters into contact with those like him. Then one studies him for the first time, and one believes one sees the seed of the vices and virtues of his mature age forming in him.
> That, if I am not mistaken, is a great error.
> Go back; examine the infant even in the arms of his mother; see the external world reflected for the first time in the still-obscure mirror of his intelligence. . . . Only then will you understand where the prejudices, habits, and passions that are going to dominate his life come from. The man is so to speak a whole in the swaddling clothes of his cradle.[33]

Of course, many have taken Tocqueville's advice and sought to understand the level of political involvement among adults by studying the civic attitudes and beliefs of the young. Democracy, by definition, requires the participation of the people. People are not, however, born with democratic predispositions, just as they are not born Communists or Socialists. Each successive generation must learn the principles and habits of what society deems appropriate for citizenship from older cohorts. Yet these principles and habits are not static. Society evolves: Wars happen. Economies transform. New media emerge. Philosophical assumptions change. And as society advances, new citizens are socialized.

The story I tell in this book is about how successive generations of students writing in seven different high school newspapers across five decades reflect the evolving norms of democratic engagement. And following the advice of Tocqueville, I tell this story through the words of some particularly influential high school students spread out across seven American cities. In choosing to focus on adolescents, I face a number of potential objections. Are not fickle youth too uncertain of themselves to know how they really feel about politics and their communities? And what good does listening to teenagers do us in the long term anyway? Shouldn't we be more focused on the adult citizens they will mature into?

The years of late adolescence may very well be the most volatile of a person's life. It is, after all, a rough transition to go from being a child to becoming an adult. Some might argue, therefore, that studying democratic engagement in young people is misguided because it produces too unstable a picture. I argue, in contrast, that while young people's attitudes may be in flux, there are two reasons why they are a useful focus for study. First, because part of my goal is to detect changes in democratic engagement across time, looking to an age cohort that is actively searching for its civic and political identities—trying them on and taking them off—will yield the richest and most subtle forms of evidence available. Political scientists Richard Niemi and Mary Hepburn have argued as much in suggesting that those concerned with how people come to develop their own personal understanding of democratic engagement should "focus on political learning in the years of most rapid change to adultlike learning capabilities and adult attitudes."[34] If one wants to detect change, adolescents are a good place to go looking.

A second reason for studying young adults is that despite the reality that young people's attitudes and opinions may fluctuate considerably, there is plenty of evidence to suggest their core beliefs have already begun to take root by early adolescence. Citing the works of psychologists Jean Piaget, Erik Erikson, and Harry Stack Sullivan, education professor and director of the Stanford Center on Adolescence William Damon has made just this assertion, arguing that for young people the "specific beliefs and commitments, of course, may change over the subsequent years, but the initial formulation of them during adolescence always has ranked as a key landmark of human development."[35] While the empirical evidence for the long-term stability of political behaviors and attitudes learned in adolescence has met with considerable challenge in recent years, a number of notable studies continue to offer support for such a claim. For instance, political behavior scholars Kent Jennings and Laura Stoker have conducted one longitudinal study with data reaching back to 1965. Their long-term analysis of life-cycle effects on democratic engagement led them to the conclusion that "as people move into the life situations of middle age that evoke or require civic engagement, they draw on the predispositions and skills set in place at an earlier time. Pre-adult experiences do eventually matter."[36] Others have more recently found further evidence of these long-term democratic habits, especially as they relate to political attitudes across an individual's life cycle.[37] So strong is the evidence for long-term stability in democratic engagement that Peter Levine summed up one recent survey of the research thusly: "The basic pattern is consistent: those who participate in politics or community affairs or leadership roles at age fifteen or twenty-two are much more likely to be involved at age thirty or fifty."[38] Looking at how young people have come to understand democratic engagement may help explain the larger national political picture today and, possibly, how things may look in the near future.

Given that they are actively learning the democratic attitudes and behaviors that will guide them throughout their lives, studying young adults is an ideal way to discover the changing norms of political and civic engagement. Their volatility at a time when they are beginning to form their core democratic values helps reveal the subtle changes taking place across time as each new cohort gives way to the next. Thinking of young adults in terms of cohorts or generations, however, has its own set of detractors. And while I do not break down the young people in this book into preconceived generational categories, choosing instead to allow the differences to emerge naturally from the research, it is important to note that each generation does share some collective understandings of the political and civic world around them. Social scientists have offered ample empirical evidence for this generational thesis.[39] As Levine has recently summated, the research clearly reveals that "generations share durable civic and political characteristics attributable to the political and cultural situation that prevailed when they were young."[40] These shared generational worldviews emerge, moreover, from a number of influences. As one group of social scientists argues, these influences include the formal and informal political socialization that takes place on a daily basis through education, media consumption, and interactions with others. The shared worldview is also a result of various events (e.g., major political scandals, military conflicts, etc.) that occur during a cohort's adolescence, and it is more broadly contingent upon major changes in society writ large (e.g., major scientific advances, the introduction of new communications technologies, etc.). The opinions and behaviors of a cohort can be so cohesive that "generations, much like individuals, can develop their own distinct 'personalities.'"[41] To use "American youth" as a collective noun, then, is to speak of individual cohorts of young people who have much in common.

It is, however, equally problematic to conceptualize generations of American youth as somehow separate from one another. The American youth of today or any other time are not, despite what many of them might want to believe, completely unique. It is, after all, the natural folly of impatient youth to race headlong into growing older. A great many fifteen-year-olds are always already going on twenty-five, which is nothing more than to note that each new generation of young adults is greatly influenced by those a few years their elder—at least those older youth who have been deemed cool enough to emulate. This process is what one of the foremost sociologists of child development, William Corsaro, refers to as "interpretive reproduction."[42] As children and adolescents grow, they are constantly adopting the norms and behaviors they see in their older peers. In many ways, then, each new generation of young people in the United States represents a new chapter in the evolving story of American youth. To understand the youth of today, we must turn back a few chapters to the youth who came before.

Thus, listening to what American youth have been saying about their political and civic selves over the past five decades can go a long way toward helping us understand the changing nature of democratic engagement in the United States. As it stands now, we have done a poor job of listening. Instead, researchers concerned with the nation's political and civic health spend most of their time talking about what is wrong with America's youth. It seems that young adults are more often a crisis to be dealt with than a group to be listened to. To get a sense of this pervasive and long-standing attitude toward young people, at least in the United States, one need only glance at a sampling of books written on the subject:

- *Generations Lost: Pop Culture and Youth in Crisis*, by Timothy W. Quinnan (2002)
- *Youth Crisis: Growing Up in the High-Risk Society*, by Nanette J. Davis (1999)
- *America's Youth in Crisis: Challenges and Options for Programs and Policies*, by Richard M. Lerner (1994)
- *Suburban Youth in Cultural Crisis*, by Ralph W. Larkin (1979)
- *Youth, the American Crisis*, by James Haywood Collins (1972)
- *Crisis in Youth Culture*, by Nicholas Von Hoffman (1967)

The American obsession with the crisis of American youth is not even relatively new. For instance, traveling around the nation and talking with young people for four months in 1936 led journalist Maxine Davis to pen *The Lost Generation: A Portrait of American Youth Today*. As a reviewer of the book in *The ANNALS of the American Academy of Political and Social Science* summated that same year, Davis reported that adolescents in the 1930s were in a state of "complete nihilism [as] they sit and wait in vegetable passivity."[43] One does not really listen to nihilistic vegetables.

But American youth are not in crisis—at least no more today than a hundred years ago. They are not something that one must solve. Young people are, however, actively engaged in learning what it means to be an adult. And part of being an adult in a democratic state is being a citizen of that state. The adolescent years are, therefore, a stage of embryonic development into adult citizenhood. My purpose in this book is to examine this incubation process in one important subset of American youth.

How the World Has Been Changing

In his historical study of citizenship in the United States, sociologist Michael Schudson strongly dispels the notion that democratic engagement has been declining. Instead, as he notes in the opening sentences of his conclusion, "Citizenship in the United States has not disappeared. It has not even declined. It has, inevitably, changed."[44] How could it not? As national boundaries changed, wars were fought, populations increased, political rights spread, education expanded, and a myriad of other developments occurred, how could one expect that the norms of democratic engagement would not transform along the way?

Although my historical focus is far more limited than Schudson's, the changes in young Americans' democratic engagement that I detail below did not occur in isolation from the larger societal transformations that took place during the same period of time. Given my focus on high school students from 1965 through 2010, it is necessary to offer a glimpse into the societal changes of the last half of the twentieth century. While there is no reason to exaggerate this case, a student entering high school in 1965 would have been living in a very different world than one entering high school in the final years of the first decade of the twenty-first century. Each of the observations below is, of course, the subject of entire fields of research. What I offer here is simply a brief sketch of a few of the many changes that have influenced new generations of young people to come to know their worlds in very different ways than those who came before them.

Communications

It is difficult to overstate how different the communications environment was for a young person in the 1960s compared to a young adult in the early 2000s. The list of new communication technologies and mass media changes is long. A student in 1965, although not without choices, would have had a limited amount of communication technologies available to her. If she wanted to communicate with someone outside face-to-face communication, her only options would have been to post a letter through the U.S. postal service or phone the other person from a land-based line. Anyone outside of her local area would have taken days to reach by mail or been subject to relatively high long-distance fees. News would have come almost exclusively from newspapers, a few newsmagazines, radio news programming, and nightly television newscasts. Listening to music outside live venues required either a radio or record player (eight-track tapes were not even introduced until 1965). Visual media would have most likely been viewed on a black-and-white television that could have received on average five channels. Movie theaters or bulky video projectors in schools would have been the only likely ways to see films. While the young adult in 1965 would certainly not have felt she was communications deprived, her communications environment would come to seem quite antiquated to a young person growing up at the start of the twenty-first century.

Over the course of the five decades this study spans, a whole host of changes completely transformed the communications world. The early 1970s saw the introduction of both VCRs and cable television. The first personal stereo (the Sony Walkman) hit the market in 1979, and personal computers were introduced in 1981. CNN began reporting news twenty-four hours a day in 1980, and the number of channels the average household received increased to almost 19 in 1985 before ballooning to more than 100 by 2003. Mobile phones began to emerge in the 1980s, and the Internet, which began being used commercially in the late 1980s and started to see widespread public use by the mid-1990s, was being used regularly by approximately 84 percent of children in their homes by early January 2008.[45] Records gave way to eight-track, then cassette tape, then compact disc, before becoming digitized in MP3 format; movies went from being shown at theaters to being rented at local stores to being downloaded online.

During the same period, people moved from simply writing letters and phoning one another to sending text messages, writing e-mails, and instant messaging online. Compared to the average young person in 1965, the young adult of today has far more mediated options and communications mobility. Whether for good or ill, young adults entering high school in the early 2000s were living in a much larger, more fast-paced, and increasingly more individualized media environment than any of their predecessors would have known.

Culture

At the time of this writing, there is a great deal of arguing in academic and political circles about the cultural wars currently being fought in the United States. Struggles between red states (Republican/conservative) and blue states (Democratic/progressive) are debated ad nauseum. The reality is that the cultural wars are grossly overblown by media personalities and political pundits, and measuring cultural values themselves has long been a thorny endeavor. Even trickier is measuring cultural changes across time. Still, it seems fair to argue that some national cultural values are different today than they were five decades ago. For instance, thanks in large part to several hard-fought (and as yet still unfinished) social movements, attitudes toward women, African Americans, and homosexuals have become far more liberal and tolerant. Perhaps the easiest way to see these cultural changes in the United States is to look to the American political landscape. The 89th Congress (1965–67) had only 2 women in the Senate and 11 women and 2 African Americans in the House of Representatives. By comparison, the 108th Congress (2003–5) included 77 female members (14 in the Senate, 63 in the House) as well as 40 African American and 3 openly gay men and women in the House. While still not the numbers some advocate for, the trend demonstrates a basic change in the societal attitudes toward women and minorities.

Outside the political landscape, American popular culture offers another way to see the cultural shifts that took place between 1965 and 2010. The most popular shows in 1965 (e.g., *Bonanza*, *The Lucy Show*, *The Andy Griffith Show*, and *The Beverly Hillbillies*) presented a relatively racially homogeneous world in which crime was rarely violent and women were never in bed (unless perhaps they were sick). The most popular shows, outside of reality television, in 2009 (e.g., *NCIS*, *House*, *Desperate Housewives*, and *Grey's Anatomy*) offered a world with far more racial diversity and a great deal more explicit sex and violent crime. A similar trend can certainly be seen in music. The Billboard Hot 100 number-three-selling single for 1965 was the Rolling Stones' "(I Can't Get No) Satisfaction," which primarily protested commercialization. The song also included the then controversial line "I can't get no girl reaction." The 2010 Billboard top-rated single of the year, by contrast, was "Tik Tok" by Ke$ha, which featured the memorable lines "I'm talking about everybody getting crunk, crunk / Boys tryin' to touch my junk, junk." For young people entering school in the final year of this study, then, their cultural world looked far different than that of young adults in the mid-1960s. For better or worse, American culture changed a great deal over these five decades.

Globalization

Put simply, the world has been getting smaller over the past century. While soldiers, explorers, and tradesmen had been traveling great distances around the world for centuries, the twentieth century brought with it technological and scientific advances that made it increasingly easier for the average individual to travel to far-reaching places and communicate with peoples vastly different from themselves. In recent decades, there has been a "widening and deepening of the international flows of trade, capital, technology, and information within a single integrated global market."[46] These transportation and telecommunications advances have had both personal and political consequences. For the individual, globalization has led to a sense of cosmopolitanism that has replaced, in many cases, a sense of local connectedness. "World citizens" have replaced ordinary community members. Politically, globalization has changed how the world does business and has brought into question the nation-state and its viability as a governing institution. Global corporations continue to gain greater amounts of political capital at the same time nation-states struggle to compete in a changing world. While the fear that corporations, rather than nation-states, are running the world seems too often exaggerated, it is difficult not to acknowledge that large international companies are increasingly gaining economic and cultural influence across national borders. The young person in the United States today is very likely to listen to music from South America (e.g., Shakira), dress in clothing from Europe (e.g., Gucci), and drive cars from Asia (e.g., Toyota).

Young people in the 1960s were not, of course, unaware of the impact of global issues on the United States. With events such as the Russian launching of Sputnik in 1957 and the ongoing Vietnam War throughout the decade,

American high school students in 1965 knew something about international issues. However, the youth of today are far more intimately enmeshed in the larger world than earlier generations as a whole. This point is made by Harvard education scholars Marcelo Suárez-Orozco and Desirée Baolian Qin-Hilliard, who argue that "the forces of globalization are taxing youth, families, and education systems worldwide. . . . Youth growing up today will be linked to economic realities, social processes, technological and media innovations, and cultural flows that traverse national boundaries with ever greater momentum."[47] From growing global corporations to an increasingly international media environment, young people today are finding their lives more interconnected with people from around the globe. Taking this interrelation into account is important in assessing the changing nature of youth democratic engagement.

Suburbanization

The history of the United States in the second half of the twentieth century is certainly one of suburbanization. While the American people were clearly moving toward suburban environments before 1950, this trend only increased after World War II. Faced with the changing economic realities of a nation that had moved from an agricultural- to an industrial-based society, the American people quickly abandoned their rural roots. And concerned with crime and overcrowding, they also left American cities in droves. Their convergence in new suburban communities was helped, according to urban planning scholar David Soule, by the U.S. government. The suburban growth that followed World War II would not have been possible, in fact, without the government's willingness to give returning veterans cheap housing loans or without the 1956 Interstate and Defense Highway Act, which eventually created the nation's intricate highway systems.[48] Spurred by these developments, the growth of American suburban communities quickly accelerated. As historians Kevin Kruse and Thomas Sugrue have recently put it, "The rise and dominance of suburbia in America after the Second World War is inescapable. In 1950, a quarter of all Americans lived in suburbs; in 1960, a full third; and by 1990, a solid majority."[49] American youth are, by and large, suburban youth. The result of this suburban dominance is that the American landscape quickly became filled with things that make suburban life manageable—automobiles, chain restaurants, strip malls, and big-box stores. This new landscape surely affected the lives of the young people who increasingly came to find themselves living in suburbia.

Economics

A student graduating from high school in the 1960s entered a much different economic environment than a student graduating at the start of the twenty-first century. Due in part to the technological and global changes mentioned above, the young people of the last fifty years have, for instance, had to learn new types of career skills as the U.S. economy transitioned from an industrial economy to a service economy. Economic scholars George Kozmetsky and Piyu Yue have tracked this changing economic structure between 1950 and 2000, summing up the transition thusly: "The leading sectors for economic growth in the United States have moved away from the industries associated with the Third Industrial Revolution, such as the automobile, electricity, and chemical industries, to the industries of information technology and services." This has led, Kozmetsky and Yue argue, to the "fall of the working class and the rise of the creative and innovative class."[50] Moreover, these new classes of workers have led many more young people today to seek postsecondary education to attain the necessary skills required in new service-based industries and the knowledge required for high-tech jobs. The increasing pressure on high school students to continue their education can easily be demonstrated by noting the increasing number of Americans awarded bachelor's degrees—from fewer than 1 in 10 in 1960 to 1 in 4 in 2000.[51] Simply to compete in the job market, young people found they needed postsecondary education. And while they were struggling to learn the quickly changing knowledge and skills that accompanied the nation's economic transition, they also had to face the uncertainty of long-term career security. A high school student in the 1960s would have been entering a workforce structured around individuals changing career paths no more than once or twice across the adult life cycle. A high school student in the early 2000s would have had no such illusions, as he could expect to change careers up to half a dozen times during his life.

At a broader level, the economic differences between young people today and those entering the workforce in the late 1960s might best be understood in relation to three indices—personal wealth, income inequality, and financial security. Put simply, young people today have, on average, greater wealth than their peers from earlier generations, but they also live in a world of greater income inequality and far more financial insecurity. Making sense of the first two indices—wealth and inequality—Yale political scientist Jacob Hacker has noted that "Americans at all points on the income ladder have gotten richer—just not at equal rates—and during this same time period, our economy has expanded handsomely." So while today's youth live in a more economically prosperous era, not everyone has benefited equally from the new wealth. More important, today's young adults also live in a world of greater financial insecurity—a world in which job layoffs, health care crises, and economic downturns can suddenly and drastically change a person's financial well-being.[52] Indeed, so different is today's economic environment that Richard Sennett has suggested it has created a new type of ideal individual, devoid of a coherent life narrative and a set of experiences through which work helps make meaning.[53] Today's young adults might have more money to spend, but they also have to learn to work in a world of less economic certainty and greater class division.

Demographics

The United States underwent great shifts in its demographic makeup during the last half of the twentieth century. Comparing the 1960 U.S. Census to the one in 2000, it is relatively easy to track these changes. Between 1960 and 2000, the number of people living in the United States increased by more than half, as the nation's population ballooned from 180 million to 280 million. Racially, the nation also became less white during these years; the percentage of the U.S. population that is Caucasian decreased from 88.5 to 75 percent, with much of the difference made up by Hispanics and Latinos. That the nation has become more racially diverse does not, however, mean that the average young person now engages people of different races more often than he would have half a century ago. While initial school integration occurred during the 1960s and 1970s, there is some evidence suggesting a growing trend toward the resegregation of schools in more recent years.[54] While interracial contact may be on the decline, it is nevertheless difficult to imagine that the average young person today would not be more aware of the racial diversity surrounding him than a young adult living in the 1950s. From magazine advertisements to television shows, young people today are certainly presented with an image of a more racially diverse society.

In addition to becoming more racially diverse, the American people got older. The median age increased by five years—from 30.3 to 35.3 years old. And while they were getting older, U.S. citizens were also becoming more educated, with the percentage of the American people twenty-five years and older holding at least a high school diploma doubling from 41 percent in 1960 to 80 percent in 2000. Given these changes, it is safe to say that a young person in the early 2000s would have been living in a world filled with more people, who were, on average, more racially diverse, older, and more educated than they would have been forty years earlier. While it may be true that today's youth seem to have less respect for their elders, actually engage people of different races less often, and suffer from the declining quality of education, they are, nevertheless, living in a much different America than were the youth of almost half a century ago.

Conclusion

A great deal changed in the United States as the twentieth century drew to a close and the twenty-first century began. The broad, sweeping observations offered above do not begin to cover all of the changes that occurred between 1965 and 2010. Each of the foregoing observations does, however, offer concrete examples of the societal changes that would certainly have influenced the socializing processes of American youth. Have these changes been positive or negative? Yes and no. The same cultural value shifts that have opened doors for women and minorities have also made casual sex and violence more socially normative. The same economic trends that have decreased job security have also increased the overall national standard of living. The same globalizing forces that may have caused a loss in local cohesion have led to a greater awareness of global concerns. Change is always Janus-faced. Still, one might wonder, have these changes led to better democratic citizens? For the most part, the short answer seems to be no—our democracy is worse off today than it was before or perhaps ever has been. Taking the negative stance is the easy, polemical answer. I prefer to leave the polemics to others. I do not, however, mean to offer unbridled optimism either. The U.S. citizenry and American democracy itself are not better or worse; they are simply different than they used to be. Change is both natural and inevitable.

This book embraces change as the expected result of time and experience. As the years have passed, the American people have learned from one another, and newer generations have adapted these lessons to fit the new experiences of the evolving world around them. But amid this natural evolution, some things have remained the same. One of the unchanged facets of the United States is the belief in democracy and the need to continue to foster new generations of democratic citizens. At his 2009 inauguration on a cold January afternoon in Washington, D.C., President Barack

Obama acknowledged the inevitability of change. He talked, specifically, of the nation's journey. And he, too, offered a source of stability:

> Our challenges may be new. The instruments with which we meet them may be new. But those values upon which our success depends—hard work and honesty, courage and fair play, tolerance and curiosity, loyalty and patriotism—these things are old. These things are true. They have been the quiet force of progress throughout our history. What is demanded then is a return to these truths. What is required of us now is a new era of responsibility—a recognition, on the part of every American, that we have duties to ourselves, our nation and the world; duties that we do not grudgingly accept but rather seize gladly, firm in the knowledge that there is nothing so satisfying to the spirit, so defining of our character, than giving our all to a difficult task. This is the price and the promise of citizenship.

President Obama understood that the United States he had been elected to lead was different than the United States of earlier eras. Both the challenges facing the nation and the tools used to deal with those challenges were new. But Obama also understood that at the heart of the United States, old and new, was its commitment to democracy. What he failed to understand was that it might not be possible to return to the democratic truths of an earlier time. That is the nature of change—it makes going back to the way things were before truly impossible.

The American democracy cannot go back to the way things were. It will inevitably continue to move forward. The best we can do now, then, is to assess the state of democratic engagement in the United States as it stands today. And I believe the only way to really get a sense of what democratic citizenship looks like today is to put it in the context of how it got to be this way. This introductory chapter has set out my reasons for believing this. I have suggested that the picture of what we think we know about young people is confusing—a portrait predicated upon an idealized democratic model that may never have existed. Given the uncertainty of the democratic picture presented by social scientists over the past couple decades, I have argued that we need to reassess what we know about the state of America's democratic health by paying attention to the nation's youth—specifically, what they have had to say for themselves about their political and civic beliefs across time. And, finally, I have assumed that examining the discourse of young adults in the United States over time will present a story of changing democratic norms, influenced by the evolving American society in which young adults learn to be citizens. Understanding these changes will, I believe, help us understand how we got to this point in our democratic history and offer some clues as to where things might be headed.

The following chapters tell the story of how the beliefs and norms that some American youth associate with democratic engagement changed in the waning years of the twentieth century and what these young citizens came to look like at the beginning of the twenty-first century. First, chapter 2 offers some context for understanding modern American high schools and the young people who inhabit them, introduces the seven high schools chosen for this study, and explains how I go about listening to American youth in the high school newspapers they produce for one another. Chapters 3 through 6 each tell a different story of how young adults have adapted their democratic engagement to fit the changing society in which they live. Finally, chapter 7 returns to some of the key themes raised in this opening chapter as it pulls together the primary strands of change presented throughout the book. It offers a final picture of what democratic engagement looks like today and where it seems to be pointed in the future.

Some may be tempted to take the evidence offered in the following chapters as an indictment against one aspect of American society or another. Some may want to argue that one social institution or another (e.g., free market capitalism, mass media, etc.) is the central problem of a modern democratic crisis. Others may view the way the young people in this study say they have come to understand their political and civic roles as evidence that young people themselves have increasingly become the problem, because American culture has become too relaxed or the American public school system too soft. I suspect that by the end of this book one might find any number of places to point a finger. I believe, however, that pointing fingers does very little good in the long run. Instead, I offer one hand to American youth and the other to the academics, politicians, and social activists who keep arguing that American democracy is failing. In the end, I hope the story I tell helps the former rethink their methods of democratic engagement and the latter think of new ways to help young adults more fully embrace the democratic experiment that is the United States.

2

AMERICAN HIGH SCHOOL:

TEENAGERS AND SCHOLASTIC JOURNALISM

In the 1985 film *The Breakfast Club*, writer and director John Hughes tells the story of five high school students suffering through a full day of Saturday detention overseen by the school's principal, Richard Vernon. The high school is located in a fictitious Illinois suburban community, and each of the (all white) students clearly represents a different segment of the high school population. Each student actually defines him- or herself as one of five distinctive types—a criminal, a princess, a brain, an athlete, and a basket case. As the movie progresses, however, all of them come to believe they are not so different from one another, eventually realizing they share more in common than they could have imagined when their day of detention began. Principal Vernon does not, it seems, see the five young adults as that different from one another either. In fact, in a conversation with the school janitor, Vernon reveals exactly how he views the students he is paid to oversee: "You think about this: When you get old, these kids—when I get old—they're gonna be runnin' the country. . . . Now this is the thought that wakes me up in the middle of the night. That when I get older, these kids are gonna take care of me." The janitor's response sums up the fear many adults have of American youth: "I wouldn't count on it." As Vernon contemplates this statement, the film cuts to students sitting around the library discussing the status of their virginity.

The American people have long had a deep-seated fear that their youth were not up to the demanding task of running the nation. In popular culture, this fear has been explored through countless television shows and movies dealing with teenagers during their high school years. On film, this exploration has frequently taken the form of a subgenre of high school dramas in which an idealistic teacher challenges and transforms his or her often underprivileged students. Such films include *Blackboard Jungle* (1955); *To Sir, with Love* (1967); *Stand and Deliver* (1988); *Dead Poets Society* (1989); *Dangerous Minds* (1995); and *Freedom Writers* (2007). In another form, movie depictions of high school have followed the pattern of *The Breakfast Club*, exploring the social and cultural complications of adolescence. This second genre has included such notable movies as *Grease* (1978); *Fast Times at Ridgemont High* (1982); *Pretty in Pink* (1986); *Boyz in the Hood* (1991); *Dazed and Confused* (1993); and *Juno* (2007). In addition to movies, rarely has there been a time in which at least one major television show was not devoted to the lives of high school–aged young people.[1] Every American generation has been raised on at least one televised drama detailing the travails of adolescents and their conflicts with adults who often struggle to make them better. Over the years, such television shows have included *Leave It to Beaver*; *Welcome Back, Kotter*; *Family Ties*; *Beverly Hills 90210*; *Dawson's Creek*; *That 70's Show*; and *Friday Night Lights*. These shows have certainly gotten grittier over the years, but the general theme has remained the same: young people must survive adolescence and be transformed into respectable adults. If our popular culture is any indication, the American people have a great deal of anxiety about helping their young become productive adult citizens.

Since the end of the nineteenth century, the arduous task of transforming young people into responsible adults has increasingly fallen on the shoulders of teachers who work in the American educational system. For more than a half century now, the overwhelming majority of adolescents in the United States have done a good bit of their growing up in public schools. Despite recent governmental policies allowing families to use federal school vouchers to send their children to private schools, the U.S. Department of Education noted in a June 2008 report that, in fact, 87 percent of all school-age children in grades K–12 still attend public schools.[2] So if one wants to get a better understanding of the changing nature of democratic engagement, as seen through the eyes of American youth, the public school system seems to be the place to look. This chapter outlines exactly where and how I plan to pay attention to youth in public schools.

This book is about how the democratic assumptions of successive generations of American youth changed between 1965 and 2010, as evidenced by the archived newspapers of seven high schools from metropolitan areas around the country: Houston, Texas; Kansas City, Missouri; Newton, Massachusetts; Phoenix, Arizona; Pittsburgh, Pennsylvania; Portland, Oregon; and Washington, D.C. Its primary focus is on how the American youth who participated in these newspapers talked about politics, community, and citizenship across time. Such a focus leads to several important questions: Can one really compare a high school in 1965 to a high school today? Are not high school students more worried about sex and their favorite bands than about political issues and community concerns? Who are the students who typically get involved with their high school newspapers? What can one really expect to learn from high school newspapers? What can reading seven high school newspapers teach anyone about youth democratic engagement?

This chapter offers answers to each of these questions. First, I describe modern American public high schools and the young people who inhabit them. Then I turn more specifically to the nature of scholastic journalism and the high school newspaper itself as a forum for democratic deliberation. Finally, I introduce the seven high schools from which the newspapers were archived and offer an explanation of the assumptions guiding my analysis of these papers.

The American Educational System

When those concerned with the education of American youth look to the nation's public school system and suggest what it should be doing, it often seems as though they are staring at a Rorschach inkblot test—they see what they want to see. For some, public schools are supposed to be teaching young people the social norms and expectations of a pluralist society.[3] For others, public schools should allow the individual student to learn what his strengths are and then work toward allowing those individual strengths to flourish.[4] Some argue America's public school system should be primarily concerned with turning out young adults with the skills and knowledge necessary to advance the American workforce.[5] Others argue the nation's schools need to be preparing all students for postsecondary schooling.[6] Still others suggest the goal of schools should be to create engaged citizens.[7] In many schools around the country, administrators are trying to do all of these things at once. Overall, then, the American people expect their schools to do a great deal.

The demanding expectations of today's public schools result, in large part, from the educational assumptions and hopes they have inherited from an earlier time. As education historian Diane Ravitch has pointed out, however, this inheritance is a complicated mix of various ideological assumptions. The most celebrated educational founders and reformers in U.S. history have had very different views of what the goals of public schools should be. Writing at the turn of the nineteenth century, Noah Webster supposed that schools could be used to socialize youth into American citizens and strengthen the nation's identity; Thomas Jefferson believed, in contrast, that public education could be used to enlighten the masses and help them resist the tyrannical tendency of the powerful. Half a century later, Horace Mann, the founder of the American common school, thought that schools were best suited for allowing individuals to find their own strengths so that they might better develop the still transforming national economy.[8] John Dewey argued in the early years of the twentieth century that education's social function could best serve the people by teaching them how to better communicate and interrelate with diverse groups of others in a democratic style of interaction.[9] In 1953, Robert Hutchins suggested schools should "produce responsible citizens" by offering every individual a liberal education that could help develop his or her intellectual abilities.[10] E. D. Hirsch has more recently argued that American schools have a greater responsibility to teach students a shared cultural literacy.[11] While these examples cover the historical expanse of the United States, they do not, of course, represent every voice that has sought educational reform. Yet they do clearly indicate the varied ideological assumptions today's educational system continues to grapple with. Public schools are tasked with strengthening everything from American identity to individual identity, and from the national economy to democratic citizenship. Add to this burden the struggle over how best to do any one of these things and it is amazing that the U.S. educational system has not imploded. Thankfully, it endures.

Too often lost in the educational and political debates about the role of education in the United States, however, are the schools and students themselves. Learning does not take place only through reading textbooks, writing reports, and taking tests. Students are educated, especially as democratic citizens, through the forms and structures that make up their school surroundings. John Dewey made this argument when he asserted "that the only way in which adults consciously control the kind of education which the immature get is by controlling the environment in which they act, and hence think and feel. We never educate directly, but indirectly by means of the environment."[12] So what does the environment in which the vast majority of American adolescents are educated look like?

The American High School

To understand how the American public high school became what it is today, one might look at the evolution of secondary education throughout three major historical eras. The first era, which roughly covered the years 1880 to 1930, was characterized by the transformation of education from a private privilege to a public good. Prior to 1880, the limited educational opportunities that did exist were primarily restricted to private education for wealthy young men preparing for college and professional careers. After the American Civil War and Reconstruction, quick industrial expansion required a more educated class of professional men. The public school system emerged as the way to fill this new educational need. While the majority of American youth were not yet regularly attending schools at the turn of the century, "about nine in ten" of those young adults who did attend did so through a growing public education system.[13] By the start of the twentieth century, Diane Ravitch has argued, "it was generally accepted that public education should be provided by the state at public expense and that the purposes of democracy were served best by offering a common academic education to children for as long as they were willing and able to stay in school."[14] This public education model had taken root by 1900, leading increasing numbers of white youth to get some education outside of the home during the first few decades of the twentieth century. The transition was so complete that one education scholar has concluded that in this initial era "the American high school was transformed from an elite, private institution into a public one attended by white children en masse."[15]

If the first era of American public education can be understood in terms of transformation, the second era, from 1930 to 1965, was one of expansion. In the middle of the twentieth century, both the number of adolescents attending school and the inclusiveness of the public school system increased exponentially. According to Ravitch, approximately 50 percent of young adults were attending school in 1930. Over the next few decades, this percentage rose dramatically to almost 80 percent of teenagers.[16] Of course, while these numbers are certainly optimistic, they do not tell the whole story of the American public education system during the 1940s and 1950s. Public schooling may have been approaching universality, but education in America was far from equal. Unpacking Ravitch's own assessment makes this point clearly. The 80 percent she identifies around midcentury includes the racial disparity in 1950, when approximately 85 percent of white adolescents were attending school, as compared to less than 75 percent of nonwhite youth.[17] It was not until May 17, 1954, that the U.S. Supreme Court unanimously rejected the myth of "separate but equal" education as inherently unequal. As Chief Justice Earl Warren put it, both asking and answering the central question, "Does segregation of children in public schools solely on the basis of race, even though the physical facilities and other 'tangible' factors may be equal, deprive the children of the minority group of equal educational opportunities? We believe that it does."[18] While the Supreme Court changed the law in 1954, several years passed before the American people had to fully face the issue of desegregation in their public schools. It was not until the fall of 1957 that the images of sixteen-year-old Elizabeth Eckford being turned away from Little Rock Central High School shocked the American people into a new cultural understanding of race and education.[19] To say the events of the 1950s did away with educational inequality would be erroneous, but one can safely acknowledge that those years did force open the doors of public schools to many students who would have been alienated in practice before then. By 1965, the first year of this study, 93 percent of fourteen- to seventeen-year-olds were enrolled in schools, including 91 percent of blacks and other minorities.[20]

Since 1965, the percentage of high school–aged adolescents enrolled in school has remained above 90 percent, reaching over 96 percent in the early 1990s before dropping slightly thereafter. Among these students, there has also been only a relatively modest improvement in the percentage of high school dropouts.[21] By the first year of this study, then, the American public secondary school system was well formed. Indeed, from an institutional perspective, walking into a high school in 1965 would not have seemed much different than walking into one today. To be sure, some of the academic subjects have changed, the media and teaching equipment are different, and the students' clothes and hairstyles are quite distinct, but the concept of high school is very similar. That is, the high school in 1965 and 2010 would most likely be one within the comprehensive model. Indeed, one can identify the third era of American public high schools as having been dominated by comprehensiveness—the attempt to offer increasingly more educational and extracurricular opportunities for an increasingly diverse range of students.

In 1959, James Conant, former president of Harvard University and U.S. ambassador to Germany, published *The American High School Today*. Based on a study funded through a Carnegie Corporation of New York grant, the book was "widely influential in its time."[22] Resulting from his assessment of more than one hundred high schools, Conant's primary argument was an unwavering and enthusiastic endorsement for the emerging comprehensive model of secondary education. According to Conant, the goal of American public schooling was to provide the means for young adults to attain the "twin ideals of equality of opportunity and equality of status."[23] To do this, he believed, secondary schools should be comprehensive in both size and educational opportunities. In other words, they were supposed to be able to bring together a diverse group of students, give them all a good general education, offer numerous extracurricular choices to advance their talents, and present advanced students with appropriate challenges. As educational sociologist Floyd Hammack has recently summarized, Conant "thought that truly democratic schools would offer a variety of curricula, leading to different occupational careers. Students would be sorted among these courses and programs according to their performance, inclinations, and ambitions."[24] Following Conant's strong endorsement, the comprehensive high school became the dominant form of American secondary schooling.

Most high schools in the United States today and all seven schools in this study are comprehensive. Most secondary schools, that is, have well over eight hundred students of varying educational ability, a wide-ranging curriculum, and a host of student athletics and organizations. So large are these comprehensive high schools that they very much resemble small, self-contained democratic communities. While students are not sovereign in their schools, the comprehensive high school is itself modeled upon a democratic commitment to equality and opportunity.[25] In fact, one of the biggest complaints against the comprehensive high school has been that it places too much choice in the hands of students.[26] Despite these criticisms, high school students today still have a great deal of opportunity. At one of the schools in this study (Grant High School in Portland, Oregon), for instance, students can take classes on everything from social skills to literature and film, from jazz ensemble to advanced placement psychology. Outside of the classroom, students can join any number of clubs, including chemistry club, chess club, and Latino club. They can also join the drill team, football team, and swimming team. All of this choice is made possible for the approximately 1,800 students by a large staff, which includes 4 administrators, 77 teachers, 5 counselors, 2 security guards, and numerous other support personnel (e.g., a testing coordinator, librarians, administrative assistants, and custodial staff). This small army of adults works to provide the many academic, social, and athletic options deemed necessary for each student to achieve his or her potential. So while students may not have the power to self-govern in their high schools, the opportunities they are given and the choices they make most assuredly allow them at least a modicum of self-efficacy within their school communities.

The American Teenager

In addition to being large, multifaceted institutions greatly resembling small communities, high schools in the United States are populated with adolescents. This is no banal observation. In chapter 1, I discussed what we think we know about how young adults behave as emerging citizens;

here I describe what young people in high school are—teenagers. While the teenage years are often difficult for those living through them, they can be just as confusing for those trying to study teenagers themselves.

An important distinction must be made between the *teen* years and the *teenager*. The word "teen" simply refers to anyone between the ages of thirteen and nineteen. It has been in use for centuries. Teenagers are, however, a more recent phenomenon, as clearly indicated by the fact that the word "teen-ager" was coined in 1941.[27] The idea that there may be something uniquely special about the teen years was, of course, not new to the mid-twentieth century. As the most common time for the onset of puberty, the teen years were identified by Jean-Jacques Rousseau in his 1762 educational treatise *Émile* as "a second birth" characterized by "a change of temper, frequent outbreaks of anger, a perpetual stirring of the mind."[28] Similarly, American psychologist and educator G. Stanley Hall wrote of the teen years as a "marvelous new birth" in his ambitious 1904 work *Adolescence*.[29] More than Rousseau, Hall's work was the first to clearly identify "the elongated hiatus between childhood and adulthood."[30] It was not so much a description of the societal norm as it was an envisioning of what was to become the teenager. That Hall's work proved popular and influential in American education may certainly have helped lead to the educational changes of the early twentieth century, but the teenager as a truly unique social category came decades after his conceptualization of adolescence.

The educational changes described above and Hall's conceptualization of adolescence would, however, play a central role in the creation of this social category. As changes occurred in how, where, and with whom teens spent their time, adolescence was transformed and a new social identity was invented. Cultural critic Thomas Hine has recently explored teenagers as a "social invention," concluding, "Like the Hoover Dam, the American teenager was a New Deal project, a massive redirection of energy." Hine's point is that the many millions of young people in their teen years who were competing for work with older adults during worsening economic times were redirected into the quickly expanded American public school system. The American high school, that is, played a central role in the creation of the socially constructed teenager. Hine explains, "What was new about the idea of the teenager . . . was the assumption that all young people, regardless of their class, location, or ethnicity, should have essentially the same experience, spent with people exactly their age, in an environment defined by high school and pop culture."[31] What high schools did was to change the focus of the teen years, which had hitherto been spent either beginning adulthood through entering the workforce or staying at home to help with family. In lieu of these two traditional options, high schools gave teenaged youth a unique space in which to interact with one another outside of the family context but without the necessary responsibilities of survival inherent in entering the workforce. Through this interaction, these youth began to find they had much in common. This realization, as Grace Palladino puts it in her history of teenagers, "revolutionized the very concept of growing up." She explains further, "As high schools claimed a larger proportion of teenage youth during the 1930s, . . . high school students assumed a measure of personal freedom and generational independence that challenged traditional notions of parental authority and respect."[32] Increasingly gathered together in high schools, American youth learned what they shared in common and in what ways they differed from others. They became teenagers.

While the high school played a significant role in sectioning off a large portion of American youth into their own self-contained communities, the social construction of teenagers would not have been possible without the consumerization of adolescence. As cultural critic and historian Jon Savage has shown in his exploration of the creation of youth culture, the arrival of the teenager coincided with the realization by some that there was money to be made on this new group. Perhaps the forerunner of this commercialization was the magazine *Seventeen*, launched in September 1944. As Savage notes, *Seventeen* was produced out of a "deep-seated conviction that high school girls needed a magazine of their own," and it "treated adolescents as quasi-adults" and as a commercial commodity.[33] This shift toward thinking of teenagers as a marketing segment was cemented within the next decade as more and more adolescents began attending high school regularly and the post–World War II economic boom gave parents and their teenagers more money to spend on the necessities of teenage culture. By the early 1950s, young adults were being sold their teenage identity through everything from music to fashion to food. Since the 1950s, teenagers have continued to play a major role in the U.S. economy as fashion designers, Hollywood producers, video game creators, and entertainers work tirelessly to sell a youth culture to adolescents. Born out of societal change, teenagers have become a mainstay of American culture.

While the teenager as a socially constructed identity may have become commonplace in the United States and most other Western cultures, these young people are rarely understood by their elders. It has become routine for older generations to look at teenagers and youth culture and marvel at their strangeness. Today, many adults have a difficult time remembering what it was like to be a teenager. As educational scholars Sharon

Nichols and Thomas Good have succinctly put it, "The further adults are from high school, the fuzzier high school memories become."[34] At times, adolescence is remembered longingly as a peaceful time of life when responsibilities were few and possibilities many. Middle-aged adults faced with the burdens of family, a career, and impending old age often reimagine how much easier their life was when they were teenagers. At other times, adolescence is described as a turbulent period of great anxiety and change. If the former image of "teenagerness" is romanticized for its serenity, the latter is equally romanticized as chaotic. Cultural critic Peter Marin's image of adolescence in an influential 1971 essay sums up this chaotic romanticism in rather vivid terms:

> It is precisely at this point, adolescence, when the rush of energies, that sea-sex, gravitation, the thrust of the ego up through the layers of childhood, makes itself felt, that the person is once more like an infant. . . . He is in a sense born again, a fresh identity beset inside and out by the rush of new experience. . . . In this condition, with these needs, the adolescent is like a primitive man, an apocalyptic primitive; he exists for the moment in that stage of single vision in which myth is still the raw stuff of being.[35]

While Marin is inclined to feel sympathetic toward adolescents over the pains of their rebirth, his description of the "apocalyptic" teenager struggling through the turmoil and excitement of a new identity formation clearly indicates a view of the teenage years as chaotic.

Those with more level heads understand that being a teenager is neither so serene nor so chaotic. It is, however, a time of change, a transition between childhood and adulthood. Such transitioning can surely be, as developmental psychologist Erik Erikson once wrote, a stormy experience,[36] which is to express rather simply that adolescence is filled with ups and downs. And why would it not be? As teenagers clearly begin to emerge from the confines placed on most children, they are gradually given more freedoms and more responsibilities. Even in their schooling, they begin to play a more active role in deciding what classes to take and which to avoid. At the same time, teenagers are not considered full adults. These mixed signals are perhaps most easily seen in the legal age requirements for various actions: finding part-time employment (14 years old), getting a driver's license (16), consenting to sex (varies by state from 14 to 18), buying cigarettes (18), marrying without parental consent (18), voting (18), and buying alcohol (21). That teenagers can get a job and consent to sexual intercourse seven years before they can buy a glass of wine demonstrates just how confusing society's expectations of them are. Trying to navigate such conflicting messages might drive anyone to act in strange ways on occasion, not even factoring in the biological changes that occur during the teen years.

Besides these confusing expectations, American teenagers have a great deal else to contend with. In addition to 180 days of school, numerous extracurricular activities, part-time jobs, social engagements, household responsibilities, and family obligations, teenagers are busy forming their identity foundations. As sociologist Pamela Perry has put it, adolescence is "the time when youth must face the fact of impending adult status and embody the rules, values, and roles the society calls them to fulfill. That embodiment translates, in part, into the quest for personal and collective identities outside of the family."[37] To understand just how important the high school years are for teenage identity formation, a number of scholars have sought out young adults in their own environments through ethnographic fieldwork. These researchers have found that teenagers live within a complex social structure of various identity expectations. Thus, they are often busy building, tearing down, and rebuilding their identities. Such identity construction includes coming to terms with gendered and racial categories.[38] In addition to these well-researched identity markers, other scholars have done more nuanced work to examine the ways in which teenagers in high school navigate the more complex layers of class structure.

While there are certainly power dynamics at play in questions over gendered, sexual, and racial identities, work focusing on the important class struggles of high school students demonstrates something more integral to the study of young adults: teenagers are complex political animals who learn to internalize their society's norms. To miss this point is to fail to see the importance of teenagers in adopting and transforming the American political landscape writ large. As linguistics scholar Penelope Eckert argues in her analysis of the ways in which teenagers discursively practice social categories, there is a "complex relation between social structure and learning."[39] Students learn as much (if not more) from the organization of the high school as they do from teacher instruction and books, and the organization of schools is largely created through larger societal expectations. These societal structures are so normalized that, as anthropologist Douglas Foley found in his ethnographic analysis of one Texas high school, complex social and class categorizing even occurs at high school football games—both on and off the field. Foley argues, moreover, that these social categories are ways in which teenagers learn the class distinctions integral to capitalistic culture, and they are also ways in which some young people struggle against these norms. As Foley discovered when he attended the ten-year reunion of one of the high school classes he observed, these class distinctions can have lasting effects.[40] Sociologist Murray Milner echoes Foley's observations and argues further that what makes the struggle over status distinctions so important for teenagers is that the negotiation of these categories may be where they find the most power.[41] As Milner notes, these social status struggles are highly political affairs.

The American high school is a community of teenagers struggling with one another through the process of becoming adults. Both high schools and teenagers are, furthermore, ambiguous cultural sites through which the American people struggle to maintain and strengthen various aspects of U.S. society. It should thus be no wonder that America's educational system and adolescents are so often described in terms of crisis. How could either live up to so many different expectations? And yet the United States endures as one of the strongest nations in the world. One cannot help but think we are doing something right. Perhaps some credit should go to young people themselves.

The Deliberative Impulse

High schools and the teenagers who inhabit them are far more complex than many people believe. The high school helped create teenagers, and the new idea of the American teenager helped transform the high school into the dominant comprehensive form that still exists today. Moreover, the high school is more community-like than is often realized, and teenagers are far more political than they are given credit for. These assertions have been true since the 1960s. As I argued in chapter 1, it is also true that the world in which teenagers have been becoming adults over the past half century has been changing a great deal. Understanding how some young adults at seven American high schools have adapted their political and civic attitudes to this changing world is the purpose of this book. Given this goal, how does one find a way to track and explore this adaptation?

A political scientist might go about this project through an analysis of survey responses given annually or periodically by young people. A cultural critic could explore the evolution of popular culture and fashion for clues. And a sociologist might track changes in school organizations, economic indices, and family structure. As a rhetorical scholar, I prefer to look at discourse—what young people have to say for themselves about their under-standings of democratic engagement. Using this method, one immediately confronts the popular assumption that young people do not talk about politics. This, I believe, is an erroneous assumption. While not all young people seem eager to talk politics, plenty of them find such matters worth their attention. They may not discuss the topic in obvious ways, but if one pays close attention one can find ample discussions of political and civic matters. Indeed, many young people have what might be understood as a deliberative impulse—a natural desire to discuss and debate the important issues of the day. These deliberations may be informal; they may even be in need of a good class on rhetoric and argumentation. They are, however, real attempts of teenagers to struggle with one another about issues relevant to their public lives. From classroom discussions to the messages on their T-shirts, American youth are very much engaged in many forms of demo-cratic deliberation.

One common site where some young people debate political and civic issues is the high school newspaper. Mainstream news media has been understood in recent years as mediated deliberation, and high school newspapers should be no exception to this conceptualization.[42] In fact, the less formal structure of high school newspapers makes them all the more deliberative, and they are perhaps the only place to find teenagers talking about democratic engagement across time. As the nonpartisan Freedom Forum noted in its book about high school journalism in the early 1990s,

> For in the absence of any other vehicle, the high school newspaper offers the voice of America's young people within their own time: It chronicles the condition of scholastic life: the hopes, fears, and gripes of students, their victories and their failures, and the teen-driven triage that determines who is 'in' and 'out' or just plain overlooked. From the magnificent to the murky and the mundane, the newspapers that serve the nation's high schools and their students form a touchstone, interpreting and connecting a generation that most often is overlooked by the professional media.[43]

More than chronicling school experience, high school newspapers also record the larger democratic deliberation of American youth. In the pages of these newspapers, one indeed finds the magnificent and the mundane hopes and gripes of young adults. Unfortunately, these rhetorical struggles are rarely taken seriously by scholars.

While high school newspapers are most assuredly overseen by at least one teacher/advisor, the intriguing aspect of these newspapers is that they are a site where students communicate attitudes and beliefs about democratic engagement directly to their peers. Furthermore, while many high school newspapers may attempt to model themselves after national newspapers, they lack the resources and, more importantly, the highly practiced routines of the modern press. Instead, one finds articles in high school newspapers to be quite fresh and spontaneous—personal narratives and testimonials about how young people view the political process and their civic responsibilities. It is for these reasons of transparency that I have chosen high school newspapers as my database in this study.

While there have been a number of instructional books written about high school journalism,[44] every high school deals with its student newspaper in its own way. Perhaps one of the most troubling aspects of high school journalism across the country is how inconsistently schools view its importance. This inconsistency can be seen in three ways. First, journalism programs are often some of the first courses to be cut during budgeting crises. In the comprehensive high school model described above, schools and school districts are constantly renegotiating what courses and activities to include and which to eliminate. As journalism courses are often seen as electives, they often struggle for administrative support. In their work on the First Amendment in civic education, one group of scholars argued in 2008 that "student journalism has yet to become a fixture in the high school curriculum in most schools. . . . Moreover, among the schools that do not offer a student newspaper, as many as 40 percent have dropped their student paper within the last five years."[45] Second, even in schools where journalism courses are taught, there is little consistency in the treatment of such courses. According to a Freedom Forum survey in the early 1990s, 69 percent of schools with a journalism course treated it as either a general or language arts elective. Just over 13 percent required journalism as part of their larger English curricula, and almost 14 percent gave no credit for it at all, essentially conceptualizing journalism as an extracurricular activity. Third, there is great variance from school to school with regard to who teaches journalism classes and advises student newspapers. In fact, many newspaper advisors are not trained in journalism. As a 1991 survey of advisors revealed, over 43 percent of respondents acknowledged that their first consideration of newspaper advising occurred only after they were assigned the job by an administrator.[46] Given administrative ambivalence and underprepared teachers, high school newspapers survive, at best, through the democratic tradition in education and the energy of a few teachers and students.

My point in highlighting the inconsistent attitudes toward high school journalism generally and student newspapers specifically is not to lament the loss of these newspapers (as I write this, the entire American newspaper industry is fighting for survival against the Internet) or to admonish school administrators (most of whom, I believe, are doing the best they can under numerous institutional and societal pressures). Rather, the point is to show how fluid the standards and norms of most high school newspapers can be. Because my goal in this study is to read high school newspapers for what they reveal about the democratic imagination of the American youth writing in them, revealing such ambivalent attitudes is simply to show that student newspapers are far less institutionalized and professionalized than their elder models. This is not to say, however, that student journalists are running amok in American high schools.

It is worth noting the two major cases that have dealt with censorship in high schools over the past forty-five years. The first involved three students in a Des Moines, Iowa, school who were suspended for wearing black armbands to protest the Vietnam War. The 1969 case, *Tinker v. Des Moines Independent Community School District*, was decided in favor of the students, granting them full First Amendment rights. In its ruling on the case, the U.S. Supreme Court pointed out, "It can hardly be argued that either students or teachers shed their constitutional right to freedom of speech or expression at the schoolhouse gate."[47] In 1988, the Supreme Court offered a different verdict in *Hazelwood School District v. Kuhlmeier.* Although its ruling gave school administrators greater power to censor school-sponsored publications, the court was careful to add that this censorship did not apply to publications that were "public forums of student expression."[48] While requiring school officials to show educationally related cause for censoring any student publication, the ruling has widely been interpreted as allowing schools a great deal of latitude. In addition to these federal cases, a number of states, including Kansas and Massachusetts, have passed laws giving student publications greater freedom. While some argue that high school newspapers are still overly censored by administrators and self-censored by the students themselves,[49] there is plenty of counterevidence that much depends on the individual schools and their administrations. As journalism professor Thomas Dickson has noted, about 79 percent of newspaper advisors and 73 percent of student editors questioned in 1992 claimed that an advisor had never told an editor that he or she could not run a story, and over 60 percent of these respondents acknowledged that administrators do not read the newspaper before it is printed and distributed.[50]

Even if students are given some freedom in their journalistic endeavors, it would be misleading to suggest they are not aware of their potential readers. Unlike writing in a diary or on an anonymous blog, student journalists would be aware of their writing being made public in a school newspaper, where school administrators, teachers, and even parents might read it. The school newspaper does not, therefore, represent the innermost secrets and desires of young adults. It represents what these young people believe is acceptable to discuss in an open, public forum targeted primarily at their peers. The news that finds its way into high school newspapers is primarily a product of what young people want to say about the world around them, written within the social and institutional norms they are still in the process of learning. Being aware of what is and is not appropriate in a public discussion of political and civic concerns is part of the democratic process itself.

Although high school newspapers offer a consistent, longitudinal forum for young adults to discuss their civic and political concerns, not all high school students work as student journalists or submit articles and editorials to their school newspaper. Whether run as an elective course or extracurricular activity, most high school newspapers are staffed by self-selecting students. A student might join her newspaper staff for any number of reasons. She might have a real interest in writing and journalism, whereas another student might join so that he can spend more time with a friend or favorite teacher. Moreover, Jack Dvorak, one of very few scholars who study high school journalism, has found that the recruitment methods used to put together a publication staff range from choosing students through an application process to an advisor picking students he or she knows. Among the students who do join their school's newspaper, there is also evidence that minority students are slightly underrepresented.[51] Given the self-selecting nature of high school journalists and the racial disparity on publication staffs, it is not possible to argue that the students writing for this study's seven high school newspapers are representative of the entire student body in their respective schools. Such a limitation does not, however, reduce the importance of the students whose words do appear in this book.

High school journalists are an important subset of American youth for two reasons. First, they are keenly aware of their primary audience. As much as these young journalists might be trying to follow professional news norms, they are also teenagers who want to fit in with their peers. What they choose to write about and how they craft their stories are both going to be influenced by what they imagine their peers would find acceptable. Perhaps even more so than other students, a high school journalist has to be aware of his peers as a group with shared cultural norms and ideas. So although high school journalists may not be statistically representative of youth writ large, they do reflect the primary audience to whom they are writing.

The second reason high school journalists are important is that there is evidence to suggest these students may grow up to be information leaders and more involved citizens. One recent study, for instance, found that students who worked on their school newspaper or yearbook earned higher grades in their final year of high school, had higher overall grade point averages, and scored higher on the ACT assessment test than did students who did not participate in these activities. This trend was recorded as early as 1987.[52] In addition to receiving higher grades, high school journalists are "significantly more likely to be extremely or very interested in following news and current events" than their peers.[53] They are also, as noted in a 2008 report prepared for the Newspaper Association of America Foundation, "decidedly more active in student government, special interest clubs, dramatic and theater troupes, religious groups and political organizations than their non-journalism counterparts."[54] After high school, these student journalists go on to earn better grades in their freshman year of college and are more likely to choose a communications major (e.g., journalism, advertising, etc.).[55] As this research demonstrates, high school journalists are more likely to do better in school, more interested in current affairs, more connected to other groups or activities, and more likely to work in a communication-related field. The students in this study are, that is, more likely to have better political knowledge and greater social capital. They are also more likely to try to influence the political and civic attitudes of their peers, both in high school and in adulthood.

In focusing on high school newspapers, this book offers an alternative to the two dominant types of studies conducted by those concerned with American youth and their political lives—social scientific survey research of representative samples and ethnographic studies of a particular group of young adults situated at one point in time. Instead of taking either of these approaches, this book employs an analysis of seven high school newspapers produced over forty-five years to reveal the influence of social and cultural changes on the democratic lives of successive generations of students writing in these papers. Paying attention to what these young adults have been saying about the political world around them and how it has changed helps us understand how a young citizen today might come to imagine democracy and learn the norms of democratic engagement differently than her predecessors did.

Understanding these differences is important for anyone who wants to understand how the American democracy got where it is and how it might be made stronger in the future. If one seeks to pay attention to the nation's most democratically engaged young citizens as they articulate the behaviors and norms of civic and political participation they have learned, America's young journalists are obviously an important group to consider. And if one cares to understand how these student journalists represent the political world to one another and their peers, then high school newspapers are the place to look.

Reading High School Newspapers

In assessing what American youth have to say about the democracy they are socialized into, I have sought primarily to offer a historical perspective through the words of young adults themselves. Because the high school newspaper offers a natural site of youth political deliberation within a consistent framework, I chose to focus on seven high school newspapers across the United States. The selection of newspapers was limited in five ways. Each newspaper had to be from a public high school, have been in continuous publication since 1965, have an available archived collection of its issues, and represent a school currently located in a metropolitan area. The final criterion was that the seven schools be regionally diverse. In deciding that each school must be public and located in a metropolitan area, I admittedly excluded private schools and rural locations. As almost 90 percent of young people attend public schools and over 80 percent of Americans live in areas defined by the U.S. Census Bureau as metropolitan,[56] these criteria allow this study to look into the democratic lives of students who resemble the vast majority of American youth.

The following seven schools and newspapers fit these guidelines and are the core subject of the remainder of this book. Finding these seven schools proved more difficult than I initially imagined. Of the hundreds of schools I tried contacting that had been open since at least 1965, those that actually returned my phone calls or e-mail inquiries often reported at least one of three problems. Many schools, including my alma mater, had stopped producing a newspaper in recent years. Other schools had temporarily ceased to produce their newspaper in various years due to financial concerns or the lack of a willing advisor. Still other schools reported having no archive, either because it was lost or because one had never even been started.

Eventually, I did begin to find schools that fit the research design, starting with Pittsburgh's Carrick High School. From that point forward, after identifying each new school, I adjusted further searches for archives with regard to regional variation. The region in which it proved most difficult to find a representative newspaper was the Deep South. Given that I attended high school in the suburbs outside Atlanta, Georgia, this was personally frustrating. Eventually, I had to hope that the southern political flavor I found in Washington, D.C., and Houston, Texas, would suffice. After six months of searching and several failed trips to schools whose newspaper advisors had erroneously promised far more than was actually available, I settled on the following seven locations.

Oak Park High School is one of four high schools in the North Kansas City School District. It is located less than twenty minutes north of downtown Kansas City, Missouri, in a middle-class suburb of ranch houses where the median family income is currently just under $50,000. The school opened in the fall of 1965 and began publishing its newspaper, *Northmen's Log*, within a month. Oak Park High's attendance has, following the norm for many of the schools in this study, declined over the years, from a high of 2,450 students in 1969[57] to 1,530 in 2009, the same year the district's fourth high school was opened to help deal with overcrowding. Much like the surrounding area, the school is overwhelmingly made up of white students. While there is no reliable data on the school's racial composition during the early years of this study, *Northmen's Log* contained no obvious images of minorities until the late 1970s, and one civil rights report showed that in 1977 the entire North Kansas City School District served only 105 black students out of a total student population of 20,338.[58] In more recent years for which reliable data is available, it is clear that Oak Park High has continued to have a largely white student population. In 1991, 92 percent of the 1,857 students were white, with the remaining students being African American, Hispanic, Asian, and American Indian.[59] It was not until a new school opened in the 2008–9 school year that the student population changed. Following the drawing of new school boundaries, Oak Park High's student population dropped to 78 percent white, with African American students increasing to 10 percent and Hispanic students to 9 percent. The Oak Park students—or "Oakies," as they are called—are therefore the most homogenous group of students throughout the forty-five years of this study. Moreover, unlike most of the newspapers in the study, *Northmen's Log* seems to have made no major changes to its format over its more than forty-year history. It has consistently published twelve to thirteen issues per year, never sacrificing its quality.

Washington High School, which opened its doors in the fall of 1955, is located just north of Phoenix, Arizona, in the working-class suburb of Glendale. The neighborhoods around the school are the second poorest of the seven locations covered in this study. While the school's population topped more than 2,200 students in 1971, that number declined to 1,204 students before increasing again to its current enrollment of 1,616. Much like Kansas City's Oak Park High, Washington High School was predominantly white during the early years of this study, and it remained so in 1991 (again the earliest year of reliable data), when the school was over 80 percent white. In more recent years, however, Washington High has become a minority-majority school. Fifty-five percent of the student population was Hispanic by 2008, with white students dropping to 25 percent and African American students composing 11 percent. The remainder of the students are identified as "more than one race," Asian, or American Indian. These numbers represent a dramatic overall change in the student population. The *Rampage*, the title of which has undergone three variations, began in 1955 as the *Ram Page* and has been published continuously since that time. Over the years of this study, the *Rampage*'s biggest change has been with regard to its publishing frequency. While the students consistently publish about sixty pages per year, the number of issues declined from sixteen in 1970–71 to just four in 2001–2. More recently, the school began publishing six issues a year, and *Rampage* was even named one of the top three high school newspapers in the state by the Arizona State Interscholastic Press Association in 2008.

With a median annual household income of almost $100,000, Newton South High School, which opened in 1950, is the wealthiest of all the schools in this study. Located in Newton Centre, Massachusetts, just three miles from Boston College, Newton South High feels more like a college campus than a high school, and with approximately 90 percent of recent graduating seniors continuing on to four-year colleges each year, this impression seems appropriate. Although the students have always been predominantly white and remain so today (at approximately 70 percent), the school also now has the largest population of Asian students (around 17 percent) in this study. These recent numbers reflect a slight shift from two decades earlier, when the student population was 82 percent white and 10 percent Asian. While solid data is not available, the school's newspaper, the *Denebola*, reveals a serious concern about racial tensions in the earliest years of this study, although it does not show a great deal of diversity. By 1968, the student editorial board of the paper was already urging "that a mandatory unit on black history be included as part of the United

States History or Contemporary Society course."[60] In 1970, the paper was reporting racial tensions in the school, noting that "the thirty-nine blacks at Newton High are, more than anyone else, conscious of the fact that they are a minority."[61] While the students at Newton South High may have been mostly white throughout the years, they have always seemed aware of the minority students at their school. Moreover, as the student population has grown—from 1,400 students in 1983 to 1,761 today—so too has the *Denebola*. During the 1966–67 school year, the *Denebola* published 66 pages. In 1970–71, it almost doubled to 114 pages before nearly doubling in size again to 198 pages in 1998–99. The final edition of 2005 had the same dimensions as the *New York Times* and was a full 60 pages long. The *Denebola*, which has been published since 1950, is the most professional-looking newspaper in this study. It currently even has its own website, www.denebolaonline.net.

Woodrow Wilson Senior High School is one of two schools in this study that have multiple security guards and a metal detector at their only unlocked entrance. Located in Washington, D.C., just four miles northwest of the White House, the school is also one of three minority-majority schools in the study. Over 50 percent of the current students are African American—a major increase from the predominantly white student base of the late 1960s. This racial shift was largely a result of aggressive integration in the 1960s and 1970s. As reported in its newspaper, the *Beacon*, in October 1980, Wilson High went from being 99 percent white in 1955 to 17 percent white in 1980, with white students composing 25 percent of the student body in 2008. Indeed, the school appears to have been largely integrated by the early years of this study, as evidenced in the *Beacon*. By the spring of 1970, racial strife could be detected when "about 400 students (practically all black) assembled in the auditorium" to protest school inequality.[62] In December of that year, the paper referred to Wilson High as "an integrated school, an unusual, precious, fragile organism, attacked from many sides."[63] Wilson High's economic makeup is, moreover, deceiving to any passersby. While the surrounding, mostly white neighborhood has a median family income of over $80,000, the school's students come from the poorer surrounding neighborhoods. As more and more students have chosen to take advantage of the district's out-of-boundary enrollment options over the past decade, the wealthier families have pulled their children out of the increasingly troubled school. The *Beacon* has suffered along with Wilson High, as the newspaper's quality and frequency have declined in recent years. With all that the school's students must contend with in their lives, this seems understandable.

Used as the filming location for the 1998 independent film *Rushmore,* Mirabeau B. Lamar High School is located inside the loop near downtown Houston, Texas. While the school had 2,040 students in 1967, it has become overcrowded today with more than 3,000 students, making it the largest high school in the Houston Independent School District (and in this study). Lamar High School is also the most diverse school in this study. In 2008, the student population was 34 percent Hispanic, 34 percent white, and 27 percent African American—numbers consistent with those reported in 1991. Thus, no ethnic group makes up a majority. This was not always the case at Lamar High, where Houston was still fighting desegregation in 1965.[64] Exact numbers for the late 1960s are impossible to calculate since the district counted Hispanic students as white through 1970,[65] but the school's newspaper, the *Lancer,* presents images of only white students in those early years. However, change seemed to happen quickly. In February 1972, an African American male graced the cover of the *Lancer,* and six out of twelve class officers were African American as of spring 1974.[66] The student population today is, moreover, made up of middle-class students, with 37 percent on the school's reduced-cost lunch program. Lamar High School's newspaper took a decidedly downward turn in the mid-1990s and was abandoned altogether in 2000. In its place, the school began publishing a quarterly news magazine, *Lamar Life,* in full, glossy color. Published four times a year, the new *Lamar Life* resembles a strange blending of *Newsweek* and *Teen Vogue.*

Carrick High School is located just a few miles south of downtown Pittsburgh, Pennsylvania, up a long, winding road through a poor, working-class neighborhood befitting the city's steel town image. The school fits in well. With a median family income of less than $30,000 a year, its student population is the poorest in this study. It is also the smallest. All of the approximately one thousand students must walk through one of two metal detectors located at the front entrance—the only doors open during the school day—which is where one can also find the security office with its camera-monitoring station and three security guards. While Carrick High was integrated by 1965, it has slowly but increasingly become more racially balanced over the years between white and African American students. In 1976, black students made up 13.1 percent of the student body.[67] In 1991, they composed 21 percent and in 2008 had reached 39 percent of all students. Given the racial division, it is little wonder that there have been a number of racial incidents over the years, and school violence seems to be the norm. During my visit to Carrick High, a fight broke out in the library, and I was told that teachers routinely had to rush to stairwells between each class period for the safety of the students. With all of this to worry about, I was surprised to find that the school's newspaper, *Carrickulum*, was going through a resurgence of sorts as a new, young advisor seemed to be breathing life into it. Given that the paper's quality and production had been sporadic over the previous two decades, this new attention was much needed.

Built in 1924, Ulysses S. Grant High School in Portland, Oregon, is the oldest school in this study. Grant High looks like it belongs in Portland; the large, faded-brick building is decidedly practical, which is probably one reason it was chosen as the filming location for *Mr. Holland's Opus* in 1995. With a student population that has fluctuated between 1,500 and 1,800 students in the past few decades, it is currently the largest school in Portland with 1,553 students. The racial makeup of Grant High has been rather consistent over the past forty-five years, as the school was integrated by 1965 and was located in an African American area of Portland. By 1976, the student body was 31 percent African American.[68] In 1991, the school's African American population had dropped slightly to 27 percent before dipping again in 1998 to 23 percent. Asian students have been the third-largest group, accounting for around 6–7 percent of the overall student body. While it is not unusual to see faculty advisors to high school newspapers come and go with some frequency, Grant High's *Grantonian* is the exception in that it has had only three advisors between 1965 and 2010. The paper has therefore remained consistently strong throughout the years of this study, producing more than ten issues and one hundred pages every year. More recently, the school took a different direction with its news publication: as of fall 2011, it now publishes *Grant Magazine*, which can be accessed online at www.thegrantmag.com.

While all are comprehensive and located in metropolitan areas, the high schools in this study have a number of intriguing differences. In terms of economic makeup, it is hard to imagine two metropolitan schools being more different than Pittsburgh's Carrick High and Boston's Newton South High. From the quality of school resources to the clothes on students' backs, the divide between working-class life for Carrick's students and the upper-middle-class life of Newton South's students could not be more apparent. The seven schools also offer a great degree of racial diversity, which has been fairly consistent in five of them. Phoenix's Washington High and Houston's Lamar High are the two exceptions, but even Lamar seems to have been quickly integrated in the early 1970s at levels that have remained fairly consistent since then. In terms of the racial differences, Wilson High, Lamar, and Carrick all have large numbers of African American students, and Lamar and Washington have sizable Hispanic populations. Politically, Newton South and Grant High students appeared more liberal, as one might expect from liberal-leaning coastal states, while Oak Park High and Washington students seemed, in general, more conservative. Given these differences, finding similarities in the ways students from most or all of these schools write about political and civic matters would suggest these similarities reflect the ways social and cultural changes that transcend local differences have influenced the norms of democratic engagement learned by these young people.

In the spring of 2005, I traveled to each of the seven high schools in this study armed with a digital camera, taking individual photographs of every page of every available issue between fall 1965 and spring 2005. The more than sixteen thousand photos were subsequently uploaded and organized into a digital archive. Since then, this archived database has been supplemented with additional campus visits and access to the online versions of several of the high school newspapers through the spring of 2010.

I read these newspapers in an attempt to understand how the students themselves have deliberated about the political and civic problems in their lives and to understand how their attitudes and assumptions about democratic engagement have changed over the past five decades. In working through this large archive, I focused my attention on textual changes that revealed themselves over time in all of the newspapers, admittedly sacrificing the exceptional for the normative. Additionally, I was guided by two basic assumptions that have already been discussed above: (1) democratic engagement has, instead of increasing or declining, simply and obviously changed, and (2) such changes are detectable through a textual analysis of the ways in which young people write about politics and community. These assumptions led me to ask rather open questions. Instead of asking, for example, why young people vote at such anemic rates in local elections, I asked where the young people in this study locate community. Instead of asking whether young people feel more or less politically efficacious, I asked where these young adults find political power. As an alternative to asking whether American youth are more or less cynical, I asked where these young journalists seem to get their political attitudes. And as an alternative to measuring their social capital, I asked who these young people identify with in their communities. Such open questions are, I believe, more fundamental to an honest reassessment of how democratic engagement has been changing in the United States over the last half century. While not everything I discovered may be seen as positive for democracy, much of it does counter many widely held assumptions about young adults, and I believe all of it makes sense within the larger cultural forces that have influenced how the country's youth come to understand their civic and political lives.

Conclusion

As adults, we too often dismiss the importance and complexity of teenagers and the primary world they inhabit—the American public high school. Teenagers are too often viewed as either too apathetic or too hyperbolical, too listless or too spastic. We deride their cultural tastes as trivial and belittle their utopian ideals as silly. American public high schools, too, are understood to be of little consequence. We complain that these schools are failing our youth and then get angry when they have the gall to give our children failing grades. We often point to inept teachers and outdated teaching materials as the source of the problem, but then we scoff at the idea of allotting more of our tax dollars for a system that does no good to begin with. We love our children but could do without teenagers; we love the idea of education but care little for schools.

As researchers, we too often cling to traditional forms of thought because these are our institutional and disciplinary norms. We measure the way things are today against the way things were before. When it comes to scientific advances, we often think of past achievements as antiquated in comparison to present ones. Who today can look back at a Commodore 64 without feeling at least a tinge of amusement at its green screen and 64 kilobytes of RAM, in contrast to new, sleek iPhones with color touch screens and 32 gigabytes of memory? And who will look back at the previous question twenty years hence and not smile? When it comes to traditional mores, we too often seem to take the opposite tack. We look at the playful, political irony that youth find so appealing and define it as cynicism, and we find the unwillingness of young people to align themselves with one religious sect or another as a loss of value. Whether we see more or less, we are always finding that today does not measure up to yesterday, and the fact that we often misremember the way things used to be is too often of little consequence.

Dismissing American youth and clinging to old notions of democratic engagement will not do. If we are to take the health of our democracy seriously, we must take American youth seriously on their own terms. The path ahead, then, requires that we begin to listen to what some of these young people have been saying about their political and civic attitudes as they have been learning them. As John Dewey reminds us,

> We are born organic beings associated with others, but we are not born members of a community. . . . Everything which is distinctively human is learned, not native, even though it could not be learned without native structures which mark man off from other animals. To learn in a human way and to human effect is not just to acquire added skill through refinement of original capacities. To learn to be human is to develop through the give-and-take of communication an effective sense of being an individually distinctive member of a community; one who understands and appreciates its beliefs, desires and methods, and who contributes to a further conversion of organic powers into human resources and values.[69]

As democracy is most certainly distinctively human, we need to do a better job of understanding what our young people have been learning. And as democracy is something that must not simply be known but also practiced, we must pay attention to what young people have been adding to the conversation. The following chapters begin the process of paying close attention to what some of America's more democratically inclined youth have to say about democracy and how this talk has changed over time.

3

DISLOCATED COSMOPOLITANS

In January 1845, the U.S. Congress decided to officially mandate a federal Election Day. Following the well-established tradition of early November voting, and seeking to avoid any conflict with the Catholic Church's observance of All Saints' Day each November 1, Congress devised the simple formula that the presidential election was to be held on the first Tuesday following the first Monday in November during even-numbered years. This formula was extended to elections of members of the House of Representatives in March 1875 and to the U.S. Senate in 1913. Since then, most states have moved their statewide elections to coincide with Election Day. At the time of this writing, forty-five of the fifty U.S. state governors are elected during federal elections. Every other year, then, the American people are asked to cast ballots in early November for candidates ranging from the president of the United States to local state representatives.

While Election Day may be an institutional norm, not all election days are equal. There is a rather sharp difference between the election in which the U.S. president is chosen and those in which he is not. The disparity is one of voter turnout. Fewer people cast ballots during nonpresidential general elections than presidential general elections. While this gap in voter turnout has been the norm for almost a century now, it has widened in recent years. Using an admittedly crude formula for calculating the difference in voter turnout percentage in a nonpresidential general election versus the succeeding presidential general election, fig. 1 shows the steady increase in this disparity. Comparing the difference in voter turnout in the 1966 and 1968 elections to that in 2006 and 2008, we can see that in the past forty years the gap has almost doubled, from 12.8 percent (48.7 percent in 1966; 61.5 percent in 1968) to 21 percent (41.3 percent in 2006; 62.3 percent in 2008). The comparable data from the mid-1930s and mid-1940s reveal that the difference between the two types of general elections fluctuated from around 11 to 12 percent, making the most recent figures all the more startling. Simply put, the American people seem increasingly reluctant to vote during nonpresidential elections.

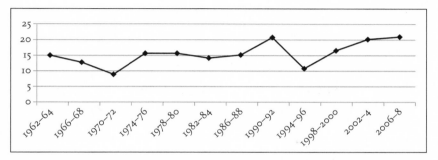

Fig. 1   The difference in VEP turnout (%) for presidential versus nonpresidential general elections, 1962–2008

SOURCE: National data from 1962 to 2000 come from Michael P. McDonald and Samuel L. Popkin, "The Myth of the Vanishing Voter," *American Political Science Review* 95, no. 4 (2001): 963–74. For national data between 2002 and 2008, see Michael P. McDonald, "Voter Turnout," *United States Elections Project* (blog), http://elections.gmu.edu/voter_turnout.htm.

Like most issues related to voting in the United States, the voter turnout disparity between presidential and nonpresidential general elections is even more alarming among younger Americans. Among the voting-eligible population (VEP) of eighteen- to twenty- nine-year-olds, the difference was 26.5 percent between 2002 (22.5 percent)[1] and 2004 (49 percent)[2] and 25.6 percent between 2006 (25.5 percent) and 2008 (51.1 percent). Although any number of factors influence voter turnout in any individual election (e.g., particular candidates, economic factors, etc.), the voter turnout data reveal clearly that while roughly half of eligible younger Americans vote during presidential elections, only a quarter of them can be bothered to vote during nonpresidential elections. That is, 75 percent of eligible American voters between the ages of eighteen and twenty-nine do not cast ballots for their U.S. senators and representatives or for their state governors and congresspersons. In a republic founded on the idea of political represen-tation, such numbers should be cause for serious alarm. So why are the numbers what they are to begin with? While others might point to cam-paign funding that benefits the presidential contest or to an increasing belief that people's nomadic lives keep them from establishing local roots, I point to a more fundamental problem facing local politics: people, especially young people, simply do not view local and statewide politics as particularly pertinent to their lives.

To answer the above question, in this chapter I investigate what commu-nities young people in the United States identify with and how these iden-tifications changed across the five decades of this study. Specifically, I ask the following questions: Where do the young people writing for their high school newspapers locate their political communities? With what different types of community do they identify? How have their community identifications changed across time? By looking closely at where the young people in this study locate community, I show the discursive changes in community identification that have emerged as they adapted to an increasingly globalized world. These shifts make sense, I argue, in light of the postmodern globalization that has taken place over the last fifty or sixty years. These young people are, quite simply, responding to their changing world. In the end, I argue that the shifts in where young people locate their primary political communities may be both good (in the benefits of cosmopolitan attitudes) and bad (in the dangers of too much distance for democratic engagement).

Community and Identity

Questions about democracy and its size are as old as democratic thought. Both Plato and Aristotle grappled with this issue and offered fairly similar answers. In his rather precise calculation, Plato offered a firm number of 5,040 citizen-farmers and their families and slaves as the optimal population for a democratic community.[3] Reluctant to be so specific, Aristotle suggested there must be a limit in population size for effective democratic government: "Most people think that if a state is to be happy it has to be great, . . . but they do not know how to judge greatness and smallness in a state." Aristotle's implication is obvious—size does not equal greatness when it comes to democracy. To make this point clearer, Aristotle ultimately argued,

> The activities of a state are those of the rulers and those of the ruled, and the functions of the ruler are decision and direction. In order to give decisions on matters of justice, and for the purpose of distributing offices on merit, it is necessary that the citizens should know each other and know what kind of people they are. Where this condition does not exist, both decisions and appointments of office are bound to suffer, because it is not just in either of these matters to proceed haphazardly, which is clearly what does happen where the population is excessive.[4]

According to Aristotle, the larger the population the more chaotic and disorganized politics becomes. Quality and quantity are in reverse proportion to each other.

However, with the advancement of agriculture and medicine over the centuries since Aristotle's time, the world's quantity could not be so easily limited. Faced with the age-old problem of democracy and size in the New World, the American founders decided upon a federal republic and a system of representation. As Benedict Anderson has pointed out, the very idea of the federal republic would not have been truly possible without the changes of the seventeenth and eighteenth centuries that led to the very formation of the nation-state. By the time the founders sat down to form their new government, however, several changes (e.g., cultural, economical, and communicative) had drastically enlarged the possible scope, both in land mass and in population, of a democratically based society.[5] To adapt democracy to the growth in population and to allay the concerns of many "antifederalists" who feared a king-like president and an overly strong federal government, the members of the Constitutional Convention devised a system of representation. Championed by the Federalist Alexander Hamilton, the representative system not only overcame the problem of a large population but literally turned the growing population into a democratic asset. As Hamilton wrote in Federalist Paper 10, "As each representative will be chosen by a greater number of citizens in the large than in the small republic, it will be more difficult for unworthy candidates to practice with success the vicious arts by which elections are too often carried."[6] Regardless of whether Hamilton's optimistic argument has always been true, he and the other Federalists won the day, and the American federal republic was born on the back of the representative system. Over the next two centuries, the United States continued to grow and, with the exception of the Civil War, was able to sustain its growth while maintaining the democratic republican model of federal government.

Despite the representative system, political scientists today continue to grapple with the issue of democracy and size. In a nation whose population has more than quadrupled in just over one hundred years, from 76 million in 1900 to an estimated 310 million in 2010, it is little wonder that size is often seen as one of the most difficult hurdles to a more engaged democratic society. Writing in the mid-1920s and contemplating the democratic thought of earlier times, American philosopher John Dewey remarked that "the notion of maintaining a unified state, even nominally self-governing, over a country as extended as the United States and consisting of a large and racially diversified population would have seemed the wildest of fancies."[7] Dewey did not believe that the "unified state" was being maintained particularly well in the early part of the twentieth century. He argued that the strengthening of such an expansive and populous nation required a flourishing network of local communities where face-to-face communication was the primary mode of democratic engagement. Similarly, Robert Dahl, speaking to the American Political Science Association in 1967, argued, "The evidence seems to me to support the conclusion that the all-round optimum size for a contemporary American city is probably somewhere between 50,000 and 200,000, which, even taking the larger figure, may be within the threshold for wide civic participation."[8] More recently, political scientist Kevin O'Leary has proposed a complete revamping of the representative system in the United States, contending that the American people have become far too many to be represented by 435 members in the House of Representatives.[9] O'Leary suggests spreading democracy downward, creating a large National Assembly and People's House. For each of the 435 members of the House, 100 people from their district would meet, in-person and virtually, to assist the representative with his or her decision making. These 43,500 individuals would, presumably, be able to connect more readily with the rest of the American people.

What Dewey, Dahl, and O'Leary have acknowledged with their emphasis on democracy and population is the belief that people will feel more politically efficacious the smaller their political community. Such reasoning follows the economic theory of democracy developed by Anthony Downs in the 1950s. According to Downs, the average person making a rational decision about voting in today's democratic societies would measure the benefits gained from casting a ballot against the amount of effort necessary to do so.[10] In most communities with large populations, the "cost" of even a simple act such as voting far outweighs the potential benefit that might be gained or the possibility that one's vote will actually influence election outcomes. Understood as a rational choice, voting is not worth the effort. Nor, perhaps, is any form of traditional political participation—writing a letter to the editor, calling an elected official, or joining in the activities of a campaign—given the size of most major metropolitan areas the American people now inhabit.

While there is certainly something to be said for size and efficacy, what these scholars have misunderstood is that in a representative system of government what matters is not only the size of the population but also how strongly one identifies with her community. No matter how small the political community, an individual may very well abstain from participating in its governance if she does not feel a sense of identification with the town and the other people who live there. By contrast, people do vote for presidential candidates in the United States today—a nation with more than 300 million people—although they live in states where the outcome of the election is known weeks in advance of actual balloting. These people surely do so because they identify with something—democratic principles, the United States of America, a political party, or even an individual candidate. We therefore need to think of identification when we think of democratic participation.

There has, perhaps, been no single word explored more thoroughly in rhetorical and political theory over the past fifty years than "identity." To study identity is to attempt to understand how an individual comes to recognize a set of characteristics shared with another person, group, or ideal. Identity is not something one is born with, although inherited bodily features can surely lend themselves to different identities later. Rather, identity is something agreed upon or forced upon people as they age. It begins with an awareness of others and is then transformed as people negotiate identities with others. Identity, that is, is a social construction. It is neither given naturally nor produced solely by the individual. As political sociologist Craig Calhoun has said, "Recognition is at the heart of the matter. . . . Identity turns on the interrelated problems of self-recognition and recognition of others."[11] Identity comes into being when one attempts to position herself in relation to others. As a result, the possibilities for identification in the late modern world are limitless. Political scientist Amy Gutmann puts it thusly: "Individuals identify in groups around their gender, race, ethnicity, nationality, class, sexual orientation, age, physical ability, and ideology."[12]

More than a simple categorization system, identity—the identification with some place or people or idea—is a prerequisite to any act of democratic engagement. Actions that are performed without the influence of collective identities, that is, are not really human actions at all. Through a shared set of characteristics, one forms beliefs that dictate how one acts. As political philosopher Kwame Anthony Appiah has summarized this idea, "What I do intentionally is dependent on what I think I am doing." What I think I am doing is, moreover, dependent upon the kind of person I think I am and the "behavior appropriate to a person of that kind."[13] One acts—or performs, in the words of Erving Goffman—through the identities with which she identifies.[14] Rhetorical scholars know this lesson well, thanks to the work of Kenneth Burke.

With regard to identity, Kenneth Burke did two things worth noting here: he rooted rhetoric in identification and showed that action comes out of an understanding of shared identification. As for the first insight, he writes, "A is not identical with his colleague, B. But insofar as their interests are joined, A is identified with B. Or he may identify himself with B even when their interests are not joined, if he assumes that they are, or is persuaded to believe so."[15] It is through this process of identification that persuasion—the ability to change one's beliefs, values, and behavior—takes place.[16] Even more important, however, is the realization that action, the result of persuasion, can only take place once an identity is constituted. As Burke puts this in *A Grammar of Motives*, people's "judgments are based upon assumptions as to what constitutes the scenic background of their acts. The quality of the situation in which we act qualifies our act—and so, behind a judgment, there lies, explicitly or implicitly, the concept of a constitution that sub-stantiates the judgment."[17] An action is the result of a judgment, which is based on a constitution. As rhetorical scholar Dana Anderson has helpfully pointed out, for Burke these constitutions can be understood as identities when discussing individuals rather than other entities.[18] Rhetorical theorist Barry Brummett summarizes Burke's notion of identification by observ-ing that, for Burke, "identification occurs when people perceive that their interests are joined, and that they share ways of thinking and valuing. This sharing is embodied in shared ways of speaking."[19] In addition to speaking, one might include action in all of its symbolic forms.

Voting, like all methods of democratic engagement, is a symbolic human action that requires identification with something. This identification may take the form, as stated above, of an ideological belief in a system or a party, a sense of association with some individual, or a feeling of connection to some place. Living in a particular place does not, however, mean that an individual will automatically identify with it. One might (as hard as it is to believe) live just off the Boston Common in the heart of Boston, Massachusetts, but read the *New York Times*, root for the New York Yankees, and prefer tomato-based clam chowder to cream-based. This does not mean that she will be uninflu-enced by her immediate surroundings, but it does suggest that she will be less likely to become politically engaged in Boston politics if she does not identify as a Bostonian. The political community with which one identifies will largely dictate *where* one acts politically, even if it does not suggest *if* one will act politically.

Over the past half century, the young journalists deliberating in their high school newspapers have written about political community in ever-larger geographical locations. While each new generation of these young adults has continued to live in towns and cities with provincial governments and local customs, they have increasingly come to identify with the political community at the national and international levels. They more often think of themselves as Americans or global citizens than as Portlanders or

Houstonians. This centrifugal expansion of political community has not been without its consequences for democratic engagement. Understanding these changes, then, is a worthwhile endeavor. Tracking where the high school students in this study have located their primary political communities over the past forty-five years illustrates the way in which these changes have occurred.

Neglecting the Local

This study looks at high school newspapers, which are designed to report the news of the schools in which they are published. As such, the school itself is the most salient political community represented in these newspapers. They deal primarily with information involving administrators, teachers, and students, and no single topic is more discussed than the recurring concern about a lack of school spirit, which is really a concern about whether students are identifying with their school. While this news is important to examine, the students' relationships to their school communities are not the focus of this chapter. I focus here on the communities in which these schools and their students are situated. Looking at these school newspapers, one quickly notices that news from outside the school makes it in as well. The object of this chapter, then, is to uncover where the young people in this study locate democratic politics.

Beginning with the most immediate political unit outside the school—the one that has been praised as the ideal since Plato and Aristotle—it becomes apparent that the young people in this study largely stopped writing about their local communities over the past five decades. This implies, of course, that these young people once did write of their more immediate geographical locations. Indeed they did. Looking back to the late 1960s and early 1970s, it is clear that young people were quite aware of the local polis.

The young people writing for their high school newspapers during that time were clearly aware of their local communities as sites of political struggle. This was especially true for local issues particularly salient to youth. When the state of Massachusetts raised the legal driving age in the late 1960s, for instance, Newton South High School's *Denebola* saw fit to publish an article on the new requirements: "Starting at the beginning of 1967, no one may obtain a driver's license until he reaches 16 ½ and then only if he has completed a classroom Drivers Ed course, in addition to six hours of on-the-road instruction and six hours of backseat observation either from his high school or an accredited driving school."[20] In the spring of 1972, the students at Wilson High School in Washington, D.C., seemed excited to report that "plans were announced to establish a Youth and Government program for the District. This program would bring an elected youth mayor, youth city council member, and youth board of education to the District Building to represent the youth of the city."[21] And the students on staff at Washington High School's *Ram Page* in Phoenix, Arizona, wrote a half-page story in 1968 on a local curfew change:

> Familiar to all is the pastime of cruising Central Avenue. Students of all schools and ages participate and often stop to indulge in sport activities such as mild riots at the various drive-ins. . . . Then came the crack-down and consequential curfew. The immediate results were evident to anyone who took a drive down the stretch of Central Avenue between Camelback and Thomas. The only source of activity is at Der Wienerschnitzel and even it is reduced to a tiny percentage of its former inhabitants. . . . In spite of strict police control of the Central Strip, certain young adult elements still cling to their haunts even though the majority of their followers are at home. Since the curfew applies mainly to minors of high school and early college age, the young adult finds himself strangely alone after curfew and heads home.[22]

These are all stories about local politics and how they immediately impact young people in these communities. Laws affect community culture, political decisions increase local opportunities, city ordinances change tradition—and each of these factors influences civic life. That the students are aware of these issues and feel the need to report them indicates their awareness of community politics.

In addition to these local youth issues, the young people in this era demonstrated an awareness of larger political issues in the cities where they lived—issues that did not have such an obvious connection to youth. Wilson High School's *Beacon* offered one such story in 1968, discussing a local community group dedicated to helping African Americans: "Eighteen months ago, Pride Inc. was a dream. Today, according to its members and its leaders, Pride has become an integral part of Washington's black community."[23] One reporter at the *Ram Page* wrote about a local hippie gathering in 1967: "The 'hippies' gathered at Tempe Beach for Phoenix's latest 'thing,' a love-in. There were no policemen in uniform, but there must have been some plainclothesmen. They could just as well have stayed home, because the love-in was exactly that—a love in."[24] And in Pittsburgh the staff of Carrick High School's *Carrickulum* reported on the mayor's 1969 conference: "The Twenty-Fourth Mayor's Highway Safety Conference was held this year, on December 8, at the William Penn Hotel with a special teen session taking place that afternoon."[25] This last example demonstrates not only young people's acknowledgement of larger issues but also local administrators' willingness to listen to youth. During the late 1960s and early 1970s, the young people represented in these newspapers were inclined to cover local political issues even if those issues were rather removed from their lives. This inclination is particularly striking given the limited amount of room allotted to news coverage in each newspaper.

Young people were also connected to their local communities through local elected officials. While many of the articles discussing local and state-wide politicians tended to focus on their visits to the school, their appearance in the school newspaper is still noteworthy. During the first decade of this study, local officials appeared in a wide array of situations:

> Gubernatorial and senatorial candidates were featured in this week's political forum series. Speaking to students were Tom McCall and Robert Duncan.[26]

> "Washington D.C. is a wondrous seat of government with many, many interesting and historical sights, but Phoenix is a wonderful place to live." This was Mr. Eldred Spain's last impression of the Nation's capital where he spent the summer in the employment of Representative John Rhodes.[27]

> Wednesday March 23rd marks the day of the election for the first non-voting Congressional delegate for D.C. The delegate will not have the right to vote on the House floor, however, he will vote in committee.[28]

> As voters would have it, Rev. Walter E. Fauntroy, Democratic candidate, overcame his opponents in a major upset, getting 58% of all votes cast in the election for nonvoting delegate for the District. His nearest adversary, John Nevius, managed to gather 25%.[29]

> George Bush, the speaker for commencement, was elected to his first term in the U.S. House of Representatives in 1966 by a five percent

margin. He was the Republican candidate for the new seventh congressional District seat in Harris County, Texas, and is the first Republican
ever to represent the county and the city of Houston.[30]

One might think that high school students reporting about political
issues and agents in their local communities is not all that striking. However,
such coverage contrasts with its overwhelming absence in subsequent
years. While local officials most surely still visit schools and deliver speeches
at important youth events, the newspapers in this study stopped considering such events newsworthy. Young people, quite simply, quit talking with
one another about their local environs as *political* communities. Although
the occasional story about a local political issue that directly affected youth
was still reported from time to time, the frequency with which such stories
appeared took a sharp downturn in the mid-1970s. Issues of broader
political importance in the local communities disappeared altogether.
Gone, too, were references to local and statewide officials, except when
the political agent had drawn national attention. The students themselves
seemed to be aware of these trends. According to a 1986 *Denebola* survey of
the students at Newton South High School, only 40 percent could correctly
identify the name of their U.S. representative from a list of choices.[31] Over
the middle years of this study, young people stopped seeing the importance
of local politics and, in some cases, lost touch with their local communities
completely.

A clear indication of the waning interest in local concerns among high
school students can be seen by simply looking at the number of published
articles on such matters. Examining *Northmen's Log*, the newspaper of Oak
Park High School in Kansas City, it is easy to detect the change over time
by comparing two school years. During the 1970–71 school year, *Northmen's
Log* published twenty-one articles discussing local and state political and
civic issues in its total ninety-six pages. These articles touched on everything from a visit from John Danforth during his failed first attempt to win
one of Missouri's U.S. Senate seats to why "voters turned down a proposed
$.85 increase in the operating levy for the NKC school district."[32] Even when
covering a traveling carnival visiting the area, one young journalist found
it normal to include information about the carnival's economic benefit for
the local community.[33] For these students, local political and civic concerns
were apparent. By contrast, the students writing for *Northmen's Log* during
the 1990–91 school year produced only ten articles on local politics despite

having ten more pages to fill. Although these articles included important issues such as the election of Kansas City's first black mayor and a proposed nearby landfill, the fact that these students published fewer than half the number of articles than their predecessors did twenty years earlier suggests a clear change in attitude about the importance of local and statewide issues.[34]

What was true of the young journalists at Oak Park High School in north Kansas City was also true of the students writing at Newton South High School just outside of Boston. Over the course of the 1970–71 school year, the *Denebola* staff published twenty-four articles on local and state politics. These articles ranged from a front-page piece about a local mayoral candidate that appeared in the year's first issue to a story about the building code problems for a local community building, which had been discussed during a town meeting.[35] Throughout the year's total 120 pages, local issues seemed a routine concern. Twenty years later, *Denebola* students could muster only thirteen articles on local and state issues despite publishing a full 180 pages during the 1990–91 school year. That is, while producing 50 percent more pages, students in the early 1990s wrote half the number of locally and state-focused articles. These articles included three pieces on the state's gubernatorial race and one on concerns about state House budget cuts.[36] In just twenty years, then, the ties of students in both Kansas City and Boston to the democratic workings of their local environs had diminished dramatically.

Nowhere is this loss of identification with local communities more obvious than in later articles bemoaning the disconnection. While infrequent, stories promoting students' reconnection with the local community are telling. For example, in *Carrickulum*, a 1988 article reported on one teacher's desire to acquaint students with their local community when, "on October 18, The Scholars 4 English classes toured Pittsburgh to familiarize themselves with some of the city's geography, history and culture."[37] According to their teacher, the students at Carrick High School needed to reconnect with their city and its long history. And even as early as 1979, reporters for *Grantonian*, the newspaper of Grant High School, found it imperative to offer their classmates a two-page spread on what the Portland area had to offer. Beneath the headline "Reporters Find Portland Does Have 'Places to Go and People to See'" were brief articles on local cruising, Portland's disco scene, skiing, and how to have fun in the city on little money.[38] In both of these instances, the attempts to get readers to take notice of their cities indicates that a few students were keenly aware that their peers had already lost touch with local circumstances.

In terms of local politics, matters seem even worse. One recent article from Newton South High School's *Denebola* reflects the common sentiment among the few young people who would like their peers to pay more attention to their local government. The editorial, written by the paper's senior staff, begins with the admission that "comparatively few students pay attention to local politics and the workings of the municipal government." The editorial then goes on to describe some of the issues and the candidates included on the local ballot for mayor, aldermen, and the school committee. To make the issues even more salient to their peers, the senior staff offers the following argument: "Especially now, when Newton must address the [Newton North High School] construction, the turf fields at South, and other issues of health care and economy, the upcoming election is of vital importance. The School Committee elections in particular will touch students, since the Committee is responsible for policies that have direct effects on the schools and their policies. The mayoral and alderman elections will also affect students, indirectly through tax and housing policies, as well as city laws and regulations." Having laid out several reasons for why readers should feel a personal connection to local politics, the editorial then makes one final appeal to "encourage students to appreciate the democratic election process." The senior staff argues, "Not all cities have completely elective processes for legislative bodies or educational boards, and Newton residents should realize and make the most of their opportunity to directly elect representatives."[39] That these young editorialists worked so hard to urge their peers to pay attention to local politics suggests they were under the impression that their peers did not. Given the rest of the evidence presented thus far in this chapter, their assumption seems to have been correct.

In short, while the city-state polis may be the democratic ideal, it no longer attracted the attention of the high school journalists in this study. It has not piqued their interest for several decades now. From Washington, D.C., and Boston to Phoenix and Portland, these young adults decided that local initiatives, city government officials, and community problems were not worth their time or energy. But to assume they quit paying attention to politics altogether would be a mistake. Instead, the time they might have spent on local politics was given over to other political arenas. Increasingly, the American youth in this study turned their attention to national politics.

Focus on the Nation

Standing in front of the Virginia legislature on June 5, 1788, Patrick Henry—the very same man who once roused an audience to war with his now infamous declaration on liberty and death—questioned the legitimacy of the new federal government. As Henry put it with his gift for the rhetorical flourish, "The question turns, sir, on that poor little thing—the expression, We, the *people*, instead of the *states*, of America." Henry's primary concern was that the federal government's power was sure to supersede that of the states, and that the newly established presidency would reign supreme. Henry went so far as to exclaim, "Away with your President! we shall have a king."[40] For Henry, the better system was to keep the locus of power, and by extension the people themselves, rooted within smaller and more controllable states. Henry, in the end, lost this argument.

By contrast, the Federalists feared factions, perhaps more than anything else. Given the large size of the new United States, the Federalists had to argue that it was not too large for one centralized government. They also had to bring together newly liberated peoples under the new banner of the nation. To do so, the Federalists needed people to connect with the country, and this meant getting them to think outside their local communities. This was the point made by President George Washington (with the help of James Madison and Alexander Hamilton) when, eight years after Patrick Henry's speech, he celebrated the federal government in his farewell address: "Citizens, by birth or choice, of a common country, that country has a right to concentrate your affections. The name of American, which belongs to you in your national capacity, must always exalt the just pride of patriotism more than any appellation derived from local discriminations. With slight shades of difference, you have the same religion, manners, habits, and political principles."[41] What is most intriguing in this statement is Washington's privileging of the national over the local. He and the Federalists concentrated their efforts on drawing the peoples of the United States into a larger political arena. Given these peoples' common language (English) and mutual enemy (the British), Washington's job was not all that difficult.[42] The American nation was well fortified by the time its first president left office. In the two centuries since his address, the United States has survived a civil war and a civil rights movement to become one of the most powerful nations in the world.

It should come as no surprise, then, that the young people writing in their school newspapers over the past forty-five years have consistently shown awareness of their American identity and the national political community. The word "American" is not difficult to find in these newspapers. Identifiers such as "Houstonian," "Portlander," "Arizonan," and "Pennsylvanian," however, very rarely appear, even when students are writing about their cities and states. What is especially surprising is how much this national focus increased throughout the 1980s and 1990s. If anything, the national identification the young adults in this study felt has only increased in the past few decades.

Nowhere is the increasing national focus of these young journalists more obvious than in regard to presidential politics. The presidential races of 1968 and 1972 were barely mentioned by the youth of that era, but by 1976 all of the newspapers were talking about Nixon's fall, Ford's failing presidency, and a peanut farmer from Georgia named Jimmy Carter. Regardless of what might have caused this clear attitudinal shift, the young journalists in this study had a strong sense of their national political community by the late 1970s. One way to identify this sense of nationalism is through young people's almost exclusive connection to the president as a political actor. As references to local and state officials decreased, references to the president and presidential candidates increased. Whether discrediting Richard Nixon,[43] defending Ronald Reagan,[44] or questioning the actions of Bill Clinton,[45] young adults have increasingly felt a clear connection to their president while largely ignoring the rest of the political actors affecting their lives. As a representative of the national political community, the president became the preeminent political actor for these young people and remained so throughout the remainder of this study's timeline.

In addition, the only political campaigns reported on in more recent high school newspapers were presidential races. For example, by 1984, the presidential race was the only one discussed in Wilson High School's Beacon. In its October issue, the top half of page 3 was dedicated to the presidential contest. The upper-left quadrant offered an editorial on the Democratic candidate Walter Mondale entitled "Why Mondale?" Another for the Republican candidate Ronald Reagan, "Why Reagan?," appeared in the upper-right quadrant. And located directly beneath these editorials was a chart reporting the results of the "Beacon Presidential Mock Election," which Mondale won with the votes of 71 percent of the 589 students polled.[46] Twenty-four years later and on the other side of the country, the same trend continued in Portland, Oregon. The October 2008 edition of Grant High School's Grantonian contained four editorials, three of which dealt with that year's presidential election.[47] One of the opinion pieces complained that little had actually been said in the most recent presidential debates between McCain and Obama, and two others dealt with vice-presidential candidate Sarah Palin—one in support of her candidacy and the other opposed to it. The fourth editorial featured twelve facts about bottled water.[48] Nothing at all appeared in the paper about many of the other items on the ballot: two city council seats, U.S. House representative, U.S. senator, and twelve state measures. Grant High and Washington High are not exceptions. Quadrennially, each of the seven newspapers represented in this study examined at least the two major candidates for president, and most even conducted some form of presidential mock election.

More illuminating is that even when students chided their peers for not participating in elections, they most often did so by highlighting the presidential race. Take, for example, the following editorial from a 1988 issue of *Carrickulum*:

> Students today seem completely oblivious to the race that is going on in our country. It is a race that can and will decide our future. It is the Presidential campaign for our 1988 elections. It is our responsibility as future participants in the political circus to become familiar with today's candidates. The issues that make up a candidate's platform are arguments that affect our lives. Do we want a strong militarily based country? Are we ready for a black President? Do we have a right to intervene in the affairs of Honduras? It's our world, and many of us in 1988 will be responsible for its future.[49]

This frustrated student cannot understand how his fellow students fail to see how the president's actions directly influence their lives. Such claims of responsibility with regard to national elections have remained consistent over the past couple decades. In a more recent *Denebola* editorial, the newspaper argued that students eighteen years of age "must register to vote" because "presidential elections are critical." To ward off any potential objections to registering and voting, the editorial goes on to point out, "Even though Massachusetts will surely vote Obama, it is your responsibility to support the issues and candidates you care about."[50] Today's young people, then, encourage their peers to vote by arguing that voting is a responsibility most closely tied to electing the president. This argument is, they believe, the one that will be most persuasive to their peers.

A recent editorial debate that appeared in *Northmen's Log* in October 2005 further illustrates the extent to which students are tied to national politics.

Under the large headline "Point Counter Point," two students offer different answers to the question "Should students stay active in the political scene?" Both students rely almost exclusively on national examples for evidence in support of their positions. Making the negative case, one young woman argues that "politics are not relevant to the high school student's life." In making her argument, she suggests the proliferation of television channels and other media make it difficult to keep up with political information, and she also posits that all of the major issues high school students might be interested in—"gay rights, the War against Terrorism and Hurricane Katrina"—are too controversial and divisive. Politics is, she concludes, worth neither the extra effort nor the risk. In making the positive case, the other student presents the following thesis: "The fact of the matter remains, in order to become a well-informed adult voter, a student needs to begin learning about his *country* and how it works." While she does briefly mention a recent local bond that affected teacher salaries, the majority of her editorial remains focused on the national level. She suggests to her peers that they listen to National Public Radio and encourages them to put forth the extra effort to stay informed despite the fact "not every channel broadcasts the President's State of the Union address like they used to."[51] She even ends her piece with the suggestion that becoming politically interested might eventually lead one to become the president of the United States. In these cases for and against being active in the political scene, the only mention of local politics is, then, in reference to a local bond that had a direct effect on the school. At no point does either student discuss local or state elected officials, nor does either student discuss any other form of political involvement. The political scene is the national scene.

In addition to presidents and presidential campaigns, the only other political actors discussed with any sort of regularity are political celebrities— the civic leaders and entertainment personalities that voice political opinions reaching a national audience. These political celebrities clearly caught the attention of the young journalists in this study. For example, a *Grantonian* editorial took umbrage with conservative radio host Rush Limbaugh in 1994 because his political views were "breeding bigotry into the minds of many Americans."[52] In Phoenix in 1996, the students at Washington High School included a list of shows they wanted to see in a two-page story about talk show television. Their number-one choice was "Howard Stern meets Rush Limbaugh for a political debate."[53] In Pittsburgh, the Senator Trent Lott controversy was given a half page of attention in the February 14, 2003, edition of *Carrickulum*, despite the fact that Lott was then a U.S. senator from Mississippi.[54] Even Christopher Reeve got students' attention as a political actor. In an October 2004 obituary, a writer for the *Denebola* spent three paragraphs discussing Reeve's acting career and family. The remaining twelve paragraphs were devoted to his work as a "political activist."[55] The fact that these political celebrities caught young people's attention should not merely highlight their celebrity status. It should, instead, highlight their attractiveness as political actors at the *national* level.

It is also important to note that the young adults in this study increasingly saw political *issues* in national terms over the past forty-five years. National-level political issues hit their political radar in the late 1970s and into the 1980s. In Wilson High School's *Beacon*, for example, the issue of gun violence was discussed in national terms in 1982. After beginning with a local city proposal, the article shifts to a similar law in Chicago. Discussing gun violence in the United States, the writer states sardonically that in 1979 "in America handguns killed 10,728 people. God Bless America."[56] In a 1987 issue of Oak Park High School's *Northmen's Log*, an article on the issue of sex education and teenage pregnancy began with four facts: "Every 2 minutes, some American teenage girl gives birth. Over 1 million American girls become pregnant each year. Ninety-six out of every 1,000 teenage girls become pregnant. The United States leads nearly all other nations of the world with teenage pregnancy and is still increasing."[57] While these numbers are distressing even today, it is noteworthy that they are national statistics. Instead of citing local pregnancy statistics, the students at Oak Park High focused on the issue as a national epidemic. Even a 1995 feature story in the *Denebola* on gender differences in science classes at Newton South High School devoted most of its space to reporting a Harvard study on gender differences and a *U.S. News and World Report* article on gender bias in schools.[58] What started out as a story about the high school's science classes quickly became a story about a national problem. By the mid-1990s, all of the issues covered in the newspapers were understood as being intricately connected to larger national issues.

The young people in this study also became keenly interested in national tragedies. While local tragedies (e.g., hurricanes, large fires, etc.) most surely occurred in each of these cities, they rarely appeared in the pages of this study's high school newspapers. But national calamities appeared in all of them. The February 14, 2003, issue of *Carrickulum*, for instance, used half of its front page to cover the tragedy of the space shuttle *Columbia*.[59] The *Northmen's Log* of May 12, 1995, devoted almost a full inside page to the Oklahoma City bombing, reporting that "the country watched, stunned at the horrific act of terrorism that struck not in Washington D.C., New York or Los Angeles, but in the nation's heartland."[60] For this writer, the bombing was a local tragedy with national implications. In Houston, Lamar High School's *Lancer* reported on the explosion of the space shuttle *Challenger* in the first two pages of its February 1986 issue, referring to the dead astronauts as American heroes, just as Ronald Reagan had defined them.[61] And all of the newspapers had something to say about the terrorist attacks of September 11, 2001. As research has consistently argued, national tragedies help a nation's citizens better understand who they are as a people. That the students in this study wrote of national tragedies while ignoring more localized events highlights their shift toward a greater identification with the nation as a primary political community.

One final thing worth highlighting about such matters is that, until the mid-1980s, even international issues and crises were discussed primarily in terms of domestic issues. Unlike later military engagements (to be discussed below), the Vietnam War was largely talked about in these high school newspapers in terms of its domestic impact. A sampling of these articles from the late 1960s highlights this point:

> We of the *Ram Page* believe in the right of free speech when someone has a legitimate reason to express his particular viewpoint, but when a bunch of "mama's boys" afraid of a little hard work start throwing babyish tantrums and defending their actions as free speech, it's time for the government to take action. The new law making it a felony to burn draft cards should be the first of many steps to curb the tactics of these so-called users of the rights of citizenship.[62]

> In view of the numerous much publicized demonstrations against America's Vietnam policy, a group of roving reporters recently asked Wilsonites their opinions on student protests. Out of the 78 polled, three-fourths were against the marches, sit-downs, petitions and draft-card burnings.[63]

> Student Opinions Vary; Draft Girls—Dodge Army; Vietnam Policy Polled[64]

> Beginning this year the Junior Red Cross is sponsoring a project to send badly needed items to the soldiers in Viet Nam. . . . Anyone wishing to contribute to this project may give items to their homeroom Red Cross representative.[65]

> Probably one of the most posing problems concerning the teenage student today is the draft. Boys especially are plagued by such questions as, "Should I enlist or wait to get drafted?"[66]

As each of these examples makes plain, students were obviously concerned about the Vietnam War, but their reportage also makes it clear that their concerns were primarily domestic in nature. While some students were surely concerned about Vietnam itself, the articles in these high school newspapers primarily focused on the fear of being drafted and the domestic issues related to protesting the war.

With national politics now being so powerful, with presidential races now being the overwhelming focus of most political media, and with community issues being seen as embryonically national in nature, it is little wonder that the young people in this study have, over the past five decades, increasingly related to national politics and a national community. Furthermore, this shift in coverage supports survey research showing that, by the mid-1980s, less than 40 percent of young people could name their U.S. congressmen or identify which party controlled the House of Representatives.[67] But young people's national focus is about more than just politicians; it is also about the political issues and community problems they believe impact their lives. As I discuss below, this may be both positive and negative for the overall health of American democracy. For now, however, what is important to note is that the overwhelming national preoccupation of the young adults in this study, coupled with major economic and mediated changes around the world, may have led them to begin identifying with an even larger political community than the nation itself.

Going Global

When discussing nation formation, Benedict Anderson argued that "what, in a positive sense, made the new communities imaginable was a half-fortuitous, but explosive, interaction between a system of production and productive relations (capitalism), and technology of communications (print), and the fatality of human linguistic diversity."[68] Anderson's argument suggests that nations result from the forces of modernity. One might then argue that the emergence of globalization occurs as a direct result of the interaction among productive relations (capitalism), newer technologies of communications (digitized), and the emergence of a universal language of capital (English). That is, globalization is a direct result of the cultural changes fortified by postmodernity.

In the past fifty to sixty years, there may have been no greater political shift than that of globalization. Put simply, the world has been getting smaller over the past century. Politically, globalization has changed the way people do business and has brought the nation-state's viability as a governing institution into question.[69] Global corporations continue to gain greater amounts of political capital even as nation-states struggle to compete in a changing world. For evidence of this trend, consider the comments of Tony Clarke, director of the Polaris Institute, during an APEC conference at the end of the twentieth century: "Of the 100 largest economies in the entire world today, 51 are individual transnational enterprises (three years ago, it was 47). Only 49 of the world's biggest economies are nation-states."[70] While such evidence does not necessarily reduce the importance of the nation-state, it does suggest that global corporations, which work within and across nation-state boundaries, may have a great deal of political power given their financial importance.

Globalization is an extension of the capitalistic concerns of international trade; it is something altogether different and altogether new. As Fredric Jameson puts it in the introduction to his book *Postmodernism, or The Cultural Logic of Late Capitalism,*

> What marks the development of the new concept over the older one . . . is not merely an emphasis on the emergence of new forms of business organization (multinationals, transnationals) beyond the monopoly stage but, above all, the vision of a world capitalist system fundamentally distinct from the older imperialism, which was little more than a rivalry between the various colonial powers. . . . Besides the forms of transnational business . . . , its features include the new international division of labor, a vertiginous new dynamic in international banking and the stock exchanges . . . , new forms of media interrelationship . . . , computers and automation, the flight of production to advanced Third World areas, along with all the more familiar social consequences, including the crisis of traditional labor, the emergence of yuppies, and gentrification on a now-global scale.[71]

Jameson's point is that globalization is not merely about nations competing in a global market. Nor is it simply about the creation of transnational corporations. Globalization is about how the average person has come to see a shrinking world. Or, put differently, globalization increasingly forces the individual—especially the individual living in a Western industrial nation— to understand his or her own life as more intimately interconnected with the lives of others thousands of miles away.

The assertion that globalization is an aspect of postmodernization is not without its critics. To think of global issues especially as they relate to economic issues is not a new endeavor. In 1848, Marx and Engels were aware of capitalism's impact on the world as a whole, arguing that "modern industry has established the world-market, for which the discovery of America paved the way. This market has given an immense development to commerce, to navigation, to communication by land."[72] Immanuel Kant showed concern for similar issues when arguing for his notion of cosmopolitan citizenship in "Perpetual Peace: A Philosophical Sketch."[73] So too did Adam Smith, who argued that the true reason to accumulate the monetary wealth of gold and silver was to send it to foreign countries in order to buy goods and wage wars.[74] And those skeptical that globalization is something new— something truly postmodern—also have empirical evidence to support their argument. Adair Turner makes the point that international trade as a percentage of gross domestic product is no higher in Britain now than it was in the nineteenth century.[75] As these authors point out, nations have been concerned with the trade of goods to foreign countries ever since nations began to exist.

But the question of postmodern globalization is not specifically one of trade and the cooperation of multiple states in pursuing capitalistic goals. As political theorist John Hoffman argues, "It is rather that there is an interconnectedness between the people of the world and this interconnectedness has been such that something new has emerged."[76] Cultural sociologist John Tomlinson echoes this assertion in discussing the importance of connectivity and proximity to globalization. His thoughts on interconnectivity in a modern, globalized world are worth quoting at length here:

> The condition of connectivity not only underwrites the notion of proximity, but places its own stamp on the way we understand global "closeness." Being connected means being close in very specific ways: the experience of proximity afforded by these connections coexists with an undeniable, stubbornly enduring physical distance between places and people in the world, which the technological and social transformations of globalization have not conjured away. In a globalized world, people in Spain really do continue to be 5,500 miles away from

people in Mexico, separated, just as the Spanish conquistadors were in the sixteenth century, by a huge, inhospitable and perilous tract of ocean. What connectivity means is that we now experience this distance in different ways. We think of such distant places as routinely accessible, either representationally through communications technology or the mass media, or physically, through the expenditure of a relatively small amount of time (and, of course, of money) on a transatlantic flight. So Mexico City is no longer meaningfully 5,500 miles from Madrid: it is eleven hours' flying time away.[77]

While people have been aware of the larger world for centuries, it is only recently that the depth of their connections to people and places around the globe has increased. Transportation and telecommunications advances have had both personal and political consequences. Largely made possible by the power of nation-states and the world's growing push toward capitalism, these advances have yielded new, and perhaps unexpected, consequences for the average person and have done so on a daily basis.

Postmodern globalization is, then, a relatively new phenomenon. Its impacts on the lives of people are only now being understood, but the global interconnectedness of the last several decades is having an effect. While the young people in this study have clearly turned their attention toward the nation, they have also made another adjustment in where they locate political community: they have identified, more and more, with the global community, a shift that began in the mid-1980s.

Acknowledging globalization's clear rhetorical impact in the 1980s is not to suggest that the young people in this study were unaware of the rest of the world before then. Their awareness of others around the globe was already apparent in the mid-1960s. This can be seen most clearly in the numerous articles about the American Field Service (AFS) international student exchange program begun in 1946. Indeed, most of the newspapers represented in this study made reference to the students in the AFS program or other foreign exchange students, as seen in the following headlines from the late 1960s and early 1970s:

- "Red Cross Sponsors Potluck Dinner to Host Foreign Exchange Students" (*Grantonian*, February 16, 1968)
- "Stan, AFS Student, Goes to Ecuador; Gerlinde, WHS's Foreign Student, Arrives in Phoenix from Austria" (*Ram Page*, September 17, 1965)

- "Assembly Presents Four AFS Students" (*Northmen's Log*, September 27, 1968)
- "South Greets Tullia Todras AFS Student" (*Denebola*, September 16, 1965)
- "Swedish Student Visits Senior Economics Class" (*Lancer*, May 5, 1966)
- "AFS Hosts Student in '73" (*Carrickulum*, May 1972)

Two of the newspapers (the *Ram Page* and *Denebola*) even offered space in each of their issues during the late 1960s for the AFS student currently attending their school to write about his or her experiences in the United States. While the attention given to AFS does indicate that American youth were clearly aware of foreign others, it also indicates that these others and their political problems had yet to become personally relevant. At least into the early 1970s, the foreign students remained different, even exotic.

In most instances during the 1960s and 1970s, the AFS students who arrived on the high school campuses in this study were largely treated as exceptional and somewhat strange. In the first issue of the 1968–69 *Grantonian*, for example, the two new AFS students were front-page news, complete with a large picture of one of them. The distance between the students' home countries and their destination could not have been made more apparent. The lead paragraph of the article begins, in fact, by highlighting that "airplanes, busses and boats were the methods of transportation used in getting our two foreign exchange students . . . from Trondheim, Norway and . . . from Rio Cuarto in the province of Cordoba, Argentina, to Portland in August."[78] The article goes on to describe in some detail the routes taken by both new students before offering any biographical information about them, placing emphasis on the exceptional distance they had to travel to get to Oregon. The student journalists writing for Oak Park High School's *Northmen's Log* in Kansas City similarly considered the arrival of four AFS students in 1968 to be front-page news, placing a picture of the students and the article about them above the newspaper's own masthead. The strangeness of the foreign students is highlighted in the story, which focuses on their introduction at a school assembly. As the second paragraph reports, "A panel [of students] attempted to single out the foreign exchange students from four groups of impersonators. The panel failed."[79] While it is not stated explicitly in the article, the student's reporting of the assembly emphasizes its primary point—that the AFS students are not that different. However, in presenting them this way, the assembly and the story demonstrate the assumption that the prevailing attitude of the Oak Park student body is, in fact, that the foreign exchange students are quite different.

Young journalists may have been fairly intrigued by peoples from around the globe in the late 1960s, but they became increasingly aware of their deeper connections with those foreign peoples by the mid-1980s. One piece highlighting this global connection was a two-page spread about Apartheid in the December 1985 issue of the *Beacon*. The story's lead emphasizes the integration of others' problems into the lives of American youth: "We read about it every morning on the front pages of our newspapers, learning of the tension and the violence. We see it every night on our televisions, witnessing the blood and the fire. It is a story and issue which has found its way into our daily thoughts and conversations, into our political beliefs and affiliations. South Africa, and its racial policy of apartheid, has become *a part of our lives.*"[80] A bit dramatic, perhaps, but the point is clear: the problems of the peoples of South Africa have implications for the young adults at Wilson High School. The same was true at Oak Park High School, where, in 1985, *Northmen's Log* dedicated a two-page, in-depth story to one student's seven-month trip to Africa.[81] In an October 1998 issue of *Grantonian*, a feature article argued that students could have their voices heard around the world through Amnesty International.[82] And in the April 2005 edition of *Lamar Life*, students on the staff devoted a two-page color spread to the Asian tsunami, beginning the story by asking their peers to "imagine being in paradise, lying on a beach, sleeping in, or taking an early morning walk when out of nowhere water comes flooding into the village."[83] The ensuing text discusses both the local impact of the tsunami and the international response to the disaster. Even as recently as February 2010, *Rampage* writers noted that the world had "come together to help the people of Haiti after a 7.0 earthquake struck their nation on January 12," leaving "over 230,000 people confirmed dead." The point of the article was to chronicle how "WHS is doing its part to lend a hand."[84] In a very similar piece published the same month on the front page of *Northmen's Log*, one student noted, "Following the Haiti earthquake on Tuesday, Jan. 12, many people around the world stepped up to help the Haitian people by sending money or providing them with basic necessities, including students and teachers from the school."[85] The more contemporary young adults writing in these high school newspapers exhibit not only an awareness of people around the world but also a good deal of empathy for those people when an international crisis makes the news. They have come to feel, that is, a sense of closeness with the international community that defies distance.

In addition to American youth's increasing concern with the political and social problems of peoples in Africa, Asia, and South America, it is equally important to note that in recent years issues once viewed as local or domestic also began to be discussed with regard to their global implications. In Washington, D.C., a 1992 *Beacon* editorial discussed a recent guest speaker, George H. W. Bush's personal physician Dr. Burton Lee, who spoke of AIDS in America and Africa, pointing to the difference in drug availability. While Dr. Lee's talk was apparently focused on "how the disease is affecting today's teenagers," some students in the audience were credited with bringing up the AIDS research in Kenya, where the disease was having a far more devastating effect.[86] In Pittsburgh, one student began a 2002 article in *Carrickulum* by stating that global warming had become a major problem ignored by the Bush administration. He ended his article with the suggestion that "no one acknowledges global warming, because if people did, they would have to change a lot in their lives." For this student, the global warming problem impacted his peers and the decisions they made, but it also very clearly "affect[ed] our world."[87] In the *Denebola*, a story in September 2004 criticized the policies of Russian president Vladimir Putin and ended by arguing that "if his dangerous reforms are not criticized, shot down, and reformed, the world faces the very realistic danger of seeing another tyrant in Russia and facing the fears it had during the Cold War all over again."[88] Even in a safe and wealthy suburb of Boston, Putin's actions were felt in a very real and powerful way. And in a 2002 *Rampage* editorial, one young woman seemed genuinely shocked by the obesity and excess of people in the United States, not because of the health of Americans but because of the contrast to people throughout the rest of the world: "Around the world in the continent of Africa over 40 million people are starving and in Russia nearly 70 percent of the overall population lives below the poverty line of $30 a month for a family of four."[89] For this concerned young student, the only way to understand America's obesity epidemic was to contextualize it in relation to the poor conditions of other parts of the world where such excess was not even available. From AIDS to obesity, then, all problems were global problems in the eyes of these students by the early 1990s.

Giving us a clearer sense of just how deeply these young people have come to believe this, one article published in a December 1998 issue of *Grantonian* exemplifies their thinking. The editorialist begins by acknowledging, "No country in history has secured so much freedom for so many people." He then quickly transitions to his larger point: "We cannot preserve the rights of the individual without regard to what it does to society and the world at large. It must stop." The student's point is that his peers need to pay more attention to a much larger issue—global overpopulation and its effect on the environment. To get them to turn their attention to this looming "apocalypse," he tells them to get over their "pet projects": "I don't give a damn about the spotted owl or Keiko [of *Free Willy* fame]. I mean all your raging against the death penalty, your shouts of indignation against abortion, your distaste of affirmative action, and your rallying cries about horrible conditions in Nike factories in Indonesia." These pet projects— national and global issues in their own right—must, he insists, take a backseat to the world's environmental health. To save the world, the worried student suggests he and his peers need to address two issues: "One is the rapid decay of our social system and any sense of right and wrong, and the other is the destruction of our actual physical world." With regard to the first concern, he states that people must find a "sense of responsibility to something greater than ourselves." As for the second issue, he argues that his peers and American society writ large are being "irresponsible as members of a global community" due to their use of SUVs and consumption of too much food.[90] Here is a student who has internalized international concerns and believes that his peers will understand his global argument.

Perhaps nothing reveals how clearly these young people view today's issues as global problems better than two stories published in the *Denebola* at different times by different authors in late 2009. Both stories dealt with homosexuality, and both tied the problems homosexuals face in gaining real equality to international issues. The first article begins by quoting the recent comments of Iranian president Mahmoud Ahmadinejad, who denied the existence of homosexuals in Iran. The young journalist goes on to say, "Unfortunately, as demonstrated by Iran, homosexuality is still not tolerated in many parts of the world." Although starting with this global perspective, the student quickly adds, "Yet, as easy as it is to condemn other countries for intolerance, it's necessary to first scrutinize America's own willingness to accept civil liberties for all people."[91] The article then compares U.S. laws regarding homosexuality with those of other nations around the world, including Canada, China, and Denmark. Appearing a month later, the second article on gay rights dealt with "a bill in the Ugandan Parliament that would criminalize homosexuality." While the article focuses specifically on the bill, its ultimate point seems to be to demonstrate the global outcry against it. The student notes, "Many worldwide organizations have condemned the bill and have called upon nations to cut Uganda off from foreign aid." He adds, moreover, that Christian leaders in the United States "released a statement on December 7 condemning the bill" and then ends the piece by noting that "many international figures including Canadian Prime Minister Stephen Harper and the United States Government have attempted to reason with President Yoweri Museveni of Uganda to seemingly no avail."[92] In both of these articles, the issue of gay rights exists outside national borders. These student journalists have been raised in a globalized world, and they seem to have internalized the language of human rights, even if they do not articulate it explicitly.

Finally, one can also see the impact of globalization in the young journalists' language about American military action following the Vietnam War. As mentioned above, the student journalists of the late 1960s primarily discussed the Vietnam War in terms of its domestic issues; this was not true for later conflicts. Starting as early as 1982, students began to consider the lives of others in foreign countries. Arguing that the United States should leave El Salvador, a *Beacon* editorialist contended that the Reagan administration supported "one of the most brutal and undemocratic regimes in Central America."[93] The editorial went on to discuss some of the problems with the El Salvadoran government. In *Rampage*, one student defended the actions of George H. W. Bush during the Gulf War by arguing that "if America does not take action to end conflict in a situation where it would disrupt world peace, it would lead to world confusion and possibly stronger conflict on a global scale."[94] Clearly filled with respect for American superiority, this student focused squarely on the international impact of military actions. And this trend only continued with the wars in Afghanistan and Iraq. The editor in chief of *Northmen's Log* wrote, "It's official. The war has consumed us. Every night at dinner, millions watch CNN, MSNBC and FOX News just to see what the United States blew up that day. But just for one minute, put yourself in a different place—Baghdad."[95] And one editorial in *Grantonian* questioned the national outpouring of patriotism following the September 11, 2001, terrorist bombings:

> Three weeks ago, it would have been in poor taste to attach an American flag to the antennae of your car. Such intense patriotism could lead one to be perceived more as a fascist than a normal U.S. citizen. However, in light of the events in New York and Washington D.C., Americans have been displaying the flag every opportunity they get. It hardly seems odd now to see a two-story red, white and blue banner

draped over the front of a house, or someone bearing an American flag t-shirt. . . . As a few of my classmates expressed, it creates an "us versus them" mentality that borders on being dangerously ethnocentric. They fear that American's are determined to seek revenge at any cost.[96]

This student expresses her concern over the national response to the terrorist attacks through an unquestionably globalized lens.

In the end, by reading school newspapers over time, one finds a group of young journalists who came to see their lives as inextricably linked to the lives of people around the world. Exhibiting far more than a mere fascination with foreign others and strange cultures, these American youth have increasingly come to perceive themselves as members of a global political community. They have not yet lost touch with their nation, but they are thinking beyond American borders. They have clearly come to understand that the political problems of the United States can have a direct impact on the lives of people living in China, Romania, or Ecuador, and vice versa. In times of crisis and conflict, moreover, their identification with peoples from all over the world as simply human is truly palpable. The young adults in this study have become, psychologically at least, global citizens.

Conclusion

This chapter has explored three places where young people might locate political community and, therefore, find the sense of shared identity that serves as the backbone of democratic engagement. I have shown, first, that the attachments of the young people in this study to local communities have largely disappeared over the past few decades. These students did not identify very deeply with their cities or care for the politics that accompanied them. Their relationship to the states in which they lived appears to have been no stronger. Instead, these young people have come to primarily identify with the nation-state, seeing themselves principally as Americans and understanding most political issues and electoral offices as national. I have also shown, however, that these young adults have increasingly become aware of politics in the larger global community. With ever-growing frequency, they see their own lives in the United States as politically interconnected to the lives of people all over the globe, clearly sensing that the world they live in has been getting smaller and smaller. This chapter, then, has been about place.

It has also been, at least tangentially, about size. While the young people quoted in this chapter may have felt a greater proximity to their fellow Americans and the global citizenry, this identification is not without its costs; it could be problematic for both democracy and citizenship. If one assumes, for example, that the cost of participating must be weighed against the expense of taking action (i.e., voting, writing a letter, etc.) and against the possibility of having a real impact on the system, one wonders how much actual participation there can be in a global community. If rational choice theory is correct, then as a community gets larger the possibility of a single person having a true impact decreases. As young people increasingly identify with the global community, that is, one might wonder what kind of efficacy they can generate as cosmopolitan citizens. The students in this study clearly showed that they were concerned about the larger world, but they rarely offered any explanation for how they were to engage the problems occurring in that world, short of donating money and material goods—an issue that will be further addressed as potentially problematic in the following chapter.

To supporters of cosmopolitanism, this chapter may very well bring good news. Concerned as they are with the conflict that local differences can create, cosmopolitans such as David Held and Kwame Anthony Appiah, even with their differing views of cosmopolitanism, might find comfort in the fact that the young people in this study have increasingly embraced the idea of living in a global village.[97] Given that both agree with Immanuel Kant's assertion that "the peoples of the earth have thus entered in varying degrees into a universal community," how could they not find young people's increasing awareness of this "universal community" to be a positive change?[98] How could they not be happy with the level of identification many of today's American youth seem to have with people all over the world?

Cosmopolitan thinkers argue that all people must come to transcend their own provincialism in favor of a more sophisticated global citizenship. This may be good and true but, one must ask, what happens to the local, democratic participation envisioned by Aristotle and Robert Dahl in an increasingly cosmopolitan world? With almost 7 billion people in the world, how does one feel a sense of political efficacy if he identifies himself as primarily a global citizen? In a perfect world, the best outcome of the changes presented in this chapter might be found in the popular slogan and bumper sticker "Think Globally, Act Locally." But the postmodern world is not perfect, and there is no real reason to believe that young people will suddenly begin reengaging their local communities in the ways that Aristotle or Dahl envisioned. If the political communities with which they identify become increasingly globalized, it may be a good thing for international business, but will it be, one must ask, a good thing for democracy?

4

REMOVED VOLUNTEERS

Presidents reflect their times. As much as any given president may frame or even change the course of American history, he is equally, if not more, constrained by the societal norms that helped him rise to power. The American people have often flirted with political outliers, but they have always eventually settled on a president who more clearly reflects their view of the world. So when a president speaks, he uses language and delivers arguments with the premise that the majority of the people understand. When one finds two presidents speaking in different terms, one can therefore presume that the country, not just the speaker, is different. Here, then, are two different presidential responses to similar national events.

On January 6, 1942, Franklin Delano Roosevelt delivered his annual message to Congress. Unlike most other State of the Union addresses, with their laundry lists of national issues and policy recommendations, Roosevelt's speech focused primarily on only one topic—the United States' response to the attack on Pearl Harbor and the larger threat of the Axis powers. In making the case for the shift from supplying "weapons of war to Britain, Russia, and China" to active American military engagement, Roosevelt noted that "modern methods of warfare make it a task not only of shooting and fighting, but an even more urgent one of working and producing." This working and producing were that "which collectively we call labor." Such labor required that the American "workers stand ready to work long hours; to turn out more in a day's work; to keep the wheels turning and the fires burning 24 hours a day and 7 days a week." In addition to more work, Roosevelt told the American people that they should expect to sacrifice their easy access to raw materials (e.g., rubber, copper, and tin) and help support the war financially through higher taxes and purchasing government bonds. Ultimately, Roosevelt noted that the call to war "means cutting luxuries and other nonessentials. In a word, it means an 'all-out' war by individual effort and family effort in a united country."

Sixty years later, George W. Bush addressed a joint session of Congress just nine days after the terrorist attacks of September 11, 2001. While there were differences between this attack and that at Pearl Harbor, Bush's speech, like Roosevelt's before him, was an explicit call to war. However, despite their similar purpose, a great deal had changed in the intervening six decades. In explaining how the War on Terror was to be waged, for instance, Bush could not help but paint a very different picture of modern warfare: "We will direct every resource at our command—every means of diplomacy, every tool of intelligence, every instrument of law enforcement, every financial influence, and every necessary weapon of war—to the disruption and to the defeat of the global terror network." Bush also described a much more limited group of people who would be actively involved in the new war—"from FBI agents to intelligence operatives to the reservists we have called to active duty." As for the American people, Bush spoke directly to them but did not ask them to make sacrifices or work long hours. Instead he told the people "to live your lives, and hug your children." He also asked them "to continue to support the victims of this tragedy with your contributions. Those who want to give can go to a central source of information, libertyunites.org." And, finally, Bush requested the people's patience and their "continued participation and confidence in the American economy."

In making the case for war, both presidents understood the American people needed to feel included in the national response to the attacks. Such unifying appeals, communication scholars Karlyn Kohrs Campbell and Kathleen Hall Jamieson tell us, are standard fare in presidential war rhetoric.[1] In constituting their audiences, both men, moreover, offered suggestions for how the people should understand themselves. Roosevelt told the American people they were needed in the factories; Bush told them they were needed at the mall. Roosevelt asked them to work hard; Bush asked them to consume avidly. Roosevelt called for sacrifice; Bush called for patience and money. Roosevelt portrayed the American people as humble, hardworking citizens; Bush portrayed them as caring but impatient consumers. The American people to whom Bush spoke in 2001 were not, it seems, the same American people Roosevelt addressed in 1942. How could they have been? Much had happened in the United States during the intervening six decades.

One might be tempted to argue that the differences in the rhetorical con-stitution of the American people demonstrated above merely represent the changing nature of warfare and two very distinct types of enemies. While these factors are important to note, they are not enough to fully explain the divergent constructions of the American people. A more fundamental explanation understands that the United States and the American people changed a great deal between World War II and the War on Terror. Just as George W. Bush knew the American people would be unlikely to accept such sacrifices as higher taxes and the rationing of sugar and gasoline, Franklin Roosevelt understood that his American people would have been insulted if told to hug their children and stand aside patiently. Both presidents were smart enough to understand their respective audiences. They had to be. As rhetorical scholar Vanessa Beasley has noted, presidents are "constrained by what they can and cannot say," and the discursive "options can be greatly compromised by cultural logics, by the facts of history, and, of course, by public opinion."[2]

By most accounts, the American people of 2001 lived in a much different economic environment than their predecessors in 1942. The very nature of the U.S. economy changed drastically, in fact, because of the post–World War II economic boom. As I will argue below, people's outlooks on money, work, and what constitutes "the good life" also shifted dramatically across this time span. These changing attitudes, in turn, influenced the ways in which people came to understand many other social relations. In terms of approaches to democratic engagement, some scholars have suggested that these attitudinal shifts led the American people to more often think of their stance toward politics from the viewpoint of a consumer rather than a citizen. Some recent scholars have gone so far as to defend and praise this new political consumerism—something they are supposedly finding with increasing frequency in the civic and political behavior of American youth. But are such claims true? Have young adults become increasingly active in politics as political consumers?

This chapter explores whether these assertions about an increasingly consumeristic approach to democratic engagement ring true for the young adults in this study. I begin by examining in more detail the changing economic shifts of the past half century, paying close attention to the implications of the transition from the production-based economic system of the post–World War II era to the consumer-based economic system of today. I then look at just how discursively focused on consumeristic concerns the student journalists in this study became over the course of the past five decades. After clearly establishing the depth of the consumer impulse evident among these modern young adults, I turn my attention to three different types of democratic engagement exhibited by the student journalists over the past half century—what are here referred to as *networked conventionalism*, *networked consumerism*, and *removed volunteering*. In the end, I suggest that while all three civic exemplars are potentially valid forms of democratic engagement, only one—removed volunteering—captures the predominant way in which the high school students wrote about the interaction of money and politics.

Postmodern Capitalism

Understanding the three models of civic engagement presented below first requires a brief explanation of the increasingly central role that money and consumerism have come to play in the lives of the American people. The argument that Americans place a great deal of importance on capitalism and material goods may seem, at first glance, self-evident. After all, Americans have long been concerned with money and its social display. Anyone who has ever read Thorstein Veblen's 1899 *The Theory of the Leisure Class* or one of the many Henry James novels from the same period (e.g., *The Bostonians* or *The Portrait of a Lady*) knows full well that the American people have been strikingly focused on material wealth since at least the Gilded Age. One can sense their fascination with it even further back in time. Alexis de Tocqueville noted in 1840, "Democracy favors the taste for physical pleasure. This taste, if it becomes excessive, soon disposes men to believe that nothing but matter exists. Materialism, in turn, spurs them on to such delights with mad impetuosity. Such is the vicious circle into which democratic nations are driven."[3] There is, according to Tocqueville, something about the freedoms made possible by democracy that leads people to become excessively concerned with the consumption of material goods. While Tocqueville ostensibly saw the seeds of a materialistic society in the middle of the nineteenth century, even he might be surprised by the level of material consumption in the United States today.

While the American people may have always been drawn to the physical pleasure of materialism, it seems to have truly spurred them on to "mad impetuosity" in the second half of the twentieth century. Indeed, this is the argument that political theorist Fredric Jameson makes in his influential work *Postmodernism, or The Cultural Logic of Late Capitalism*. According to Jameson, the beginning of the postmodern period may be marked by the rise of a new capitalism that came into being after the consumer shortages of World War II were refilled or overfilled. With increased production and growing economic wealth, the United States transitioned from a production-based economic system in which need was preeminent to a consumption-based system predicated on want or desire.[4] Late capitalism, that is, moved from a focus on the object itself to an emphasis on the act of consuming the object. It is this process of transition from need to want that has played a particularly important role in reshaping recent discussions of democratic engagement in the United States. The primary concern is that the late capitalistic shift has fundamentally changed the primary roles the American people have come to see themselves playing in the public sphere. As Zygmunt Bauman has put it succinctly, "Postmodern society engages its members primarily in their capacity as consumers rather than producers."[5] More than a simple economic shift, this focus on consumption subtly alters one's sense of community, politics, and citizenship.

That the American people became increasingly materialistic during the second half of the twentieth century is a relatively uncontroversial claim. That this increasing materialism fundamentally changed the public culture of the United States may be a less acceptable proposition for some. Harvard historian Lizabeth Cohen has argued, however, that over the past fifty years the American people have, in fact, come to see themselves as participants in a very different political and social culture. In tying this transformation in public culture to the changing norms of mass consumption, Cohen argues explicitly "that in the aftermath of World War II a fundamental shift in America's economy, politics, and culture took place, with major consequences for how Americans made a living, where they dwelled, how they interacted with others, what and how they consumed, what they expected of government, and much else."[6] What happened in the United States after World War II was no less than a "reconversion" of the booming wartime economy to an equally strong peacetime economy. While the impetus of war was enough to keep patriotic Americans working around the clock in the country's factories and manufacturing plants, how to maintain an equal level of output, so as to avoid a postwar economic slump, was less clear. The answer was found in making mass consumption an act of civic responsibility.[7] The roles of consumer and citizen were thus intertwined in ways that continue to influence how the American people come to understand their place in the public sphere. While Cohen stops short of arguing that the consumer has replaced the citizen as the central role Americans play in the public sphere, she does acknowledge that the consumer-citizen conflation has led to newer forms of democratic engagement in which "self-interested citizens increasingly view government policies like other market transactions, judging them by how well served they feel personally."[8] According to Cohen, the more central the act of consumption becomes for the American people, the more likely they will begin to understand other activities through the same framework.

Within Cohen's notion of the new consumer-citizen hybrid lies a concern that many people have about the growth in mass consumption and materialism in the United States—specifically, consuming material goods is largely a selfish act. Self-interested citizens who are only concerned about how things affect them personally are not, in the view of many, citizens at all. For some, the attitudes and behaviors of consumers are the opposite of those needed for citizens. Political theorist Benjamin Barber finds the distinction between consumers and citizens particularly salient. He believes that the citizen should be understood as "an adult, a public chooser empowered by social freedom to effect the environment of choice and the agendas by which choices are determined."[9] The citizen is a mature individual with an understanding of her place in the political and social world around her and an inherent desire to influence that world for the better. In contrast, the consumer is better represented as a child or, as Barber puts it hyperbolically, an *infantilized* individual. The infantilized person engages the public sphere in ways that mimic the modern child: he is concerned with private matters as opposed to public concerns, displays narcissistic tendencies in place of sociability, seems at ease with ignorant pleasure instead of knowledgeable happiness, and seeks immediate gratification for himself at the expense of a long-term satisfaction for the community.[10] Consumers and citizens are so at odds with each other that Barber dispels the idea of a consumers' republic—a democratic state in which citizens act productively through consumer behaviors—as "quite simply an oxymoron. Consumers cannot be sovereign, only citizens can."[11] Citizens are capable of self-governance, but consumers are little more than children unwittingly playing by the rules of the market's ideological forces.

While such exaggerated dualistic thinking may help sell books, a more levelheaded look at citizens and consumers can easily reveal that the two roles are not necessarily disjunctive.[12] One of the primary problems with the arguments that make a strict distinction between consumerism and citizenship is a tendency to root consumption in private choice and citizenship in public action. The reality is that these categories are not nearly so neat. A citizen who petitions his city council to stop a discount department store from building on land adjacent to his property may do so because he is selfishly concerned about his home value, and a consumer who buys only local meats and vegetables may do so out of a public concern for her local community. To note that citizens often make political choices based on private concerns is to do little more than acknowledge human nature, and while being selfish may not be considered a virtue, being virtuous is not a necessary requirement of citizenship—no matter what some idealists wish to think. To show, moreover, that consumers can make publicly minded decisions is to recognize the long history of consumer activism in the United States. The American people have been joining together to boycott and buycott in response to explicitly public matters ever since they became a people. Historian Lawrence Glickman has surveyed consumer activism in the United States since its founding and discovered a more symbiotic relationship between consumerism and citizenship. The very idea of consumer activism is that organized groups make a political decision to buy or not buy certain products or shop in particular stores or shopping districts. Such consumer activism is nothing new in the United States. As Glickman argues, "A more historically informed vantage might suggest that citizenship has not moved from one side to the other. It has always been practiced in both realms, although, to be sure, at times, including the recent past, the emphasis has been weighted toward the consumerist side."[13] The American people have long mixed consumerism and citizenship to influence, either positively or negatively, the world around them.

Although the roles of citizen and consumer are not mutually exclusive, even Glickman acknowledges that in recent decades the consumeristic attitude has been more dominant than one based on traditional forms of citizenship. One senses in Glickman's concession his acceptance that consumerism as a political act is fine so long as it is tempered by the values of citizenship. However, there is some apprehension that the role of consumer may become increasingly central to how the American people engage the public sphere. And this concern is never more salient than when America's young people are involved.

Young adults in the United States have increasingly grown up in a consumer environment—an atmosphere decidedly different than that of their predecessors. This is the argument sociologist Juliet Schor makes when she points out that while children have a long history as consumers, the sheer pervasiveness of consumerism and the early marketing focus on young people construct a very different consumer world for youth today.[14] From parents feeling obligated to buy infants a variety of toys to teenagers spending their parents' and their own money on everything from the newest video games to the latest fashions, American youth control a substantial piece of the U.S. economy. By some accounts, they have become the core of the nation's financial health. As Schor argues, "Kids and teens are now the epicenter of American consumer culture. They command attention, creativity, and dollars of advertisers. Their tastes drive market trends. Their opinions shape brand strategy."[15] According to one recent study, American children between two and fourteen years old influence over $500 billion in annual household spending.[16] Teenagers in 2002 personally spent $170 billion.[17] For American youth, then, being a consumer is simply a natural part of life today, and they have increasingly come to see the greater ability to consume as synonymous with greater levels of actual happiness.[18] Given these trends, it is little wonder that some scholars have found the balance between consumerism and citizenship leaning toward the former in recent years. But is this true? Do the seven high school newspapers in this study reveal a similar trend? And, if so, how might these changes have influenced the ways in which the young journalists chose to write about democratically engaging the world around them?

Growing Up Consumers

Before exploring how late capitalism may have changed democratic engagement in the United States for the young people in this study, it is necessary to establish that the seven high school newspapers elucidate just how prevalent consumer concerns have become for more recent generations. The following analysis shows that these young journalists have clearly become enmeshed in consumer society. While this may seem unsurprising given the above discussion, the following textual exemplars reveal just how entangled these young people have become with money and materialism.

The clearest way to see the rise in consumerism represented in this study's newspapers is to simply compare the number of articles dealing with financial issues across the years. Looking at Washington High School's *Ram Page*, for example, even a casual observer can detect the change. In a six-page December 1965 edition, the only article on financial matters was about a local community fund-raising project. After explaining that a number of groups in Phoenix had been working to save Camelback Mountain, a local landmark, from erosion, the writer reported that "the teenagers are also contributing to this project in their own way. The high schools have their own committees, which will try to earn the most money for the project. The high school which earns the most money will be awarded an engraved plaque."[19] Apart from this one article, the only other reference to fiscal issues is to the cost of a ticket for the winter formal—$2.50.[20] In late 1965, the students of Washington High School were not consumed with pocketbook issues.

Jumping ahead almost forty years, it is clear how much materialism had come to dominate the lives of American youth. The twelve-page December 19, 2002, issue of *Rampage*, for example, contained seven articles dealing directly with financial issues:

- "Universities Raise Tuition"
- "Purple Nets Prize" (reporting a student's monetary prize from an M&M's contest)
- "Check Your Checks" (about fees at the school's bookstore)
- "Looking at Head-to-Toe Fashions"
- "'Tis the Season to Go Shopping"
- "Bobby Miranda's 1967 Chevy Impala" (focusing on the value of his remodeled car)
- "Starvation in Some Places, Obesity in Others" (discussing the global economic divide)

In addition to these seven articles, even a story about a canned food drive was reduced to its monetary aspect. The paper reported that the winning class in the recent contest owed its success to three seniors "who alone brought in over 3,000 cans and spent almost $140."[21] Regardless of what they are talking about—world hunger, cars, or Christmas—today's young journalists seem to reflect an overwhelming concern with what things are worth and how one's wealth should be displayed. There is, however, more going on in the lives of these young people than simple awareness of monetary influences. Indeed, the money seems far less important than those things it buys and the meanings derived from those things.

Nowhere is this complex attitude toward materialism more apparent than in the area of fashion. Clothes and style have long been important to many people in the United States. Thorstein Veblen pointed out that Americans loved showing off their newfound wealth through fashion in his economic critique over a hundred years ago.[22] Benjamin Franklin noted the importance of dressing for success in his autobiography, published posthumously in 1791.[23] Over the past four decades, however, many of the American youth represented in this study have come to see the consumption of fashion as increasingly central to their lives.

The young journalists of the late 1960s and early 1970s were also concerned with fashion, but their discussion of clothing avoids the talk of money and brands indicative of more recent youth. The articles that made it into these earlier newspapers were instead marked primarily by two characteristics—questions about what is socially proper and the irrelevance of brand names. A 1966 editorial in the *Ram Page* explicitly made these points when arguing that the female fashions of the time were not "suited" for Phoenix girls.[24] While the article derides go-go boots and tight bell-bottom pants, it does so in only general terms of what the student feels is appropriate. Calling the new fashions "ridiculous," the editorial argues that go-go boots are unpractical "since it hardly ever rains in Phoenix"; that new sweaters are "so tight, and the prints so wild that one would think the girl wearing the outfit was tattooed"; and that bell-bottom pants look "molded on." Here, clearly, is an editorialist worried about young women dressing immodestly, but there is no concern with money or brands. In a similar 1967 front-page *Lancer* article, one fashion reporter wrote about what was proper for the successful man heading off to college. Talking of dark suits, vests, overcoats, and umbrellas, the article clearly encouraged young men to opt for a traditional look.[25] And while it did discuss fabric materials and costs, there was no mention of name brands or even of specific retailers. In a 1971 issue of *Grantonian*, a writer arguing for individual choice in clothing spent the first half of his article discussing the proper clothing for young people. With regard to female teachers wearing pants, he concluded that "there have been questions whether these [pants] are proper or not but the final analysis is left up to the individual."[26] No brands were mentioned in this article either, with the emphasis being placed on not pressuring people to adopt specific fashion choices. Even a 1967 *Northmen's Log* article emphasizing the "Twiggy" fad avoided discussing the new clothing style materialistically, choosing instead to talk more broadly about the style's universality: "The wild, wild, way out stripes are one of the biggest evidences of the 'Twiggy' look at Oak Park this year. All sizes and shapes of girls are seen in all styles and varieties of the many new creations of the Twiggy fashion plate."[27] Although all of these stories dealt specifically with fashion, they primarily focused on the functional quality of the products described.

For the high school journalists in the 1980s, clothing as a social marker took on a whole new meaning, with these young people increasingly regarding material goods as an outward sign of a particular lifestyle—a notion that becomes something of a politics in and of itself. To recognize that there is a politics to the stylistic choices one makes is, of course, to note the symbolic value of fashion. As Mike Featherstone argues, using the symbolic value of fashion to one's advantage can be empowering: "Rather than unreflexively adopting a lifestyle, through tradition or habit, the new heroes of consumer culture make lifestyle a life project and display their individuality and sense of style in the particularity of the assemblage of goods, clothes, practices, experiences, appearance and bodily dispositions they design together into a lifestyle."[28] Featherstone points to this shift among young people—the new heroes of consumer culture. From such a perspective, clothing is no longer simply a fashionable necessity but an outward sign of a particular lifestyle and, hence, of a particular politics. That is, lifestyle becomes the social packaging used to gain power within one's groups and to distance oneself from others via branding.[29] Lifestyle becomes a group identifier and, therefore, an integral part of community life.

Among the young people in this study, the move to a lifestyle of consumerism could not be more apparent. By 1984, these trends were already manifesting themselves at Wilson High School in Washington, D.C. An article about two young designers in the October issue of the *Beacon* opened by simply asserting, "Many teenagers thrive on purchasing fashionable and expensive clothing." The writer then moves on to discuss the students' work for a local designer, Satiny, focusing on their sources of inspiration—brands such as Calvin Klein, Giorgio Armani, and Perry Ellis. After exploring the career hopes of the two designers, the article ends by stating, "Regardless of the direction that their careers take them, John and Steve will almost certainly have careers in fashion. Don't be surprised if you are wearing Sullivan jeans and a Fitzgerald jacket in a few years."[30] The matter-of-fact tone is striking and the point quite clear. As early as the 1980s, many of the young people in this study had begun to internalize a fetish for fashion and style, and they felt their peers would find such matters worth reading in their high school newspapers. This trend toward consumerism expanded exponentially thereafter.

Wherever one looks in these high school newspapers, fashion is an obviously important material aspect of the students' lives. From a fashion show fund-raiser at Grant High School in Portland[31] to a discussion of how different types of students—goths, skaters, and preps—should dress,[32] the need to understand and engage in commodity fetishism could not be clearer. And those who seem to engage in the highest level of fashion get the most rewards. In Phoenix, for instance, the *Rampage* featured some of the latest 2002 winter clothes, including in a fashion spread the "Senior class president [who] is flaunting his look a like Justin Timberlake jacket from Gap for a whoppin $185," and a senior basketball star who "is sporting his Chicago Bulls warm-ups. He purchased them from the Sports Cage for $75."[33] The student president received two points for being cool since his jacket was both from the Gap clothing store and also connected to a major popular culture idol, while the basketball star was praised for wearing an iconic symbol of his sport. Each student was represented as being successful in school and hence worthy of emulation. During the following school year, the new class president received similar attention as a model for an article on head-to-toe fashion, wearing a "trendy Guess shirt" and a pair of Kenneth Cole shoes.[34]

Nowhere is this commodity fetishism more apparent, however, than in *Lamar Life*. As mentioned in chapter 2, Lamar High School's newspaper moved to a magazine format in the fall of 2003, and this colorful and glossy publication took fashion coverage to a whole new level. A two-page spread on fashion appeared in the winter 2004 edition. On the left page is an interview with a local student who has begun designing his own T-shirts (which entails buying solid-colored shirts and hand-painting them). The right page offers a short article on women's fall fashions, accompanied by ample pictures of new clothes and their respective prices. These pictures include an Abercrombie and Fitch Renee Houndstooth peacoat for $149, a Gap Boucle wrap coat for $128, and a Banana Republic pavé flower brooch for $38.[35] The spring 2004 issue follows suit by presenting another two-page spread offering fashion tips for girls on one page and for guys on the other.[36] The summer 2005 issue, however, pushes this focus even further with a four-page color spread on summer fashion, featuring students in sexual, flirty poses that mimic the images in fashion magazines. The spread includes nine pictures and no more than sixty words.[37] These young people are clearly offering a repackaged image of the consumer world that has captured them, and they are doing so for the benefit of their peers. That these teenagers would perform such commodity fetishism in the pages of their high school magazine reveals how natural such behavior seems to them.

The young adults in this study have clearly become enmeshed in consumerism. Their personal choices in the area of fashion are particularly relevant to how they conceived of group identity and the power dynamics in their high schools. Neoliberals and fashion designers might well be proud of having helped produce a consumer force of more than 32 million teenagers by the turn of the century—a force that spends over $100 billion a year on themselves. Community activists, however, may be less optimistic about this trend, since it coincides with decreasing levels of political participation. Many concerned about the civic health of the United States cannot help but see an inverse relationship between higher levels of consumerism and lower levels of democratic engagement. Whether good or bad, the young people in this study have certainly exhibited more consumeristic attitudes and behaviors over the past forty-five years.

Networked Conventionals

While the young people studied here were clearly consumed by consumption, this does not necessarily mean that deep-rooted materialism affected their democratic engagement, either positively or negatively. To assess such possible changes, one needs to look at where money meets matters of political action. Doing so requires a brief examination of whether the young people in this study ever seemed to enact a more traditional form of citizenship in which money is of little concern or consequence.

At the end of the 1900s, the political system in the United States was, by many accounts, cobbled together by political parties and corruption. Individuals did not vote according to political issues but according to party affiliations, and votes were often paid for by local party bosses. Politics was most certainly a passionate enterprise, but it was not a serious one for most citizens. The Progressive movement sought to change that. According to Michael Schudson, "Progressive Era politics instructed people in a citizenship of intelligence rather than passionate intensity. Political participation became less a relationship to party than a relationship to the state, less a connection to community than to principles and issues. The voter who kept up with the news read less to bask in the glow of his party's achievements than to peruse reports on the various issues, politicians, and parties of the day."[38] These changes created what Schudson refers to as the age of the informed citizen. The possibility of the emergence of the informed citizen resulted from several Progressive policies, including the secret ballot, stricter campaign regulations, and an emphasis on the Constitution as an educational instrument. Today, this model of citizenship is one that many scholars promote, since it highlights a network of citizens working together as voters and places political power in the hands of conventional political institutions.

While Schudson argues that a new rights-based citizenship began to emerge in the 1960s, the *networked conventional* still serves as a civic archetype today. Simply put, the networked conventional's primary duties as a citizen are to stay informed about political issues and to participate in traditional forms of political engagement. She is networked since her concern with political information keeps her abreast of her community and its troubles. She is conventional because she believes that the community and its institutions offer the best opportunity for fixing problems. Personal issues remain largely private, and work is about being a productive laborer. As Schudson notes, this model of citizenship has been waning, eclipsed by newer forms of democratic engagement. Based on the textual evidence in high school newspapers, Schudson's argument appears to be correct.

Beginning with the late 1960s, the last vestiges of the networked conventional remained a dominant attitude among the young journalists. In the early years of this study, most political and social problems that young people encountered were discussed in terms of their impact on the community. Such trends are evidenced everywhere in the high school newspapers. Even a problem such as parking became an issue about what it means to act as a good member of the community, as this excerpt from a 1967 article at Oak Park High School demonstrates:

> There is a possibility that Oakies will not have to purchase parking stickers in the future. Mr. Little explained that if students would treat a car as a means of transportation only, there would be no reason for any student to pay a parking fee. He added if the students would drive with courtesy and not interfere with the bus or pedestrian traffic there would be no need for parking regulations. . . . There is always the 5% who take advantage of the freedoms offered the student body as a whole. This minority acts in such a childish manner as to sometimes cause the privileges of the rest of the students to be revoked.[39]

The issue of parking stickers and restrictions is not a financial matter; it is instead a matter of acting responsibly. Four decades later, a similar issue was reported with no reference to collective responsibility. In an April 2005 article at Lamar High School, the towing of cars was discussed primarily in fiduciary terms:

> In the program, once the police are notified of a stranded car, the cops authorize towing from Houston TranStar and call a tow truck. The first tow truck driver that spots the problem will ask the police for permission to tow the car away. The cost of the towing is $75 for the first five miles and $1.50 for each additional mile. If a car needs to be stored it will cost $40 for the first day and $15 for each additional day. If the costs are not paid, the car will be sold at auction after 61 days. The "six minute rule" that goes along with the Safe Clear program states that a person has six minutes to "fix" his car, or their car will be towed. . . . With a large number of Lamar students hitting the road every day, it is very important that they all know the rules—and how to fix a flat in under six minutes![40]

The students at Lamar High School in 2005 did not seem to share the community concerns of the earlier generation at Oak Park High School. They were seemingly not worried about what was best for others. Rather, they focused on the financial and individual impact of the new towing policy.

What is true for traffic issues is also true for dietary issues. In addition to school spirit, one of the more frequently discussed school issues is the state of cafeterias. Perusing the high school newspapers in this study, one can find articles and editorials about overcrowded lunchrooms and complaints about food options with yearly consistency. Although a reliable concern, the way in which such matters are discussed has changed dramatically. For instance, writing in *Grantonian*, one Portland student reported in December 1966 on the proposal "that soda pop and coffee be served to the students in the cafeteria." While the young reporter is aware that the proposal indicates that his peers want such options, he chooses to focus on the more collective concerns about health. Noting that the school district does not explicitly prohibit soda and coffee for students, he writes that it is nevertheless "the expressed recommendation of the American Dental association, the American School Service commission, and other agencies that carbonated drinks not be served to students." The young journalist goes on to explore several other options, including vending machines, which some students will take advantage of by "using 'slugs' to cheat the machines." Written as a news article, the story offers the following concluding opinion: "Therefore, not selling pop and coffee to students is apparently not a policy of useless denial but a policy of weighted evidence with the students' benefit in mind."[41] Here is, ultimately, a student's argument about why the school's decision to not serve certain beverages at lunch is best for the collective health of his peers.

Writing for the *Denebola* four and a half decades later, one Newton South High School student took up the issue of lunch in very different terms with a news article about a student petition to improve school lunches. The lead sentence sets the story's frame: "To the misfortune of many South students, a budget cut of $500,000 has cut this year's lunch menu from 11 options to five." While such a change might be framed as a concern about student health, the reporter focuses instead on what the fewer options mean for individual choice. Indeed, the words "choice" and "option" appear a total of sixteen times in the short piece. Developing the story in the second paragraph, the young journalist notes, "Students are disappointed that with the budget cuts many of their favorite lunch options have been removed. In particular, South's cafeteria no longer offers breakfast, a deli/wrap bar, a self-serve salad bar, a separate snack bar, and rarely offers the French-fry-burger option."

The article goes on to point out a possible financial concern for the cafeteria: "While the budget cuts may intend to save money, the lack of options has resulted in fewer students buying lunches as well." The article thus turns its primary focus to whether the new budget cuts are financially responsible and how students (and some faculty) feel their choices have been too severely restricted. It is only in the last sentence that health becomes an issue. Quoting the student who started the petition, the story ends, "'Students need healthy options to make the right choices.'"[42] Even here, when student health is briefly mentioned, the issue remains rooted in individual choice, not collective concern.

A similar shift can be seen in students' attitudes toward voting. The networked conventional is quite serious about becoming informed so that she can be part of the larger, networked community. This is especially true for the students in the earliest years of this study. At Oak Park High School in 1968, one student exemplified this attitude when lionizing the informed young person: "Students all over the United States are more involved in the modern world of politics than any nation's youth has ever been. . . . A citizen of the United States can't vote until he's 21. He can, though, influence others, if he's well informed and interested."[43] This young writer places a great deal of importance on being a citizen and part of the nation's youth. There is a clear sense of collective action. And as late as 1980 the students at Wilson High School in Washington, D.C., voiced their belief in the sheer sanctity of voting, as tied to a sense of networked connection: "We, the Beacon staff, encourage active involvement in the election. We believe everyone that has registered and is of age should vote, not just because it's the American thing to do or because it makes them feel like they have a heavy responsibility which they want to prove they can handle, but because they should care. . . . The Beacon staff reiterates their belief that those who can should vote, and should choose the man who best stands for what they believe."[44] Voting, for these students, is a simple act of communal concern. Rational choice and economic concerns appear nowhere in their writing. These are students who think that young people should vote "not just" because it is their responsibility as Americans but also because they should care about their democracy. As these examples show, then, the young adults writing in the early part of this study saw democratic engagement as important for informed, networked citizens.

By the early 1990s, these attitudes were replaced by much different assumptions about voting. While they had certainly not completely abandoned the idea of informed responsibility,[45] the young people in the latter half of this study did seem to understand the act of voting in much more personalized terms. This difference is exemplified by a student who encouraged his peers to vote, while simultaneously criticizing others who tried to get young people involved. His primary reason for voting is this: "If we voted maybe television networks would cancel shows like 'Rock the Vote' and we will not have to listen to so called 'stars' tell us to vote when they probably haven't voted themselves."[46] At Newton South High School, one student exhibited great frustration with her own and her peers' political ignorance. Referring to mock elections in which she had participated in earlier years, the concerned student admits, "I know that before I cast my vote in this election, I need to have much better reasoning behind my decisions than in past elections." While she does voice a desire to make better choices, her reason for voting is ultimately very different than that of an earlier era, which emphasized the collective nature of voting. She argues, "Nobody has the right to complain about the system if they aren't doing anything to change what they don't like about it, and voting is a way of expressing what you believe, whether you vote for candidates of the main parties, those of smaller, independent parties, or even yourself, if you feel that nobody else can run the country as you'd like."[47] This student rationalizes voting as giving her the ability to express herself now and granting her the right to complain later. In a similar vein, one Oak Park High School student argued in the fall of 2008, "To me, a 17-year-old who can't vote yet, the appeal of voicing my opinion through a political election seems beyond desirable. Everyone has their complaints about politicians or politics and this is the time and place to change those things."[48] Here again, the student frames voting as a chance to voice her opinion and complain about things she does not approve of. Far removed from the rhetoric of collective responsibility, this young woman is more interested in voting as something to be personally desired.

However dominant the networked conventional attitude may have been for the students in the early years of this study, there seems to be little evidence that such collective and community-focused concerns still resonate in the pages of the high school newspapers today. Even when writing about municipal traffic problems, school petitions to increase lunch choices, and the very conventional political practice of voting, the young journalists focused primarily on individual choice. Such an emphasis on personal options and desire might suggest that many of the more contemporary young journalists have taken a more consumeristic approach to civic and political matters. Whether this is true is the subject of the next section.

Networked Consumers

One of the reasons why the young adults in this study may have come to disconnect their political concerns from community responsibility has to do with their lack of faith in others. According to political scientists Wendy Rahn and John Transue, young people in the United States have increasingly lost trust in politics and placed it in enlightened consumerism instead.[49] Borrowing a conceptual definition of materialism as a "set of centrally held beliefs about the importance of possession in one's life,"[50] they argue that an important value shaping young people's attitudes toward others is "characterized by the conjunction of nontraditional values with consumption-oriented values."[51] Through an analysis of time series survey data, Rahn and Transue find that American youth have rather quickly adopted a more materialistic view of the world that has altered their value systems and caused them to lose trust in others. Young people, according to this argument, have begun to see the social world through the competitive lenses of late capitalism.

The idea that arises from Rahn and Transue's study can be understood in terms of what is most often referred to today as political consumerism. As recently defined by Dhavan Shah and his colleagues, political consumerism is "the act of selecting among products and producers based on social, political, or ethical considerations . . . to hold companies and governments responsible for the manner in which products are produced, as well as for the nature of social and environmental consequences of this production."[52] Implicit in this definition is a two-step process: individuals have come to realize the pressures placed on them in their roles as consumers *and* have discovered that joining together with networks of other consumers is politically efficacious. While the idea of such behavior has been much discussed among scholars in recent years, there is far less evidence that such *networked consumerism* actually occurs all that often. This study's analysis of seven high school newspapers reveals that while the young people in the study have come to fully realize the pressures of materialism, they have not yet shown any consistency in responding to these pressures as consumers with like-minded others.

While it was shown above that these young journalists have increasingly become rooted in talk of consumer behavior, understanding the pressures to consume is another matter. In a number of articles, the students did, however, openly discuss these pressures. As one Pittsburgh student wrote in a December 2001 article in Carrick High School's *Carrickulum*, "Instead of borrowing mom and dad's [credit card] you can have your own. It's a material world out there, and we are all material boys and girls. . . . Credit card companies are targeting teenagers and college students to make their money. The younger generation has no idea what paying bills and working to stay afloat feels like. Our part time jobs turn into forty hours a week and our high school and college years are spent between school work, job work, and absolute stress."[53] This student admits that young people are attracted to materialism, that they have to work hard to afford their lifestyles, and that the financial/consumer world is aware of young people as an important marketing segment. Given that today's youngest generations are the most marketed-to generations ever,[54] it should be no surprise to find students becoming increasingly aware of the role young people play in the market-place, and it should be even less astonishing that they are starting to feel frustrated with the pressures of this role.

More than simply starting to understand their roles in consumer society, there is also evidence that the young people in this study were not entirely happy about this development. At Newton South High School in Boston, such concerns have become especially clear in recent years, as can be seen, for instance, in the March 2005 edition of *Denebola*. Under the large banner "Selling Adolescence," writers devoted three pages to examining how young people are targeted as consumers. One article on how trends were poisoning the school culture began by arguing that "Newton South High School can-not get enough of anything worn by a celebrity or with a brand name. These products are perpetuating the American stereotype of a stupid, gluttonous society, because all we do is waste our money and follow trends."[55] Another article explored why young people are so aggressively targeted by advertis-ers, pointing out that "it is estimated that teens spent $169 billion in 2004, a figure that includes both teens' own money as well as that given to them from their parents."[56] And a full-page piece on ten of the coolest current trends then hitting Newton South High was filled with sarcasm. Referring to *The OC*, a popular television show about wealthy high school students in California, the article states that "teens still can't get enough of watching the rich, privileged characters struggle through a life filled with angst, affairs, and alcohol." With regard to a popular new Gap vest, the writer goes on to exclaim, "That's right—$120 for a jacket without sleeves!"[57] As these stu-dents were keenly aware, they and their peers were being targeted by—and following the lead of—advertisers who would do anything for their money. Five years later, students at Newton South High continued to be concerned about the pressure to consume. After arguing that teen spending remains excessive despite a national recession, one concerned student expressed her fear in February 2010 that teens failed to understand the importance of managing their money. She contended that she and her peers needed to get smarter with their spending, stating that "financial education is vital to help teens make good decisions about their money now and in the future."[58] Thus, even students at the most affluent school in this study apparently needed help understanding the pressures of money and consumerism.

To understand just how far this pressure goes, one need only look at newspaper coverage of proms. Proms have long been a major part of spring life for high school juniors and seniors, but students' attitude toward them has changed over the past forty-five years. In the early years of this study, many proms took place in school gyms with minimal expenditures, and the prom was typically portrayed as an end-of-the-year party for juniors and seniors. The writer of a March 1967 editorial in *Denebola* illustrated this point when reporting that "the prospect of holding the Prom at the Meadows was heatedly discussed at several Class Committee meetings. It was argued that the type of Prom advocated would keep many students from attending due to a rise in cost. This would defeat the primary purpose of the Prom: To get the Whole class together for the final time."[59] An article in the May 1967 issue of the *Ram Page* struck a similar tone by pointing to what some other schools around the country were doing for the prom. The young journalist noted, for instance, that "Jay and the Americans and lobster tails are generally not considered aspects of a senior prom. Not at WHS proms, anyway."[60] While such extravagances might have just been beginning to emerge for some high schools, this student's perception is that such activities go too far. He points out, "Also uncommon . . . is the $30 seniors of Plainedge High School of Massapequa, New York, will have to cough up." For the students of the late 1960s and early 1970s in this study, then, the prom was primarily an event to bring students together for a night of fun.

Over the years, the prom has changed in character. What was clearly the exception in the early years of this study seems to have become the norm more recently. Most high schools no longer hold their dances in the gym, and most students end up spending a good deal of money on dresses, tuxedos, limousines, and five-star meals. As sociologist Amy Best has argued, the prom has become an important financial event for students, schools, and communities.[61] Its significance as a fashion show cannot be denied, and students have begun to feel the pressures. The following headlines, which were all published after 1990, demonstrate that whenever coverage of the prom appears in more recent newspapers, it is accompanied by at least one piece questioning its cost:

- "Bankruptcy Court Maybe in Near Future for Seniors" (*Carrickulum*, June 15, 1994)
- "The Perfect Prom: At What Price?" (*Rampage*, May 10, 1995)
- "Prom Dollars: What Can You Afford to Spend for Memories? Is It All Worth the Money?" (*Rampage*, May 2, 1997)
- "Is $1,000 Too Much to Ask for ONE Night of Fun?" (*Carrickulum*, May 23, 2000)
- "Facing up to Prom PRESSURE" (*Northmen's Log*, April 19, 2002)

As all of these headlines reveal, the high school students are aware of the prom's soaring cost and the pressures associated with trying to keep up with some of their peers. What is not so clear is whether they believe they can do anything about it.

For some, prom expenses have become so natural that they are encouraged. In a May 2006 editorial in *Northmen's Log*, one student argued against moving Oak Park High School's prom from the KCI Expo Center to Bartle Hall in downtown Kansas City. While the editorialist clearly wants the prom to remain at the Expo Center, her concern has nothing to do with money; she is instead worried about the new location's proximity to the school. Far from decrying the prom's financial impact, the angry senior actually takes quite the opposite stance in her concluding paragraph: "It's senior Prom and I encourage everyone to have a crazy-good time. Dress up, spend lots of money, dance until you can't stand up and then race go-carts, but please, keep Prom easy-access."[62] While this student may not have considered prom expenses to be an issue, for those who are aware of such problems, the question remains: Do they have the political efficacy needed to fight back as networked consumers?

The average individual is, indeed, faced with a growing number of choices that conflate his or her roles as citizen and consumer. If a woman walks into a local coffee shop and finds two coffees on the menu—regular Colombian supreme and a 100 percent organic fair trade—she *may* find her consumption habits (buying the cheaper Colombian coffee) in conflict with her political values (fighting the inequality of globalization). Moreover, she may share this conflict with other cosmopolitan citizens. In seeing her choice this way, she becomes a networked consumer, a persona that *may* give her a sense of efficacy. In any event, her decision is not based on her need for a caffeinated, hot beverage. She must also contend with multiple desires that underscore the postmodern shift of late capitalism. But while her proto-political action is laudable, is it the norm for today's youth?

According to a number of recent political and communication scholars, young people have begun to take a more direct consumeristic approach toward the political world around them. Today's youth are said to be demanding more from their governmental and corporate-run communities, in much the same way that consumers are demanding better products and services. As Lance Bennett argues, "Across a whole range of relations with the state, citizens now take a more explicitly consumeristic stance, expecting more direct benefits and fewer collective goods and demanding more choice in education, health care, and other areas of state services."[63] More active examples of political consumerism include, according to Bennett, the 1999 WTO protests in Seattle, the boycotting of Nike products due to the company's use of sweatshops, and the direct lobbying of Microsoft by a large network of computer users for better product standards. Bennett agrees with other researchers who have argued that young people have increasingly pulled out of traditional political action, suggesting that "when our political lens moves out beyond government, we find new forms of political expression taking shape that often channel individual identifications into surprisingly large-scale activities."[64] Included in these activities is the belief that many young adults now act as highly politicized consumers.

As Michele Micheletti defines it, political consumerism is the "consumer choice of producers and products with the goal of changing objectionable institutional or market practices."[65] And Lizabeth Cohen has referred to these same types of activity through her notion of the consumer's republic.[66] Both authors assume that many people—particularly today's consumer-savvy youth—have begun to bypass the old channels of governmental intervention in political matters. Citizens seeking to impact their communities go straight to the source of power—the corporations and financial institutions that are polluting the air, failing to provide health care and fair wages to labor, and suppressing the free speech of labor unions. They are primarily taking action through boycotts, buycotts, and individual consumer choice. The individual who consciously chooses to buy American-made products is, from these scholars' perspective, acting as a political consumer. So too is the individual who decides against buying a Liz Claiborne sweater for fear of supporting the company's use of sweatshops in Third World countries.

For many scholars, there is a built-in sense of efficacy for the political consumer. For instance, Anthony Giddens has argued that the buying power and inherent choices associated with consumerism are emancipatory.[67]

A number of scholars see this emancipation as natural. Margaret Scammell takes up the argument with matter-of-factness: "The act of consumption is becoming increasingly suffused with citizenship [which] is not dead, or dying, but found in new places, in life-politics . . . and in consumption. The site of citizens' political involvement is moving from the production side of the economy to the consumption side."[68] Micheletti and her colleagues have argued that political consumerism is quite natural in that it allows individuals to act through "consumer choice of producers and products with the goal of changing objectionable institutional or market practices."[69] And still others take the argument further to include more activist-type consumer actions, contending that "when people engage in boycotts or 'buycotts' with the aim of using the market to vent their political concerns, they are said to engage in the act of political consumerism."[70] All of these arguments rest on the assumption that one can act politically through consumerism and that the networked consumer can thereby have a real effect on the world around her.

While networked consumerism may indeed be on the rise in some quarters, there is very little textual evidence to suggest that the young journalists in this study are part of this trend. Of the seven high school newspapers, only two discussed how students can respond to societal problems as political consumers—the *Denebola*, from Boston's Newton South High School, and *Grantonian*, from Portland's Grant High School. In the *Denebola*, students discussed such issues as eating at local restaurants instead of national chain restaurants and working collectively as a school to escape the pressures of wearing expensive, brand-name clothing.[71] The students at Grant High School offered ideas for political consumers that included frequenting locally owned movie theaters instead of larger chains, not shopping at all on the day after Thanksgiving (what they referred to as "Buy Nothing Day"), and boycotting Nike due to its use of sweatshops.[72] While these articles clearly point to a sense of networked activism, they do not constitute a trend. After all, Newton South High School is located in the Newton Centre suburb of Boston, one of the wealthiest and most liberal areas of a left-leaning city. Grant High School sits in the heart of Portland, Oregon, surrounded by a counterculture of local shops, breweries, and cultural diversity. Newton South and Grant High students are clearly familiar with the networked consumerism that Lance Bennett and others have found to be on the rise, but these notions have not sunk deep roots among the young people studied here. Considering that these student journalists are some of the most politically informed and socially aware young adults in their schools, the fact that they rarely, if ever, discuss the option of political consumerism suggests it is far from the norm.

Removed Volunteers

Given that networked conventionals seem to have largely disappeared and that networked consumers are more the exception than the norm, what type of political engagement does one find among these young journalists? According to the newspapers studied here, they seem to have become a generation of *removed volunteers*. That is, the young adults writing in these newspapers over the past twenty years have adopted two primary outlets for political engagement: donating goods or money and volunteering in various organizations.

Most problems that might have once been dealt with through representative political action are now handled by collecting goods and donations. Young people in high schools around the country have long engaged in fundraising activities for a number of causes. At Grant High School in Portland, Oregon, for instance, a 1965 article praised the school's students for raising over $1,000 for the United Good Neighbor Drive.[73] In Phoenix, Arizona, the same year, the *Ram Page* reported that close to $200 had been added to the Student Council treasury during a workday drive in which students earned money "by waxing a semi-truck, washing windows, washing a car, cleaning pipe and trimming shrubbery."[74] And in Washington, D.C., the students at Wilson High School decided to sell school buttons and pom-poms to raise money for pep rally decorations instead of turning to the school's administration or local school board.[75] While all three of these examples show students raising money to benefit their organizations, the students are not giving their own money, nor are they working individually.

Throughout the 1970s and 1980s, the young people in this study continued to raise money for school organizations and local causes. What distinguishes such activities in more recent years, however, is the emphasis on students donating their own money and working individually to find ways to raise funds for good causes. The holiday season became a particularly important time to do this.

A new form of political action emerged in the 1990s and has continued into the present—students giving money directly to support causes. In October 2000, *Northmen's Log* reported, for instance, that Oak Park High School had raised well over $5,000 for United Way and that much of this came directly from students who contributed "money to the administrator's bucket they most wanted to see wear one of the ugly thrift store outfits" that had been donated for the fund-raiser.[76] At Grant High School, students were expected to pay $8 a ticket for a benefit concert held in 2003 to help fund the

Grant High School Foundation, which helped "buy back teacher salaries that [had] been eliminated by the budget cuts."[77] These students gave money to pay for their own teachers. Indeed, students donating their money to a good cause became such a norm that it even made it into some arguments against the cost of the prom. One guest columnist in the *Ram Page* explained that she did not want students to boycott the prom and could even understand "that dressing up and riding around in a limo with your friends is like being a celebrity on the way to a gala event." What concerned her was that "when a game of dress up exceeds $300, then parading around in a fantasy of adulthood becomes undesirable pretty quickly." With some measure of guilt inducement, she suggested her peers could go ahead with their expensive plans "if you are comfortable with yourself knowing your money could have supported a battered women's shelter."[78] Instead of spending on themselves excessively, this concerned student implied that her peers would be better off donating their money to help others.

The tendency of the young people in this study to donate money for political purposes was especially apparent in the wake of major tragedies. Following the terrorist attacks of September 11, 2001, for example, the students at Washington High School in Phoenix responded with the following front-page headline: "WHS Family Unites for Terror Victims: School Fundraisers Net over $3,000." Whatever else the students might have been doing as citizens in response to 9/11, they were definitely acting with their wallets. In the same issue and directly beneath a factual account of the terrorist attacks, students were given the names and numbers of eight different organizations to which they could donate money, from the New York Firefighters Fund and the American Red Cross to the National Disaster Search Dog Foundation, where donations would "assist in buying booties for the search and rescue dogs to help them walk in the glass and rubble."[79] The same emphasis was found at Oak Park High School in Kansas City, where it was reported that the average student could get involved in one of four ways: (1) by contributing to Gladfest donations, through which anyone could pay to have a friend "arrested," (2) by using the online donation services provided at helping.org, (3) by donating to the online contribution site september11fund.org, and (4) by donating blood.[80] And at Lamar High School in Houston, an article on the tsunami in Asia listed famous individuals who had made contributions: "The tsunami even has some of the hottest rock and action stars donating money to help the victims. Rock/Rap group Linkin Park gave $100,000, action star Jackie Chan gave $65,000, Sandra Bullock gave $1 million, and Michael Dell donated $1 million. HISD raised over $135,000."[81] The story ends by voicing the hope that these donations are just the beginning of the needed philanthropy and then offers a list of web-sites and organizations where further contributions can be made. In each of these instances, students are not asked to help *raise* money. They are asked to *give* of their own resources, thereby conflating financial and political activity.

Such conflation of money and politics seemed quite natural to the young people in this study whenever problems emerged, regardless of the scope of these problems. As demonstrated by one recent Newton South High School student, the assumption that donations are the key to solving the world's problems seems a foregone conclusion. Writing in the *Denebola* two months after the earthquake in Haiti struck on January 12, 2010, the concerned student noted that following the tragedy "students at Newton South High School immediately took action and began to devise tactics that they felt would raise the most money to send to the Red Cross." Over the next four paragraphs of the editorial, the student recounts some of these tactics—including collect-ing money from students as they were entering school—before turning to his central concern. He writes, "Sadly, we tend to forget the suffering and agony that occurs on a daily basis to other people outside of Newton. This is, in part, a natural tendency, but above all it is selfish." While he praises the students' original efforts to donate money, he is bothered by how quickly they have gone on with their lives, and he is, moreover, truly concerned about the continuing struggles faced by the Haitian people. The student therefore argues "that the task of helping the Haitians is not complete. We must refo-cus our efforts." To get his peers to refocus, he chastises them, "You should spend a little less time on Facebook or playing COD, and think of ways we can continue to raise money." Ultimately, he wants students to quit being selfish and to work harder to help others. Of course, wanting to help others is a noble goal, but nowhere in the article does this passionate student question larger systemic problems or the actual good the donations might do. There is no discussion of writing letters to congresspersons to increase the American government's response or of buycotting companies involved in the rescue and recovery of the Haitian people. Donating money is, simply, what should be done to help solve the problems of others. And raising the money through various charities and events becomes the way to "come together" and to "tap our full potential."[82]

It would be wrong, however, to assume that the high school students in this study eschewed involvement in their communities in nonmonetary ways. They did, in fact, become involved in community volunteering. No longer content to let the government take care of the poor (and with the decline in the modern welfare state in the United States), these young journalists sometimes advocated stepping in to fill the void. Two articles in a May 2000 issue of *Rampage*, for instance, discussed the importance of volunteering and how rewarding it can be for the individual. One of them also mentioned the practical side of volunteering—that it might help a student earn a scholarship for college.[83] An article in *Northmen's Log* in the fall of 2001 made a similar point by arguing that students had gained insight and awareness through volunteering.[84] Students at Carrick High School found volunteering at the local food drive to be a rewarding way of serving their communities: "There is nothing like the feeling that someone engages in when they are able to lend a helping hand to someone less fortunate than themselves."[85] The young activists at Grant High School likewise reported that "if you've been looking for an activity that is fun, doesn't have to take a lot of time and makes you—and others—feel good, get out there and start volunteering."[86] And the benefits of volunteering were not lost on the wealthy students at Newton South High School; an article in the *Denebola* reported that "there are many benefits of doing community service. The one that consistently keeps students involved in what they do is the satisfaction they get from seeing how their work improves the lives of others."[87] While some of these students may have been volunteering because of the recent service-learning push in public education, they also saw volunteerism as personally rewarding.

The long-term trends of volunteering may not be so promising, however. Over the past fifteen years, a number of researchers have identified the possibility of service learning as a way to get students to reengage with their communities. Sidney Verba, Kay Lehman Schlozman, and Henry Brady have, for instance, argued that adults are more likely to become politically engaged if they have been active in community-based organizations as young adults.[88] Yet other scholars have found that service learning has no discernible impact or that its impact is short-lived.[89] Some research has additionally found that those whose volunteering does impact their worldview do not necessarily see politics as an arena in which they can affect social issues.[90] In the end, young people's current spate of community volunteerism may actually be teaching them that while they may be able to help their neighbors, they cannot affect the larger political sphere.

Another concern with volunteering today is that organizations themselves have changed. Unlike the soup kitchens and American Red Cross of today, organizations during the 1950s and 1960s were more demanding of the individual and thereby created a greater sense of community networking.

Sociologist Theda Skocpol has elaborated on this point: "A civil society once centered on nationally active and locally vibrant voluntary membership federations—such as the American Legion, the Elks, and the PTA—went the way of the once-popular television program *Leave It to Beaver*. . . . By now Americans are no longer such avid joiners, although they may be organizing more civic endeavors than ever before. Professionally run advocacy groups and nonprofit institutions now dominate civic society, as people seek influence and community through a very new mix of largely memberless voluntary organizations."[91] While today's students may very well be taking on more volunteering than previous generations, the voluntary organizations demand much less from them. Instead of playing a more networked and central role in the group, these newer organizations relegate the individual to a subcontractor, thereby creating the removed volunteer identified here.

In recent years, the high school newspapers in this study have been filled with arguments about how and why students should donate money to organizations and volunteer for good causes. Their understanding of removed volunteering as central to democratic engagement is overwhelming. One recent article in Oak Park High School's *Northmen's Log* demonstrates just how dominant this theme has become. The front-page article of an October 2007 issue delved into the problem of global poverty. Arguing that the "global market system" led many Third World countries to produce goods for the pleasure of wealthier nations, the concerned student writes, "Unfortunately, this forces these poor countries to be stuck in the role of exporter, and are thus stuck as slaves to the prices the developed countries are willing to pay." Being stuck in subordinate roles, the student argues further, causes a great deal of poverty in these less developed nations. To explain why his peers should be concerned about this, the student goes on to outline the serious problems poverty causes—the spread of disease, terrorism, and environmental problems. Having laid out the severity of the issue and connected it to the lives of his peers in the American Midwest, the impassioned young journalist then offers some advice on what can be done about global poverty: "If this article has moved you to take action there are numerous organizations trying to help the impoverished. The World Bank has made it its goal to eliminate poverty and encourage development around the world." To help in this effort, the young man writes of "numerous charities," and he suggests that "students can send donations to the World Bank and write their Congressmen to urge them to take action on an important issue." While one might want to praise this student's awareness of more conventional politics, it is concerning that this more traditional form of political engagement gets only passing mention. Immediately after reminding his peers of their elected representatives, the young man returns to the importance of donations and incorporates volunteering into his advice: "Students at Oak Park have already contributed greatly to the fight against poverty. National Honor Society conducted the clothing drive and Volunteer Club organized a canned food drive."[92] In the end and despite the reference to a more traditional political action, fighting poverty—and, by extension, disease, terrorism, and global warming—requires acting as removed volunteers.

Conclusion

The story told in this chapter is a complicated one. Over the past forty-five years, the young adults in this study came to see themselves as consumers in the marketplace. The days of the networked conventional, who saw the worlds of politics and materialism as distinct from each other, have come to an end. But these same youth have not predominantly come to see themselves as networked consumers, using their personal buying choices and consumer power to influence corporate and governmental policy. Instead, they have begun to see problems and issues that might have once been handled through more traditional means (i.e., voting, letter writing, petition signing) as best dealt with by donating money and volunteering, thereby distancing themselves from the traditional political sphere.

One might argue these young people do not yet have the financial capital to engage society as networked consumers. Given enough time, it might be assumed, these young people will grow into more financially secure citizens who can then begin to engage in their communities through networked consumerism. If this were true, one could expect to see a burgeoning political force that is free of the inequalities of the past. As Anthony Giddens has argued, life politics, within which networked consumerism plays a major role, is emancipatory since it works through the creative powers of free market capitalism.[93] Might this be true for tomorrow's young people? There is reason to believe quite the opposite. Acting as a networked consumer does not require one to have considerable financial assets. Choosing to buy New Balance running shoes, which are made in America, instead of some other brand's shoes produced in Third World sweatshops is no more or less expensive for the consumer. Nor is it any more expensive to stop by the locally owned coffee shop instead of Starbucks. These young people, that is, could already be making politically motivated consumer choices. However, they appear to be doing no such thing.

Richard Sennett has recently agreed with the research reported here, arguing that "rather than just as an angry voter, we might want to consider the citizen as a consumer of politics, faced with pressures to buy." Unlike those who praise networked consumers, Sennett sees the world of consumption as essentially theatrical, since the individual is asked to consume something that he or she does not actually need. For Sennett, this requires a questionably dangerous suspension of disbelief that disempowers the individual. More problematic, he believes, is that a society based on mass consumption strips the individual of vital tools necessary for democratic citizenship. He suggests that "when citizens act like modern consumers they cease to think like craftsmen. This worry complements the policymaker's inattention, but more finely; the citizen-as-consumer can disengage when political issues become difficult or resistant."[94]

The idea here is that surplus capitalism and mass production have negated the individual's need to have a functional knowledge of *how* things work, to understand the political process. One does not need to know how a television works since it is easier to drive to Walmart and buy a new appliance than to fix the broken one sitting in the living room. As Sennett ultimately argues, "User-friendly makes a hash of democracy. Democracy requires that citizens be willing to make some effort to find out how the world around them works. . . . When democracy becomes modeled on consumption, becomes user-friendly, that will to know fades."[95] In the end, Sennett finds the consumer culture to be at odds with citizenship. Or, as Alan Aldridge has summed up the argument,

> The claim that citizens have been reduced to consumers implies a loss of political engagement. Citizenship expresses a fundamental equality, while consumerism generates and feeds on inequality. Citizens have social, economic and political rights, but they also have duties and responsibilities; consumers have merely consumer rights, and the dubious "protection" provided by regulators. Citizens engage in collective action to make society better, whereas consumers are preoccupied with improving their own individual lot. Citizens move in the public domain, consumers retreat into a private refuge. On such accounts, citizenship is not an aspect of consumerism but its antithesis.[96]

For these scholars, there is little reason to believe that networked consumerism is liberating, because the acts of citizens and consumers are at odds with each other. This more negative argument sees the rise of consumption as a central problem for the health of democratic citizenship.

The networked consumerism that some researchers have identified may actually be the dying vestiges of an older "citizen mentality." Individuals who were politically socialized as networked conventionals eventually found themselves in a changing political landscape. Forced to find new ways to engage a political community increasingly controlled by corporations and market forces, they turned to networked consumerism. Young people being raised today as consumers might, in fact, be lacking the tools of citizenship. As a result, the United States may now be harboring a nation of individually motivated citizens who fail to understand the political and collective implications of social problems and corporate issues.

As removed volunteers, the young journalists in this study have given up much of the collective political power central to civic life. Instead, they engage in politics through two avenues—by making donations to political causes and by volunteering in loose, low-membership organizations. Neither decision requires communal or networked activity. After all, each can be accomplished in complete isolation, thereby giving power to special interest community organizations, the result of which is a lowered sense of individual political efficacy. A person can donate money, but that buys little control over the impact of the donation. Similarly, the individual can volunteer but must do so within the organization's guidance and rules. The removed volunteer resembles the subcontracted employee of modern corporations—doing the company's work with no input in the process and no clear benefits from the community (e.g., health care).

Today's organizations are more than happy to promote this removed model of citizenship. Take, for example, the following "How to Help" directive to concerned individuals visiting the website of the Dana-Farber Cancer Institute: "With the support of compassionate and committed volunteers and donors like you, Dana-Farber is able to continue the progress we've made in the fight against cancer."[97] While the removed volunteer may feel good about lending a helping hand, this individual has no input in the larger mission of Dana-Farber. Even the American Red Cross has learned that lesson. As of 2006, its website featured a number of links—Donate Now, Give Blood, Tissue Donation, Volunteer, Donate Goods—as well as the following suggestions:

> Planned Giving: What is the secret to making a gift that will provide the greatest benefit to you and the American Red Cross? . . . Planned gifts

create opportunities for both the American Red Cross and our donors. Determining what gift is right for you is just as important as making the gift. There are a myriad of easy giving options from which you can choose—from naming us as a beneficiary in your will to a more complex trust arrangement.

Be a Red Cross volunteer! Helping others feels good, and helps you feel good about yourself. Your local Red Cross can work with you to provide rewarding experiences, opportunities to utilize your talents, or provide training to help you serve your community.[98]

While these appeals are heartwarming, they also suggest a managerial model of civic life. What is missing from the Red Cross website is a link to where the individual might find information about contacting U.S. senators or representatives. Nor does the website provide an assessment of government spending for disasters.

The Red Cross has pushed the point one step further. It recently teamed with the Advertising Council, America's Blood Centers, and the AABB (an international network of blood banks) to create the Blood Saves Campaign. To increase blood donations, the organizations have put together a number of advertisements depicting young people struggling over the complicated workings of government. In one, a troubled African American youth explains that she wanted to stop a company from polluting local streams and rivers. She wrote to her legislators to complain and then organized a protest, both of which led to the company's closing. This victory, however, resulted in job losses and sick children since parents had lost their health insurance. The increasingly frustrated tone of the speaker stops as the voiceover announces, "Saving the world isn't easy. Saving a life is. Donating one pint of blood can save up to three lives. Maybe even someone you know." In the end, the message is clear: let us take care of the messy business of politics. In recent years, the students studied here have clearly heard that message.

5

PROTECTIVE CRITICS

In an interview with *Time* magazine in March 2002, Bono, the lead singer of the rock band U2 and a political activist in the struggle to aid Third World countries, voiced his frustration over decades of singing politically motivated songs, which he had come to believe effected no real change in the world. Regarding his recent decision to engage in more traditional political actions, Bono explained, "I'm tired of dreaming. . . . U2 is about the impossible. Politics is the art of the possible. They're very different, and I'm resigned to that now." The difference for Bono was that while music might inform, it could not deal with the real problems on the ground. He further stated, "I learned about South America from listening to the Clash. I learned about Situationism from the Sex Pistols. But that's a long way from budget caps and dealing with a Congress that is suspicious of aid because it has been so misused."[1] For one of the biggest popular culture icons of the past few decades, then, there is a clear distinction between the worlds of politics and popular culture. Bono's assertion that politics is a science directed at what can be done is reminiscent of Harold Lasswell's well-known definition of politics—"who gets what when and how."[2] Popular culture, on the other hand, is a space in which people can dream and imagine utopia or dystopia, but it is not a place where things necessarily get done. Bono is not, of course, the first person to stumble onto this difference. Robert Frost knew it too, telling an audience in 1962 that "poetry is about grief and politics is about grievance."[3] Art seeks to understand the human social condition; politics wants to change the human social condition—for better or worse. While this distinction may have held for centuries, this chapter begins by asserting that the division is no longer as clear as it was once conceived.

A growing number of scholars across many academic fields have begun to suggest that the worlds of politics and popular culture are becoming increasingly intermingled. This is implied in political theorist John Street's observation that "when Bono . . . is granted an audience with the Pope or is invited to spend time with the U.S. president in the White House, it certainly *seems* as if the worlds of politics and popular culture are almost inseparable." Street argues that there is, in fact, a clear "currency of celebrity and fame" that creates an intersection of politics and popular culture.[4] A growing number of celebrities are becoming politicians (e.g., Ronald Reagan, Sonny Bono, Clint Eastwood, Jesse Ventura, and Arnold Schwarzenegger), and a grow- ing number of politicians are turning up in movies (e.g., John McCain in *Wedding Crashers*), television sitcoms (e.g., Al Gore on *30 Rock*), and cartoons (e.g., Tony Blair on *The Simpsons*). It seemed only natural to see Bruce Springsteen perform at a campaign stop for Barack Obama during the 2008 presidential race and to see celebrity couple Angie Harmon (actress) and Jason Sehorn (football star) deliver a speech at the 2004 Republican National Convention. Clearly, celebrities and politicians have come to find each other mutually beneficial, but it seems that the intersecting of politics and popular culture can go much further than this.

There are indications that, at least for some, politics and popular culture have blurred into one world where reality and fiction become indiscern- ible. One recent example from season 5 of NBC's television show *The West Wing* clearly illustrates this point. In episode 15, the character of White House intern Ryan Pierce recommends the closing of Fort Drum, a military base in northern New York, while covering a meeting of the Base Closing Commission for Deputy White House Chief of Staff Josh Lyman. The morning following the show's initial February 25, 2004, airing, New York's Senator Hillary Rodham Clinton and Representative John McHugh, who were then representing the congressional district in which the real Fort Drum is located, felt compelled to respond since they felt that the military base was not, in fact, in danger of being closed. Clinton and McHugh sent a letter addressed to the character of Deputy Lyman at the *West Wing* studios. The congresspersons wrote that they "want[ed] to make sure that such a rec- ommendation doesn't make it into another *West Wing* scene. It is important that all White House advisors have the most current information to respond to such flawed proposals." One day later, *USA Today* picked up the story and criticized the letter. The newspaper's article on the incident begins, "People, it's just a television show."[5] It goes on to describe the problem with the "sur- real missive": "'Dear Josh,' begins the letter from Clinton and McHugh, who are real, to Lyman, who is not." The author obviously found the exchange a bit confusing and seemed appalled at the idea that anyone might have thought the comment about Fort Drum on the show was true.

Even if one takes Senator Clinton and Representative McHugh's letter as a tongue-in-cheek publicity stunt, the incident points to the growing interconnectedness of politics and popular culture. A television network airs an episode in which fictional characters discuss the possibility of closing an actual military base, which prompts a response by real politicians, which then gets reported in the mainstream news media. Politicians (one of whom is a celebrity in her own right), a television show about a fictionalized White House (with an actor—Martin Sheen—who is an outspoken Democrat in real life), and the news media are all mixed together in a single event. What is one to make of all this? Surely Senator Clinton and Representative McHugh can tell the difference between the *real* world of politics and the *fictional* one represented on television. So why would these two presumably sane government leaders send a letter to a fictional deputy White House chief of staff regarding a proposed base closing discussed during a television show? Perhaps they were concerned that their constituents might not be able to make the distinction between a television drama and the real world. Is this true? Have today's citizens lost the ability to separate politics and popular culture? And, if so, what might the outcomes of such confusion be for the American democratic system?

This chapter begins with the assumption that politics and popular culture have indeed become entangled and that it is safe to say the resulting mélange might be affecting people's political perceptions. With this in mind, the chapter delves into the discourse of the young journalists in this study to see how their interaction with popular culture may be impacting their political and social views. It reveals that these young people have become increasingly enmeshed in the world of popular culture, and its pervasive influence has taught them to be too cool to care too much about that world. This nonchalant attitude has manifested itself in their critical take on much of what they watch and listen to, a perspective that seems to protect them from caring too much about the all too fickle world of popular culture. Given that these young journalists do not make clear distinctions between the worlds of politics and popular culture, I argue in the end that their critical attitude has carried over into the political world, where many of them have learned to be *protective critics*. To make this argument, I begin by first exploring how central popular culture has become for the young adults in this study over the past half century. As with the consumerism discussed in the previous chapter, many of these young people today seem to be overwhelmingly immersed in popular culture.

The Rising Importance of Popular Culture

While in an earlier time scholars might have legitimately attempted to argue that popular culture does not influence people's worldviews and real lives, that time has passed. Indeed, the question is no longer *whether* such effects exist but rather *how* popular culture influences people. What one reads, watches, and listens to—whether civics textbooks or graphic novels—are epistemic texts. People learn about the travails of the human heart through popular novels dealing with marriage and infidelity. They also learn the consequences of war through film. They even learn about political problems, regardless of whether they act on this knowledge, from the songs they listen to on their MP3 players. Put simply, people make sense of the world around them through the popular culture they consume.

That popular culture should be understood epistemically is something scholars have understood for decades. One of the earliest writers to make such an argument was rhetorical theorist Kenneth Burke, who contended in 1941 that all literature should be understood as extended proverbs. That is, Burke understood "literature as equipment for living."[6] His point was that people literally use the knowledge they gain from the books they read to help them live their own lives. Writing a half century later, rhetorical scholar Barry Brummett extended Burke's idea to include "electronic literature." Brummett demonstrated that even something as seemingly innocuous as a haunted house film may actually give viewers the necessary "equipment for living" through anomie.[7] Faced with an unfamiliar situation, someone could use the lessons learned from haunted house films to deal with the uncertainty of real life. Since the mid-1980s, scholars in rhetoric, communication, media studies, and a number of other academic fields have come to accept that both Burke and Brummett are correct in noting people learn from the popular culture with which they engage. To be sure, it is but one of many socializing forces they learn from, but it is nevertheless an important one to examine. In the world of politics, popular culture may have very real consequences. As communication scholars Trevor Parry-Giles and Shawn Parry-Giles have recently argued, for instance, television shows such as *The West Wing* can serve as mimetic representations of the real presidency, with very genuine implications for how viewers come to think the actual president can and should act.[8] The fact that technological changes over the past half century have made popular culture an all the more pervasive part of life only increases the need to study its influence.

One clear impact of the communications revolution of the last fifty years has been the increasing salience of popular culture in the everyday lives of individuals, particularly young adults. Popular culture is not, however, a new phenomenon. The reasons for taking it seriously as "equipment for living" can best be explained through a brief recounting of its history. Popular culture has been around for at least the past two centuries. Cultural studies scholar John Storey notes this fact while tracking the history of popular culture from folk music and art to its growing globalized reach. He argues,

> The first concept of popular culture was invented with the discovery of the folk in the late eighteenth century and in the folklore and folksong movements of the nineteenth and early twentieth centuries. Over a period of 140 years the idea of popular culture as folk culture was developed by intellectuals across Europe and the USA. They had not set out to produce a way of thinking about popular culture, but in doing what they did—whether this was seeking to promote national cultures or to develop a science of "primitive man"—the first concept of popular culture was invented.[9]

As Storey points out, studying folk culture as a way of understanding the masses of ordinary people led to the very notion of a popular culture many years later. The idea of a strictly defined popular culture was a clear response by societal elites to differentiate their own high culture from the music, art, and fiction being consumed by the masses. This is not to suggest that social class and cultural taste have not always been linked in some important ways, but it is to suggest that as the notion of a folk/popular culture came into being there was a movement to distinguish it from more aesthetically rigorous high cultures. Storey makes just this distinction when arguing, "What had changed—and this is what I mean by the invention of popular culture as the 'other' of high culture—was the institutionalization of this connection between class and culture."[10] In the late nineteenth century, Shakespeare and classical music were, Storey contends, systematically removed from mass production and reserved for consumers of high culture.

This division between high culture and popular culture, while unclear and not always strict, held for decades. It was not until the mid-1960s that a blurring of the two cultural poles became evident.[11] The American intellectual Susan Sontag termed this blurring of cultures the "new sensibility." She claimed that a new group of artists, performers, and critics had begun implementing a number of changes, thereby bringing an end to "the Matthew Arnold notion of culture, finding it historically and humanly obsolescent."[12] As Arnold had gone to great extremes in the mid-nineteenth century to argue that real culture was only that which sought to make "sweetness and light . . . prevail," Sontag rejected the distinction between real culture that was good and mass culture that duped the masses. The new sensibility was, then, a revolt against modernism's canonization of high culture. This revolt attacked "modernism's official status, its canonization in the museum and the academy, as the high culture of the modern capitalist world."[13] Writing of the final breakdown of the division between high culture and popular culture, Zygmunt Bauman points more directly at the distinction's impossibility: "The end came, therefore, both from the outside and the inside of avant-garde art. The world of the mundane refused to be kept at a distance; but the supply of sites for ever new other-worldly shelters was finally exhausted. We may say that the avant-garde arts proved to be modern in their intention, yet postmodern in their consequences (their unanticipated, yet inescapable, consequences)."[14] For Bauman, the line between the two worlds could not hold because the capitalistic masses were constantly searching for new modes of cultural exchange, which they took and adopted almost at will. Postmodernity ultimately collapsed the categorical boundaries between the two cultures, and popular culture became the only survivor. Few today bother with making distinctions between high culture and low culture. All has become popular culture.

There are, of course, still pockets of resistance, individuals and small groups holding on to the notion that they have the market cornered on high culture. Moreover, there is no reason to believe that the average American fifteen-year-old can tell the difference between Beethoven and Bach, but this is not because the cultural market is trying to systematically keep this information from her. Beethoven's music is just as available to the consumer masses as that of Madonna and Britney Spears. And this is what is meant by popular culture—any form of cultural art that is produced and marketed for mass consumption. If one were to walk into any major media store, she could find a poster reprint of Munch's *The Scream*, Beethoven's Symphony no. 9 on compact disc, and a copy of Shakespeare's *Romeo and Juliet*. She could also find hip-hop star Nas's album *God's Son*, featuring the song "I Can," which samples Beethoven's *Für Elise*, and she could purchase the 2000 martial arts film *Romeo Must Die*, loosely based on Shakespeare's tragedy.

In addition to no longer being divided between the serious and the banal, popular culture has become inescapable. Its salience, especially among young people, cannot be overstated. An entire industry of research on youth subcultures has sprung up over the past twenty years just to make sense of the influence of popular culture on the identity formation of young adults.[15] No scholar's work in this area has had greater impact than that of sociologist Henry Giroux, who has spent more than two decades studying how youth use popular culture to resist the hegemonic forces of adult society.[16] Through their styles of dress, displays of music, choices of movies and television shows, and brand accessories, today's youth have, according to Giroux, become wonderfully efficient at producing subcultural pockets of resistance. That this resistance is carried out through the use of popular culture only highlights the salience of media in the lives of many young adults. In a positive sense, young people fight with the means given them by consumerism and the mass media. In a negative sense, their forms of resistance are easily reco-opted by the very marketers and industries that youth were originally resisting. The case of punk rock in the 1970s clearly highlights this point. Just as bands such as the Sex Pistols and the Stooges began to emerge, they were quickly taken up by major record labels, which either signed the acts themselves or reproduced them in more manageable, market-friendly forms (e.g., the Go-Go's). The point in examining Giroux's work is not to highlight youth resistance but rather to demonstrate the sheer prevalence of popular culture in the lives of young people.

Even a cursory glance through the seven high school newspapers examined here reveals the growing importance of popular culture for the young journalists over the past forty-five years. During the late 1960s, very little attention was paid to popular culture in these newspapers. When popular culture did make it into the newspapers, it was often connected to the immediate community. At Washington High School in 1965, for instance, the *Ram Page* contained a rather amusing reference to early pop icons Sonny and Cher: "Sonny and Cher are living on the WHS campus in the home economic department. They're not rockin' and rollin' but they are eatin' and eatin.' Sonny and Cher, two white rats . . . are being used to show the girls the benefits of proper nutrition."[17] At Lamar High School in Houston, the students were excited to report that the Lovin' Spoonful was coming to the city in concert since it was the "Rock and Roll Sweetenr. according to *Look* magazine."[18] And at Carrick High School in Pittsburgh, one student reported on his interview with the Evergreen Blues just before the taping of a television show.[19] In all of these early instances, the popular culture references had some direct connection to the local community. These were not stories about popular culture generally; they were stories directly related to the students' community.

While the student journalists in the late 1960s may not have seen popular culture as important enough to warrant writing about, this began to change slowly over the next couple decades. The *Ram Page* presents a clear example of this phenomenon. During the early years of this study, one continues to find few references to popular culture in the newspaper, although the students did begin to engage more texts without local connections. A look at the paper during the 1970–71 school year makes this point explicitly. Of the approximately three hundred articles spread out across fifty-six pages, only five dealt with popular culture. In the October 23, 1970, issue, one student reported on the deaths of two well-known rock stars, writing, "Her name was Janis, and his was Jimi. Although they were two of the biggest money makers in their field, the world will not remember Janis Joplin and Jimi Hendrix only as rock superstars, but as victims of drug overdoses."[20] Two months later, another student reported on his date at a Linda Ronstadt and Neil Diamond concert.[21] Although the headline proclaims that Diamond received a standing ovation from the audience, the article is primarily about the student being late to the show, arguing with ushers about torn tickets, missing Ronstadt's opening performance, and having to deal with two girls in front of him who were blocking his view. In addition to these two stories, the newspaper included three movie reviews. In January 1971, one student reviewed the movie *Love Story*, which starred Ryan O'Neal and "the beautiful brunette, Ali MacGraw."[22] Two months later, another student reviewed *Ryan's Daughter* and *Little Big Man*.[23] The final movie review of the year appeared in the March 23 issue, focusing on Pat Boone in *The Cross and the Switchblade* and Timothy Dalton in *Wuthering Heights*. As the newspaper did not have clearly demarcated sections, these popular culture stories and reviews were interspersed with the rest of the news the students found important enough to report.

Over the next two decades, the students at Washington High School continued to write sporadically about popular culture. The March 1, 1974, issue of the *Ram Page* offered no coverage of popular culture, while the next issue presented one review about the controversy surrounding *The Exorcist*, which "opened the day after Christmas." The student focused on how foolish she thought some moviegoers were for having "claimed they were possessed by the Devil after seeing the film."[24] Similarly, in the October 1980 issue, the young journalists at Washington High School published only one piece on popular culture—a review of the George Burns comedy *Oh, God! Book II*.[25] While the review primarily recounted the movie's plot, it was, perhaps more importantly, located on the editorial page next to a piece encouraging young people to "exercise your right to vote."[26] The following issue in the fall of 1980 contained no articles devoted to popular culture at all.

The sporadic reporting of popular culture changed dramatically by the early 1990s. At Washington High School, the shift toward a greater focus on popular culture took place in the fall of 1990. That year's December issue contained almost half a page of movie reviews. Beneath the headline "Movie Review: What's Hot and What's Not," students offered separate starred reviews of *Memphis Belle*; *Look Who's Talking, Too*; *Edward Scissorhands*; and *Home Alone*. Below the four movie reviews, two other students wrote a review of Billy Joel's "latest appearance in Phoenix at the new Desert Sky Pavilion on the ninth of November."[27] One month later, the two young critics returned with four film reviews focused on Valentine's Day themes.[28] The March 1991 issue went even further, with one article reviewing a Marty Stuart concert, one piece on the state of country music, two film critic reviews of two movies, and an additional student review of the film *The Doors*.[29] By the early 1990s, then, the *Rampage* staff had come to devote far more of its paper's space to popular culture. And in 1995 it began giving an entire page of its then ten-page issues to the section "Entertainment," which offered reviews and news related to movies, music, and television shows.

The same trend can be found in the other high school newspapers represented in this study. Each began with little discussion of popular culture in the mid-1960s before dramatically increasing its coverage in the early 1990s. The eight-page December 1966 issue of Wilson High School's *Beacon* featured only one such article, an interview with *Temptations* member Melvin Franklin.[30] Three years later, there was little change. The October 1969 issue also contained one story—a review of *The Learning Tree*, "the first American movie written, produced, and directed by a black man."[31] By the early 1970s, the amount and type of popular culture included in the newspaper began to change. In the June 1971 issue, the newspaper presented—in addition to an interview with *Doonesbury* creator Gary Trudeau[32]—a movie review of Woody Allen's *Bananas*, which the reviewer judged as offering "a lot of laughs, something we all can use."[33] Over the next two years, movie reviews appeared sporadically, and by 1972 the student reporters had also begun reviewing albums. The May 1972 issue, for instance, reviewed three records—a posthumously released Jimi Hendrix album as well as albums by the Beatles and Little Richard. Within a couple of years, the newspaper started providing a half page of popular culture reporting, including the "Critic's Corner," which appeared in March 1974 with a review of *The Exorcist* and several other movies lumped together as part of the "Karate-Kung-fu craze."[34] Over the next decade and a half, things remained remarkably the same. By the mid-1990s, however, popular culture had taken an even stronger foothold. Instead of devoting two or three stories and reviews to movies and records, the *Beacon* staff began publishing them more extensively as well as including satirical cartoons and horoscopes. Thus, like the young journalists at Washington High School in Phoenix, the students at Wilson High School in Washington, D.C., began to mimic the arts and entertainment sections of adult newspapers—with more emphasis on the entertainment.

Beginning in the early 1970s, then, references to popular culture began to slowly multiply. These articles, moreover, no longer needed a direct, local connection to justify their appearance in the newspaper. By late 1972, this change could be seen in Carrick High School's *Carrickulum*, where a regular "Musical Notes" column focused on reviewing new albums.[35] By the fall of 1974, the students at Oak Park High School had already begun setting aside three-quarters of a page for arts and entertainment articles in each issue of *Northmen's Log*. Even Newton South High School's *Denebola*—the last newspaper in this study to begin featuring reviews of music and movies—started running a fairly regular record review column and occasional movie reviews by the fall of 1973. By the mid-1970s, therefore, all seven school newspapers were routinely publishing movie and album reviews.

The amount of popular culture that made its way into these high school newspapers over the next few decades is startling. This is especially evident in one issue of Grant High School's *Grantonian*. In 1992, the newspaper consisted of eight pages—two pages each of news and sports, and one page each of features, editorials, opinions, and entertainment. The November 20 issue contained a number of stories, including a piece on a new teen health clinic and an assessment of fall sports.[36] It was also filled with references to popular culture. For instance, a humorous story on what to anticipate in the new Democratic administration included references to popular psychic Jeanne Dixon, Elvis, and the entertainment news show *Inside Edition*.[37] One article focused on two students who spent twelve hours as extras on a movie set at a Portland club, and another offered a positive review of a new techno band called the Utah Saints.[38] In addition, there were three film-related stories and an opinion page that was mostly devoted to director Spike Lee and his latest film, *Malcolm X*.[39] There was also an editorial blasting NBA players for forcing Magic Johnson to leave the Los Angeles Lakers after he admitted to having contracted the HIV virus.[40] In all, eight articles—almost half the newspaper—were devoted to a wide array of popular culture.

Presumably, there was an increase in the salience of popular culture in the lives of the young journalists in this study over the last forty-five years. This is not a groundbreaking observation, but it is important. Naturally, this study cannot begin to measure how much popular culture was being consumed by these students outside of the simple increase in newspaper space allotted to its coverage, but this increase in newspaper coverage was surely representative of a larger trend. The student reporters and their advisors clearly found that devoting more space to articles related to movies, music, and celebrities was what the student body expected of them. And this is important since more time spent on popular culture means less time spent on other issues. However, it is one thing to note the increased salience of popular culture *in* the lives of these young people, but quite another to understand the impact of popular culture *on* them. This latter calculation requires paying attention not to *what* is being talked about but to *how* it is being discussed.

A Generation of Critics

A popular assumption about the more recent generations of young people in the United States—often referred to as Generations X and Y—holds that they have become overwhelmingly cynical, negative, pessimistic, and jaded. Of course, young people often rebel during their teen years in an effort to achieve self-autonomy and separate themselves from their parents, and it is no wonder that parents often find this behavior troublesome or irritating. Recent generations of young people, however, seem to have become more cynical than ever before—or so the assumption goes. In 1993, the *Washington Post* described Generation Xers as "crybabies" and then told them to "grow up."[41] Richard Linklater's 1991 independent film *Slacker* portrayed an entire generation of young adults whose cynicism had caused them to disengage from mainstream society. According to many, this mindset remains strongly entrenched. In a recent online editorial for the media company Real Clear Politics, one commentator described the young people attending comedians Jon Stewart and Stephen Colbert's "Rally to Restore Sanity and/or Fear" in October 2010 as being on a "march toward cynicism."[42] Whether in the news media or popular culture itself, young people entering high school after 1975 have been depicted as cynics. Are such claims true? Have American youth become too cynical for their own good? Have they become too detached for a healthy democracy?

While many of today's young people may appear more pessimistic and scornful than previous generations, the high school newspapers in this study suggest at least some of them are not necessarily so cynical. That is, the contemporary young journalists studied here were far more engaged than any cynic would ever be. These students were not, however, willing to take everything at face value. In fact, they exhibited a great deal of skepticism. Such doubting does not make them cynics, but it does suggest a far more critical stance toward the world around them than their predecessors may have been comfortable displaying. This critical attitude, I argue in this section, was learned through their engagement with popular culture.

Unlike removed cynicism, being a critic requires one to pay attention to the world around him. It also demands that one have something to say about that world. A cynic may stand above society and mock it without engaging it, but the critic must engage the world to get a sense of what is wrong. Raymond Williams nicely captures the critical mindset when observing, "Criticism has become a very difficult word, because although its predominant general use is of fault finding, it has an underlying sense of judgment and a very confusing specialized sense, in relation to art and literature, which depends on assumptions that may now be breaking down."[43] It is at this point of a breakdown between faultfinding and art and literary criticism that new forms of critical engagement with popular culture may best be understood. Thus, the three main concepts to take from Williams are (1) that criticism is primarily about finding fault in something, (2) that there is a sense of judgment tied up in being a critic, and (3) that the specialized notion of the artistic or literary critic no longer holds.

Formalized criticism of the arts cannot flourish if the division between popular culture and high art has been largely erased over the past several decades. What is important to note here, therefore, is the negativity of the other two concepts in Williams's sense of criticism. The modern critic looks primarily for negative aspects of the criticized object when passing judgment on it. Noting what is wrong with something has become, for the modern critic, more important than any other aspect of judgment. Looking at the high school newspaper reviews of popular culture across the past forty-five years shows that this negativity fits rather well with the sensibilities of the young people studied here.

The young journalists in this study have not always been critics. At Grant High School in 1971, for instance, one student reviewed a new "electric western" and a young actor, Don Johnson. The student devoted much of his attention to the actor's impact in the movie, which depicted the lives of two gunfighters: "To make a long story short, the pair end up by fighting each other, which is ironic because they were such close friends."[44] One gets the impression the reviewer is not very impressed with the movie, but the tone of his criticism is largely simplistic. It is as if he wants to review the movie without passing judgment on it, to comment on it without criticizing. At Wilson High School in 1975, another student offered a similar review of a movie based on the Who's psychedelic rock opera *Tommy*: "All in all, 'Tommy' is a unique film—one should go prepared to experience it rather than watch it. Whether or not it merited the massive opening night party thrown in the New York subway is debatable, but it is definitely a movie not to be ignored."[45] Again, one gets the sense the student reviewer did not quite understand what to do with the movie, and she did not know how to judge it in the manner of her successors. Both of these reviewers appear naïve in their criticisms and polite in their judgments. Such attitudes were soon to disappear.

By the start of the 1980s, the level of criticism among the student reporters began to rise as they picked up more complex ways of critiquing popular culture. In 1981, one reviewer at Grant High School took a multifaceted approach to reviewing the horror film sequel *Halloween II*. The student covered the acting of Jamie Lee Curtis and pointed to serious problems with the writing and directing of the movie before reaching his conclusion: "It turned out more like one of the carbon copy rip-offs of 'Halloween' that were churned out to cash in on its initial success such as 'The Boogeyman,' 'Prom Night,' 'Terror Train,' and countless other exploitation pictures. Overall 'Halloween II' is only worthy of a viewing for the curious, but it may be a big disappointment for fans of John Carpenter and of the original 'Halloween.'"[46] This review includes, among other things, a comparison to a list of other films, and it ties the reviewer to the fandom of the original movie and its director. Both of these moves clearly demonstrate the author's knowledge of the horror film industry. The review also points to his assumption that he can tell the difference between a good movie and weaker carbon copies. While the article still has a sense of naiveté, written by a reviewer still learning the art of criticism, this young critic does take a clear judgmental position on the movie. For the serious horror film connoisseur, *Halloween II* is unfulfilling.

Throughout the mid-1980s, this sort of criticism was the norm. The students offered a wide array of movie reviews, and each one rather benignly mimicked adult reviewing styles, as the following three examples demonstrate:

> The acting is excellent. McClain and Winger proved their acting talents, once again. Because of the fine acting, by the end of the movie you feel like you really know these people. Hopefully *Terms of Endearment* will get an Oscar Nomination, it definitely deserves one.[47]

> Garry Marshall, who has given us such infamous television shows as "Laverne & Shirley" and "Mork & Mindy," has not created a concise, amusing comedy/drama in the same genre as, let's say, *The Graduate*. Don't be deceived by the title of *The Flamingo Kid*; behind the glitz of the ostentatious beach club setting lies a sophisticated discussion of success, wealth, and happiness.[48]

> The latest chapter in the Rocky Balboa saga opened nationwide on Wednesday. *Rocky* is the "rags-to-riches" story about a man from the ghettos working his way up to become a heavy weight boxer, later the World Boxing Champion. . . . I found *Rocky IV* a well-done movie.[49]

Of these three examples, the harshest criticism comes from the review of *The Flamingo Kid* when the writer asserts that Matt Dillon cannot really act. Otherwise, the critical reviews from the 1980s were not very critical at all. Still, it is clear from each of these reviews whether the student liked or disliked the movie. *Terms of Endearment* deserves an Oscar nomination, *The Flamingo Kid* is more sophisticated than one might think, and *Rocky IV* is well done. All positive reviews, but all judgments nevertheless.

By the 1990s, there was a very different tone to the newspapers' popular culture criticisms, as seen in the movie reviews below. Whatever timidity existed before, these reviewers were not the least bit afraid of saying what they did not like about the movies they reviewed, and they did so in no uncertain terms:

> If you've seen *Titanic* or *Armageddon*, you've seen *Pearl Harbor*. It's simply one more recycled plotline to add to the archives. The equation is a fairly simple one: add a rugged group of working class heroes to an overly dramatic love story, mix it all in with some sort of crisis (historical or not) and multiply it by three hours of fantastic explosions, and Blammo!—movie in a can.[50]

About every thirty minutes, something bad would happen to a big satellite dish. This dish made it possible for five men to talk to Neil Armstrong. It was the biggest dish in the world and was located in Australia in a sheep field. I could hardly stay awake, so I suggest that you save your money and your time and not see this horrible movie [*The Dish*].[51]

"The Beach" is a visually stunning film that is sabotaged by the lack of clear issues and a weak plot. . . . My initial reaction to "The Beach" was that it was a movie with the depth of an Abercrombie and Fitch catalogue.[52]

Each of these reviews works off the same critical pattern in which the reviewer finds nothing in the film worthwhile. *Pearl Harbor* is unoriginal, *The Dish* is boring, and *The Beach* is empty. Each review also posits the reviewer as somehow too savvy for the material being examined. These are indeed very critical reviews. They find fault, pass judgment, and show no signs of a reviewer who is afraid that he or she does not have the requisite skills necessary to offer such criticism.

It seems, then, that as the young people in this study became more immersed in popular culture they also became archly critical. This was not only the case with movies. It happened just as dramatically with music. While earlier music reviews were either neutral or positive pieces, later reviews became quite biting. Mandy Moore's music was alleged to be filled with "generic and often cheesy lyrics,"[53] Will Smith was said to lose his touch with "unfitting lyrics and monotonous beats,"[54] and even the punk band 311 was said to have sunk to a new low.[55] For communication scholar John Sloop, this move toward increasingly negative criticism comes as no surprise since mainstream "popular music criticism encourages an aesthetic that is celebratory toward cynical self-reflectiveness and musical commodification."[56] Sloop's observation suggests that it somehow became cool to knowingly make fun of the popular culture one consumes. That young people, as heavy consumers of popular culture, learned this negative critical stance from outlets such as MTV and *Rolling Stone* magazine seems only natural in retrospect.

It is worth noting that not all the popular culture reviews of more recent years were this negative. Movies were often praised for having good direction, actors for acting well, and bands for playing enjoyable music. Christian pop singer Steven Curtis Chapman wrote inspiring music, with "each song deliver[ing] an incredible message."[57] The popular teen television series *Friday Night Lights* showed "more depth" than one young woman had anticipated.[58] Even a romantic comedy such as the 2010 *Valentine's Day* could be "sure to jerk a few tears while at the same time making you fall out of your seat laughing."[59] While such reviews do appear, the young reporters in this study lavished the most praise on shows that emulated the critical attitude within popular culture itself. One Oak Park High School student offered an example of this high praise when he applauded the biting and satirical comedy of shock jock Howard Stern: "I thought that *Private Parts* was definitely the most vulgar and distasteful movie, with every scene packed with many racial slurs and sexual references. It was these very same obscene jokes that made the movie absolutely hysterical."[60] And a Carrick High School reviewer seemed to genuinely lament the cancellation of one of MTV's most popular programs of the 1990s: "The years keep on going by, and things start to get worse and worse. Can't we go back to the good old days when things were good? Back when 'Beavis and Butthead' was on the air. 'Beavis and Butthead' is arguably the greatest show in the 90's."[61] What ties these two pieces of popular culture together, of course, is their disparaging attitude toward society and media. As Steven Best and Douglas Kellner point out, the characters Beavis and Butt-Head truly exemplified their era: "Mentally challenged though they are, Beavis and Butt-Head are very shrewd in their own element, as they play the role of media critic and construct their Manichean world of cool versus sucks. They rarely are viscerally attached to and numbed by TV; rather, they engage in an ongoing critical and deconstructive analysis that exposes pretentiousness, mocks advertisements, and even decodes the pornographic content of many music videos."[62]

In a sense, popular culture icons such as Beavis and Butt-Head, Howard Stern, Bart Simpson, the Southpark kids, and the cast of *Saturday Night Live* serve as exemplars of the critical stance found in much contemporary popular culture. The young people who have grown up on such shows have learned that it is cool not to care too much. The young adults in this study have at least learned to act as if they are too cool to care too much about the mediated world of popular culture around them. Moreover, their critical take on much of the popular culture they consume seems expressly designed to help protect them from caring too much and thereby becoming uncool. Whether this critical attitude has found its way into their relationship to politics is another matter.

Mixing Politics with Popular Culture

Showing that these young journalists have become increasingly immersed in popular culture over the last forty-five years and that this immersion has led them to be more critical in their attitudes toward popular culture is only half of the argument in this chapter. In order to demonstrate that these youth have largely adopted a protective critical attitude in their democratic engagement, one must answer the following question: Has the critical attitude of some young people toward popular culture found its way into their political attitudes? Indeed it has. As I will show below, the young journalists in this study have become quite critical in their writing about all things political. They still write of politics, but they far more often do so behind the protective shield of their critical attitudes.

Perhaps the primary reason why such critical attitudes have emerged is that these young people have not clearly distinguished between popular culture and politics. For them, politics today is popular culture and popular culture is political. They seem to feel no need to discern the importance or reality of either one. A Grant High School student in Portland made the point clearly when, in October 2000, he recounted the three weeks he spent working for a carnival over the summer. As he staffed a novelty stand for most of that time, he felt as though he had "conceived some interesting trends and products that have supplanted themselves into American culture." The majority of his cultural critique focuses primarily on two popular culture fads, Pokémon and Razor Scooters, before turning to a website created to let users enter the "serial number of any U.S. [monetary] bill and follow its movement across the country." Unimpressed by this website, the student suggests that more attention be paid to a website created to track "the nation's favorite Jezebel [Monica Lewinsky] as she cavorts from place to place. Starting with Clinton's entry last term, Lewinsky has over 983 'hits' to date."[63] Writing about American culture, this student sees little reason to separate a children's multibillion-dollar toy and media franchise from a presidential sex scandal.

Indeed, many of the young journalists in this study seemed to see politicians as cultural celebrities. This trend is evident in a March 2006 issue of *Northmen's Log*. Beneath the headline "Celebrities Set Bad Example," a student editorialist begins by stating as fact that "as young Americans, we all look up to celebrities." She then quickly laments, "Not all of them provide good examples of behavior, however. There are athletes, musicians, actors,

politicians and other famous people who are just plain bad examples."
For this young woman, politicians, like athletes and actors, are just one
type of celebrity. Over the next several paragraphs, she complains of Kansas
City "Chiefs players accused of drunk driving" and "Duke lacrosse players
charged with rape." She worries about "Britney Spears going psycho" and
"rappers with videos flooded with big shaking sweaty butts." She is, in
addition, so frustrated with "ugly political campaigns" that she admits they
make her "not want to vote." While the student's complaints are most assuredly valid, what is revealing here is that she sees these athletes, musicians,
and politicians as being equal in that they are all "celebrities" young people
look up to.[64]

In another example, one student described the recent "Twitter craze" as
something that had affected all of society.[65] Her evidence of this included her
peers at Washington High School, celebrities Oprah Winfrey and Ashton
Kutcher, television networks CNN and Discovery Channel, and presidential candidates Barack Obama and John McCain. In this student's article,
an actor (Kutcher) who got his start playing a stoned high school kid on
the television sitcom *That '70s Show* gets equal billing with the future president of the United States. In a more political context, one Newton South
High School student wrote an editorial on vice presidential candidate Sarah
Palin that included several popular culture references as evidence for her
argument. Citing Palin's stated views that sex education should be offered
through abstinence-only programs or not be taught in schools at all, the editorialist argues that "sex-ed needs to be as unbiased as possible" and include
information about contraceptives. Her argument includes references to
Levi's and Abercrombie and Fitch clothing advertisements, which she suggests encourage teenage sex, and to the movie *Juno*, in which the portrayal
of a pregnant high school student "sugarcoats the harsh realities of teenage pregnancy."[66] Such evidence is used to demonstrate that Palin does not
really understand the sexual realities of teenagers, which leads this student
to sarcastically dismiss her and wish that she remained an unknown politician from Alaska.

That politics and popular culture have become increasingly intermingled in the minds of these young adults does not itself mark a new development. In the past ten years, a large corpus of research has emerged on
the subject of politics and popular culture. While some researchers have
argued that the "popularization of culture and the democratization of politics" go hand in hand[67] and that popular politics can create a rational citizen
fandom,[68] much of the research in this area has been less than positive.

John Street has pointed out, for instance, that "parties and politicians are increasingly marketing and packaging themselves to attract voters, using the same devices advertisers deploy for perfumes and cars."[69] For Street, these marketing strategies play on the emotions of citizens instead of the reason required to make sound political decisions. Darrell West and John Orman have argued that the line between celebrity and politician has largely and dangerously been erased, noting that in the 1990s "the celebrity-star system became institutionalized with politicians becoming interchangeable with other guest celebrities on television talk shows."[70] Such personalizing of politicians results, according to West and Orman, in candidates being judged too much on character and not enough on the things that should matter. John Fiske has shown that the media play a primary and biased role in the blending of the popular and political.[71] And David Swanson has more directly questioned this hybridization of political news and entertainment by arguing, "Mainstream journalism has sought to market itself to consumers in both style and substance, effecting compromises that are deplored by some of its most respected practitioners and blur its identity as distinct from other forms."[72] For all of these researchers, the blending of politics and popular culture threatens to trivialize citizens as well as political institutions. In such a scheme, politics features the aesthetics of the image rather than the rationality of ideas.

Robert Hariman has observed that aesthetics have always played a role in the world of politics, examining a number of historical political texts through the lens of classical rhetoric. In the end, Hariman suggested that in a postmodern world "style becomes an analytical category for understanding a social reality; in order to understand the social reality of politics, we can consider how a political action involves acting according to a particular political style."[73] While Hariman's argument is persuasive, it does not completely account for the mediated politics most citizens receive. Style is one thing, but the image presented through mediated channels is something altogether different. In the blending of politics and popular culture, the mediated image is the zeitgeist, and the image carries with it a separate set of concerns. Rhetorical theorist Barry Brummett argues that the power of the image has a fundamentally aesthetic value. For Brummett, the image "appeals first not to the public's powers of reason and analysis but to pleasure and entertainment, to an emotional sense of bonding or disgust with a figure."[74] Sociologist Barry Richards agrees with the assertion that politics has increasingly centered on the image, arguing that part of the explanation for low voter turnout is an "emotional deficit" created by today's political actors failing to meet the emotional needs of the electorate.[75] The argument here, then, is that modern politics—which has become heavily mediated and inextricably linked with popular culture—has become a home to the image. If this is true, one would expect to find young people talking about politics and the news media with the same negative tone they use when discussing other popular culture matters. This is, in fact, what one finds.

Just as popular culture was slow to make its way into the writings of the young journalists in this study, discussion of the news media and its role in the public sphere did not begin to emerge until the 1980s. Prior to the Watergate scandal, coverage of the Vietnam War, and the start of cable television, the students represented here had little to say about the press. When they discussed it at all, they usually focused on the raw news itself. One of the few early references to the news media, in the *Lancer*, typifies the praiseworthy attitudes of the 1960s and 1970s: "To focus the spotlight on the role the newspaper plays in protecting the people's three great freedoms—Freedom of the Press . . . Freedom of Speech . . . and Freedom of Religion, the newspaper industry proclaims one week each year as National Newspaper Week. . . . President Lyndon B. Johnson and many of the Governors of the various states will make it official with statements and proclamations."[76] The word from Houston in 1966, then, was that the news media were guardians of American rights. That same sentiment was voiced in Washington, D.C., where one student reported on his numerous visits to a local television station: "Of all the visits, election night surpassed them all. From 7:30 p.m. until early midnight, the Fellows observed activities, which provided accurate and complete election results and newscasts."[77] Given the limited number of news media outlets and the relative novelty of television, it is not surprising to find this rather respectful attitude toward the news in the early years of this study. But as the 1970s came to a close, things began to change quickly.

The discussion of mediated politics in the high school newspapers in the 1980s reveals a group of young people who were quite aware of the power and problems of the media. The following quotation from one Kansas City student's 1982 editorial about the news media clearly highlights the ability and willingness of some teenagers to question news institutions:

> It is no secret we are heavily dependent on the media. Being so dependent on the media, have we ever wondered about all the things trusty Walter Cronkite never told us? Obviously the influence of the press on it's society is significant. . . . As any other business the media is also vulnerable to bias, falsehoods and manipulation. In recent months we

have seen public officials and policy makers use the press for a variety of reasons—to advance program and policy goals, further career ambitions, create and adjust public awareness to build public support. . . . By controlling what information is and is not delivered and how the information is presented, the media can play a large role in limiting the range of interpretations that the audiences are able to make. It is not that the media is telling people "what" to think. Instead, they tell their audiences what to think "about." . . . A free press is one of the most valuable possessions a country can defend. It is the crown jewel of the freedom of speech rights. Ideally, the media is a puritan institution free of bias, falsehoods and manipulations. Realistically, the press is a human job with a big responsibility. We should reconsider before we adorn the media with the labels of "unbiased source," "the public conscience," and the "reporters of truth."[78]

This student's assessment of the press is enough to make a communication scholar proud. By pointing to people's dependence on the news media, he recognizes the press's ability to at least partially function as a fourth estate of government.[79] Writing of the ability of public officials to decide the news for media outlets, he clearly emphasizes the agenda-setting function of the press and then goes on to highlight the second-level agenda-setting function of the news media as well.[80] He even offers a glimpse of framing research in communications by arguing that the news media present a bias that can be ideologically manipulative.[81]

Although the student's understanding of the news media is praiseworthy, his tone also indicates a severe skepticism. He does not trust media outlets or the politicians who "use the press" for their own ends. Even while tempering his criticism with the assertion that the media do not in fact tell people what to think, he is concerned that they are not unbiased in what they count as news. He understands the press is a human endeavor but then suggests its humanness is exactly why he and his peers should not believe all they are told. He knows intuitively what Michael Schudson demonstrated in his 1978 book *Discovering the News*—that an objective and purely factual news media is an impossibility and that most people understand that the news is subjectively created.[82] More than anything, the Kansas City student seems to be urging his peers to actively question the validity of what the media present to them.

While the above editorial highlights the growing media savvy found among some of the young journalists in the 1980s, their peers in the

1990s became even more critically protective. A 1997 *Rampage* editorial emphasized the press's tendency to report certain news stories in a feeding-frenzy fashion: "The media has been covering many unnecessary stories. News does deserve national attention, but repeated news stories do not. The Heaven's Gate cult recently received this kind of attention."[83] This article, which goes on to talk about how the news media over-report stories that are not particularly important for democratic purposes, shows a clear disdain for reporters' choices. A *Denebola* student reporter also understood feeding frenzies and detailed the effects of such sensational journalism for her readers: "Presidential and government scandals also dominate news reports. After the success of the 1974 publishing of *All the President's Men* and the prior reporting by Bob Woodward and Carl Bernstein, networks, newspapers, and newsmagazines have been eager to find the next scandal that will lure an audience and win accolades."[84] Both of these pieces lament the news media's habit of looking for a story that catches the attention of the public and then reporting on the story for months at a time. That is, the students seem turned off by the news media's very attempts to get them to pay attention. It is as if the harder the news media work to attract their attention, the more frustrated the young people are with the news media.

In addition to what events were covered, the students had complaints about how the news media covered them. As the following example from Portland's *Grantonian* highlights, students neither appreciated nor respected media biases: "Much of the media tells us only part of the story or they avoid it all together if it doesn't fit their requirements, especially if it reflects poorly on the US government."[85] This student clearly wanted more objective reporting and a more open aspect to the media's gatekeeping function. And when it came to political coverage specifically, the young people of the 1990s had very few positive things to say. At Oak Park High School in Kansas City, a report on election coverage demonstrated young people's distaste for the news served up to them: "In fighting for shares, network news has also turned to episodic reporting, called 'horse race journalism,' in which the pollsters, campaign staff, and candidates' personalities are what is covered. The media focuses on the stories behind the campaigns instead of the issues driving them. Witness the popularity of George Stephanopolos [sic] and James Carville after the 1992 race."[86] While it may be tempting to appreciate this young person's understanding of news routines, his attitude represents an archly critical stance toward the entire news industry. Such a deeply critical attitude may be worrisome for some.

In more recent examples, the level of irritation over the news media's political coverage is palpable. One recent Newton South High School student demonstrated this frustration quite clearly. Writing in October 2008, the student began his editorial on news coverage of the presidential campaign by noting, "The media has been focusing widely on nonpolitical aspects of the race." For evidence of this nonpolitical information, he argues that "candidates' personal lives have become hot topics in the media spotlight, and gossip has begun to greatly influence the election." Citing the prevalence of such gossip in newspapers, news magazines, television shows, and Internet sites, the student worries further that "the public has begun to formulate ideas based more on the candidates' personal lives rather than their policies." Acknowledging "that modern American society has become engrossed in gossip and celebrity news," he eventually concedes, "The yield of a candidate's 'celebrity status' will be determined on Election Day."[87] For this concerned student, the news media, in all its mediated forms, is directly to blame for focusing too much on the popularity of political candidates at the expense of more substantive issues.

In addition to being so critical toward the press, the young people in this study have taken a similarly skeptical attitude toward politicians. In response to the assassination attempt on Ronald Reagan, for instance, one student at Wilson High School argued, "It is evident that the decisive factor in the president's image is that which is projected on television. Television is by far the most effective medium of communication for the population en masse. Could it not take over completely in bringing the president 'live' to the American people?"[88] While this statement suggests a questioning stance toward the sincerity of politicians and represents the beginning of a transitional attitude, ten years later the young journalists in this study had learned to be truly critical of them.

Writing about the 1992 presidential race, one Grant High School student could not find much to say about George H. W. Bush and the Republican Party other than that they were dishonest. Targeting "Young Republicans" specifically, the editorialist argued that they had been "stressing the positive, forgetting the negative, and creating their own safe haven in the upper tax brackets." More than delusionally optimistic and selfish, Republicans are simply dishonest. The student argues, in fact, that Bush offers "nothing but political rhetoric," which here means manipulative, deceptive discourse. He goes on to list his grievances: "Bush telling parents to look after their kids while he sends them to die in Iraq. Bush's mouth telling single mothers to get help while his hand vetoes bills that would provide aid. Bush standing on the 18th tee in Kennebunkport claiming that he is in touch with the middle class." Eventually, the student even turns his ire on Vice President Dan Quayle, arguing, "Bush dispatched his second-in-command to create a media sideshow/diversion by blaming Murphy Brown for the increase in single mothers."[89] Here is a *Grantonian* staff member railing against the incumbent president of the United States in his high school newspaper, accusing him and his Republican allies of lying and deception. Here, that is, is a young person feeling comfortable in his critical attitude.

Four years later, a young journalist in Phoenix took a more playful, albeit no less critical, attitude toward presidential politics. Accompanied by an image of Mickey Mouse and a banner calling for "Mickey in 1996," the editorial began, "The first and foremost question is do we re-elect President Bill Clinton or bring in the elder statesman Bob Dole? Maybe, just maybe, we should give old Ross Perot a whirl? Personally, I'd rather cast my vote for Mickey Mouse." Having named her candidate, the student explains her reasoning. She feels that "Dole and Clinton have both dodged a number of . . . issues." And although she likes what Ross Perot has to say, she admits that "with all his infamous graphs and charts one tends to get lost." Lest there be any doubt about her critical attitude, the editorialist states plainly, "Since the early days of America, the United States has been flooded with crooked politicians. The candidates for this year's election are faring no better than these stereotypes." Ultimately, she decides to go with Mickey Mouse because "I've never seen Mickey whip out a graph in the middle of a parade, or bash Donald Duck's character in an interview. No mudslinging, no empty promises, no taxes, nothing but mouse."[90]

Even when students actually focused on more local politics, their critical attitude was evident. As one Boston student demonstrated when writing about the 1998 Massachusetts gubernatorial race, no politician seemed trustworthy, and political campaigns more generally seemed a waste of time. Titling her editorial "Politicians Are Immature," the student began by recounting how Nixon lost "the first-ever televised Presidential debate" because "he looked awful that evening." Questioning the legitimacy and usefulness of televised debates, she then asks whether the debates between the two candidates for the state governor's office have "affected voters." Before exploring this question, she notes, "These two grown men certainly seemed to enjoy themselves while throwing insults back and forth. Has their desire to revisit their grade-school days changed the poll statistic at all?" While she acknowledges the mixed opinions about that, she nevertheless returns to her criticism of the candidates for being "two forty year-old men [who] act like ten year-olds." In the end, her frustration with the candidates leads her to be critical of televised debates that "knock 'Friends' off the air, . . . placing two 'grown-ups' on a large stage together and then just letting them go at it." In her final critical assessment, the young journalist argues, "If we wanted to see a grudge match we would watch WWF."[91]

As these textual exemplars demonstrate, the young journalists in this study had become truly critical of electoral politics by the early 1990s. They treated presidential elections as unreal and presidential debates as completely fake. They disparagingly equated American politics with popular culture, and they seemed to see no discernible difference in the importance of the two. According to these students, moreover, politicians are never to be trusted.

Of course, it is not unusual for citizens to make jokes at the expense of politicians or to be critical of the political process. Theodore "Teddy" Roosevelt got his nickname, after all, from a political cartoon poking fun at his unwillingness to kill a trapped bear in Louisiana. What is troubling about the above examples is how completely the authors seem to have adopted a deeply protective critical attitude, as evidenced by the pervasive tone they apparently learned from the popular culture they consumed so readily. This attitude seems to have led many of the young people in this study to question the intentions of all that is political. At Grant High School, for instance, one student even wrote an editorial attacking what he saw as a one-sided school assembly (urging support for a school bond measure) by framing the entire piece as a "Nightmare on 36th Street."[92] The writer spends most of the editorial questioning whether he has dreamed about the assembly, likening himself to the characters in the popular horror film franchise *Nightmare on Elm Street*. The piece sarcastically mixes the popular with the political and the humorous with the sarcastic. Such is the case with a great deal of the political writing in the final two decades of this study. In these ways and more, these young journalists fuse together the worlds of politics and entertainment, adopting the negative critical attitude of the latter and applying it to the former.

The above examples evoke a sense of paranoia. Everywhere they looked, these young people saw nothing they could trust—the news media could not be believed, and politicians did not have the people's best interests at heart. Given the mediated world in which they lived, this response might make sense. That is, these students may have learned to be overly skeptical of everything they saw because popular culture had taught them this lesson.

Surrealist painter Salvador Dalí referred to this phenomenon in his own work, describing his paranoiac-critical method as a "spontaneous method of irrational knowledge based on the critical and systematic objectivity of the associations and interpretations of delirious phenomena."[93] For Dalí, by simulating paranoia one can undermine a more realistic understanding of the world. As artist Marcel Jean wrote, "One can see, or persuade others to see, all sorts of shapes in a cloud: a horse, a human body, a dragon, a face, a palace, and so on. Any sight or object of the physical world can be treated in this manner. From which the proposed conclusion is that it is impossible to concede any value whatsoever to immediate reality, since it may represent or mean anything at all."[94] The idea of the paranoiac-critical method was to replace reality with an unstable image. This is, of course, exactly what mediated popular culture has been doing, with research showing that television and the news media hardly offer realistic portrayals of the world at large. Instead, they present a world of sharp negativity. It is not surprising that some young adults have trouble seeing anything but these negative images. Also unsurprising is their need to protect themselves from this mediated onslaught.

That the young people in this study have increasingly adopted a protective critical attitude toward popular political culture might not be so troubling if they had not also imported it into the civic and community realms. One young writer seemed unusually aware of such concerns in the early 1970s, arguing that this approach would do young people no good: "It is often said that Watergate has made people cynical about their government, and that young people are turning away from politics because of it. With everything from burglary to deals with ITT being uncovered in the Nixon administration it is understandable that people become disillusioned. But disillusionment does not have to lead to cynicism. . . . The government is not going to change unless we make it. Turning off from politics won't make the problems go away; it will only let the politicians do what they want."[95] More contemporary youth are nowhere near as hopeful, and the critical attitude is far more pervasive. Today, students wanting to engage their peers in civic conversation begin with the assumption that no one really cares about the matters they are addressing. They assume, that is, that the protective critical attitude has forced them to become detached and distanced from the political process:

> On Jan. 21, 1993 President-elect Bill Clinton will be inaugurated as the new President of the United States, leader of the "free world" and

all the other clichés that go along with a transfer of power. For the five people that read this column, relax, it is probably the last on politics this year.[96]

Please bear with me now; I know you are probably pretty bored with all the political propaganda and media flying all about these days, but I think I've discovered a solution. Put God in charge.[97]

Celebrities are used to promote [*Choose or Lose*] by making appearances and endorsing the program. This makes voting seem more appealing and glamorous. MTV is out to change the stereotype that adults are the only ones with real authority. . . . Many South students were not aware of the show and none had actually watched it on its normal timeslot. Although the commercials constantly play on MTV, the majority of Newton South has not yet chosen to "rock the vote."[98]

Whether disparaging presidential politics (the only national politics young people pay much attention to) or discussing the importance of voting, the students who were concerned about their political communities in the 1990s knew better than to be seen as unduly serious. They appear to have known they were fighting an uphill battle in commenting on political matters and, as a result, often deconstructed their arguments even when making them.

However, not all of the young people writing in the seven newspapers were resigned to such critical attitudes. Recent evidence suggests that some of them were concerned about the influence of popular culture on their political lives. In a *Northmen's Log* article in October 2008, for instance, one such student challenged his peers to become more informed about matters he felt were relevant to their lives. Presenting evidence from a school poll revealing that far more students could name two characters on the *South Park* cartoon than could name the governor of Missouri, he chides his peers for living "their lives feeding off worthless information." He argues that they should instead crave "knowledge that actually affects us as citizens." To emphasize his point, he even cites a popular assumption about youth: "Our generation appears to have earned its reputation for self-indulgence and ignorance."[99] Unhappy with this reputation, the concerned writer suggests that the students pay more attention to information about the nation's troubled economy and less to that about Brittney Spears. A rather angry student at Newton South High School made a related argument in the *Denebola*'s October 2007 issue: "More people know about Paris Hilton going to Rwanda than they do about what actually happened during the Rwandan genocide, or for that matter, the genocide in Darfur today." So frustrated with this apparent problem, the young woman contends that "pop culture has taken over the news to the extent that often, any random person on the street will know ten times more about the latest Hollywood divorce than they do about government." Acknowledging further in the article that the media is giving people what they seemingly want to hear about, she places blame on society itself for its infatuation with popular culture. While she is honest enough to admit that hearing "all about various celebrities' DUIs and other mishaps" is amusing, she ultimately advocates for a more informed citizenry. She argues that "by focusing a bit more on what we need to know, we could avoid seeing mug shots of a different celebrity every day."[100] Ultimately, this student hopes the news media and the public can come together to focus on matters of greater importance. As these examples demonstrate, at least some students are aware that the world they live in is saturated with popular culture, and they are not particularly happy about it. They are, moreover, willing to risk being serious about such concerns. Yet these students are very much the exception to the norm.

Conclusion

Researchers have been suggesting for many years now that the news media's role in politics plays an important part in structuring citizens' attitudes. Most notably, Joseph Cappella and Kathleen Hall Jamieson have argued that the news media's negative framing of politicians and political events has led viewers and readers to adopt a cynical posture.[101] The more cynical the news, the more cynical the citizen. This conclusion is particularly important since, as Timothy Cook has shown, over time "media strategies have become increasingly useful means for political actors to pursue governance—and become an increasing focus of their attention and their activities—as the disjuncture between the power of those actors and the expectations placed on them grows."[102] As a fourth governing institution, the news media play an integral role in how the nation is being governed.

While both of these arguments may be true, young adults do not pay much attention to the news media. In a recent national survey for the Center for Information and Research on Civic Learning and Engagement, Michael Olander reported that while young adults are still more likely to turn on their televisions to get the news than to use any other source, fewer than half of them do so more than a few times a week. Less than a third of young adults read the newspaper more than twice a week, and although they are listening to the radio and surfing the Internet, they are not using these media to gather civic information.[103] Young people are not ardent news consumers, so it is hard to imagine that their attitudes are being shaped by the news media.

This chapter has argued that the more contemporary young journalists in this study are, however, inundated with popular culture and that this saturation has led them to become excessively critical and self-protective. These young people have adopted a skeptical attitude that fits right into popular culture. How could they not do so? When Bill Clinton played the saxophone on the *Arsenio Hall Show* during his 1992 presidential campaign and when presidential hopefuls John McCain and John Kerry became regular guests on Jon Stewart's *The Daily Show*, young people could hardly help but see politics and entertainment synonymously. What is potentially troubling is that while politicians increasingly use entertainment to attract the attention of the electorate, they may also be pushing away potential voters whose critical attitudes buffer them from caring too much about bands, movies, television shows, and celebrity politicians alike.

Every generation has its own catchwords that help identify its predominant attitude. Today's generation's word is "cool." As the *Chicago Sun-Times* reported in February 2006, "Groovy is over, hip is square, far out is long gone. Don't worry, though—it's cool. 'Cool' remains the gold standard of slang in the 21st century."[104] The word is not new; even its usage as slang in modern times has a history dating back to at least the hippie movement, where "staying cool" meant not getting angry. But today's use of "cool" is different—it is rooted in popular culture. As public intellectual Malcolm Gladwell found out while reporting on the marketing practice of coolhunting, "cool" is an elusive term:

> The essence of the third rule of cool [is]: you have to be one to know one. . . . In this sense, the third rule of cool fits perfectly into the second: the second rule says that cool cannot be manufactured, only observed, and the third says that it can only be observed by those who are themselves cool. And, of course, the first rule says that it cannot accurately be observed at all, because the act of discovering cool causes cool to take flight, so if you add all three together they describe a closed loop, the hermeneutic circle of coolhunting, a phenomenon whereby not only can the uncool not see cool but cool cannot even be adequately described to them. . . . It is not possible to be cool, in other words, unless you are—in some larger sense—already cool, and so the

phenomenon that the uncool cannot see and cannot have described to them is also something that they cannot ever attain, because if they did it would no longer be cool. Coolhunting represents the ascendancy, in the marketplace, of high school.[105]

Cool is unobservable because of its transient nature, unmanufacturable because it must happen naturally, and unrepresentable because one either is or is not cool. Still, most teenagers want to be cool.

So how do they do so? Through the act of protective criticism. A critic, as noted above, does not have to be negative, but today's young journalists approach criticism by combining its analytical function with an overwhelming dose of faultfinding. This makes sense for the average young person trying to be cool in a pop-cultured world where coolness is inherently elusive. By not attaching themselves to anything in particular and perpetually tearing down everything they see, young people can feel cool, or at least feel temporarily protected. This might be perfectly harmless in a world of pop star icons where one hot trend fades into the next—Britney Spears followed by Christina Aguilera followed by Jessica Simpson followed by Katy Perry, ad nauseum.

In the world of democratic politics, the costs are higher. It is one thing for a young person to protect himself against being seen as uncool for liking an out-of-fashion pop star. It is another issue when these attitudes carry over into politics. Whether Mandy Moore is still popular enough to sell albums matters little to American democracy, but who is elected president and how government is (or is not) held accountable for its actions matter a great deal. The responsibilities of democratic civic engagement may not be cool, but they are central to the health of the nation. Ultimately, politics requires us to take risks.

That today's politicians have so readily embraced popular culture only muddles the civic landscape. Bill Clinton went on MTV for a *Choose or Lose* special during his 1992 campaign. George W. Bush visited *The Oprah Winfrey Show* and planted a kiss on Oprah's cheek in the closing months of the 2000 election. And, in 2008, Barack Obama and John McCain made the talk show rounds, visiting Oprah Winfrey, Jay Leno, David Letterman, *The View*, and *The Daily Show*. Such actions might make candidates appear cool or, at the least, seem more personable, but they do not necessarily suggest anything about their fitness for one of the most powerful positions in the world. Do young people know the difference? Do they care? These are *political* questions.

6

INDEPENDENT JOINERS

On Sunday, March 31, 1968, Martin Luther King Jr. delivered what would be his final sermon just five days before he was assassinated. Addressing a crowd of more than three thousand people at the National Cathedral in Washington, D.C., King chose as his topic the challenges facing the American people, who had to deal with three global revolutions: technology, weaponry, and human rights. King's first point was to remind his audience that "no individual can live alone." He elaborated on this a moment later: "We must all learn to live as brothers. Or we will all perish together as fools. We are tied together in the single garment of destiny, caught in an inescapable network of mutuality." The people were more than simply connected to one another; King's argument was that "whatever affects one directly affects all indirectly. For some strange reason I can never be what I ought to be until you are what you ought to be." To make his point even more explicit, King reminded the congregation of John Donne's infamous words: "'No man is an island entire of itself. Every man is a piece of the continent—a part of the main.'" King's advice for the American people in the face of global revolutions was to remember their need for one another.

On Sunday, July 15, 1979, President Jimmy Carter sat behind his desk in the Oval Office and addressed a national audience on what he repeatedly referred to as its "crisis of confidence." As the nation was dealing with gas shortages and economic uncertainty, Carter acknowledged he had spent the previous ten days talking to people from all over the United States to get to the core of the problem. Ultimately, he found that "the true problems of our nation are much deeper—deeper than gasoline lines or energy shortages, deeper even than inflation or recession." The deeper problem, according to Carter, was "a crisis that strikes at the very heart and soul of our national will. We can see the crisis in the growing doubt about the meaning of our own lives and in the loss of a unity of purpose for our nation." To fix the crisis and restore the American people's confidence, Carter first suggested that "we must face the truth, and then we can change our course. We simply must have faith in each other, faith in our ability to govern ourselves, and faith in the future of this nation." Carter's advice for the American people as they confronted this crisis was to rediscover their faith in one another and the power of their collective will.

On Thursday, February 5, 2009, newly inaugurated president Barack Obama delivered a few brief remarks at the annual National Prayer Breakfast in Washington, D.C. His focus that morning was faith. Noting that "far too often we have seen faith wielded as a tool to divide us from one another," Obama urged his audience to "remember that there is no religion whose central tenet is hate. There is no God who condones taking the life of an innocent human being." Obama's goal, therefore, was to suggest that faith could be a way to bring people together. As he had done in his much-discussed campaign speech on race, "A More Perfect Union," and would later do in his controversial commencement address at Notre Dame that same year, Obama reminded his audience of the "one law that binds all great religions together." This one overarching law was, for Obama, "the Golden Rule—the call to love one another; to understand one another; to treat with dignity and respect those with whom we share a brief moment on this Earth." Obama did not suggest, however, that the Golden Rule is easy to follow. Instead, he suggested the "simple rule" is "also one of the most challenging. For it asks each of us to take some measure of responsibility for the well-being of people we may not know or worship with or agree with on every issue." Thus, Obama's advice for the American people as they dealt with deep religious divisions was to remember the Golden Rule and take responsibility for one another.

America's political leaders always seem to be reminding the American people that they cannot live alone, separated from their fellow citizens. King told the American people they needed one another. Carter asked them to have faith in one another. Obama argued they shared a collective responsibility. Whatever the particular situation, each felt compelled to remind the people that they could not live without one another and that, moreover, they all shared some collective duty to one another. Each of these speakers, and many others as well, felt the need to remind the people that they were a people.

The American people are a multicultural plurality; their differences are many. U.S. presidents have always played an important role in constituting American identity.[1] Still, the words of King, Carter, and Obama seem to run deeper than simply reminding the people that they are all Americans. At the core, their arguments are reminders to be nice to one another, to not be selfish. They are, in short, arguments parents try to teach their children every day.

Did the American people really need to be reminded of such obvious lessons? Are they really so quick to lose faith in one another? Is a sense of community that difficult to foster and maintain in the United States?

The short answer is, apparently, yes. A slightly longer answer might be that while most people would acknowledge they cannot live alone, they might also admit they do not find it easy to live with others. Such a contradiction may be tied up with the human condition itself, but it is also very much a concern for the modern United States. After all, democracy requires that the people join together to struggle collectively for the good of their communities. In recent years, there has been a growing fear that the American people are losing their ability to be responsible for one another and to work together on shared democratic problems. Many worry that the American people no longer know how to join together and think of others when they act. From claims about hyperindividualism to fierce culture wars, the American people do not seem to be truly acting as a people.

From presidents and political leaders to community activists and political theorists, there is a widespread belief that the American people are in great danger of losing their sense of national community. At the very least, these concerned voices seem to think that the people need to be constantly reminded to be nicer to and care more about one another. Is such worry really warranted? Has the United States truly become as hyperindividualistic, even narcissistic, as so many have suggested? Is the social fabric of the United States tearing? Given the well-documented decrease in voter turnout and increase in social distrust, especially among young adults, discussed in chapter 1, it is hard not to feel that something is amiss in America. While the current concern about the strength of connectedness in the United States dates back to the post–World War II economic boom, the American people are now confronted with more contemporary challenges to community— challenges that are particularly salient among young Americans. But is there really anything to be so troubled about? Has there really been a change in how young people in the United States join together in communities with one another? Has there been, as the research on social capital suggests, a decline in the number of groups with which young individuals identify? Have today's young people truly become islands unto themselves?

While a number of researchers have attempted to answer these questions by counting group affiliations, I take a different approach, looking at how the young adults in this study talk about politics and organizations. What I find, in brief, is that while political issues have become increasingly centered on matters once relegated to the private realm, the high school newspapers examined here reveal that the young journalists are not adverse to joining groups. The types of groups they join, however, are not as other-oriented as past organizations are portrayed. In the end, I argue that these young people can be seen today as *independent joiners*—individuals who link to others for quite personal reasons. Referring to these young people this way is clearly contradictory, but it also seems accurate. In a positive sense, these students are taking care of their own needs. That seems reasonable since, as chapter 5 showed, they have lost their belief that government and other organizations will do what is necessary to help them. However, the more contemporary young journalists in this study still understand that they cannot go it completely alone. Despite the fact they are at odds with themselves, a nation of independent joiners still needs to be understood. Questions of individuals, community, and democracy are as old as democratic thought, but the challenges facing the United States today are uniquely American and temporally bound. Understanding these exceptional circumstances is the first step toward answering the above questions.

America and Individualism

In 2005, the *Atlantic Monthly* commissioned French intellectual Bernard-Henri Lévy to retrace the path of Alexis de Tocqueville, one of the earliest of a number of French observers who sought to understand America's democratic experiment. Tocqueville was also the first to find America's love of individualism troubling. He noted in 1835 that "Providence has given to each individual, whoever he may be, the degree of reason necessary for him to be able to direct himself in things that interest him exclusively. Such is the great maxim on which civil and political society in the United States rests." Tocqueville went on to question the tension found in this self-reliance when reflecting on the reasons why despotism could take hold in a democracy: "I see an innumerable crowd of like and equal men who revolve on themselves without repose, procuring the small and vulgar pleasures with which they fill their souls. Each of them, withdrawn and apart, is like a stranger to the destiny of all the others."[2] A century and a half later, Jean Baudrillard offered a harsher critique, observing that the "number of people here who think alone, sing alone, and eat and talk alone in the streets is mind-boggling. And yet they don't add up. Quite the reverse. They subtract from each other and their resemblance to one another is uncertain."[3] Just like Tocqueville and Baudrillard, Lévy was both enamored with and confused by America's individualism during his trek across the country. Noting the complexities of Social Security, Lévy wrote, "It stems from the methodical individualism that . . . aims to leave with each individual the responsibility for his fate."[4] For Lévy, there was also an absence of real community in the United States (except perhaps, as he suggests, in Seattle and Savannah), exemplified poignantly in the artificiality of Sun City, Arizona. Concerned over an isolated nation of individuals, Lévy, a self-proclaimed "anti-anti-Americanist," left the United States worried about its future.

The United States, it turns out, did not need another Frenchman to detail its ills. Its citizens have known the potential dangers of their individualism for some time now. David Reisman, for example, touched on the inner-directedness of many Americans in the 1950 intellectual classic *The Lonely Crowd.*[5] In the 1970s, Richard Sennett suggested that the American people had lost their ability to act together in *The Fall of Public Man.*[6] And Robert Bellah and his colleagues argued more than two decades ago in *Habits of the Heart* that American individualism was putting enough of a strain on community that it threatened the very social fabric of the United States:

> Perhaps the crucial change in American life has been that we have moved from the local life of the nineteenth century—in which economic and social relationships were visible and, however imperfectly, morally interpreted as parts of a larger common life—to a society vastly more interrelated and integrated economically, technically, and functionally. Yet this is a society in which the individual can only rarely and with difficulty understand himself and his activities as interrelated in morally meaningful ways with those of other, different Americans. Instead of directing cultural and individual energies toward relating the self to its larger context, the culture of manager and therapist urges a strenuous effort to make of our particular segment of life a small world of its own.

While they were concerned about America's love of individualism in the early 1980s, Bellah and his colleagues saw the problem as a true crisis more than a decade later. In the updated 1996 edition of their book, they argued, "There are, at every level of American life and in every significant group, temptations and pressures to disengage from the larger society."[7] This crisis, they believed, stemmed from a decline in social capital, a weakening of the family, a failure in local governments, and the rise of neocapitalism. In the end, they warned that American democracy could not withstand its people turning away from one another.

Although there is a long history of concern about the individualistic tendency of the American people, this concern has today reached a frenzy. A study published by a trio of sociologists in 2006 set off a small national media firestorm by arguing that "the number of people who have someone to talk to about matters that are important to them has declined dramatically, and the number of alternative discussion partners has shrunk."[8] The report generated spectacular headlines in some of the nation's leading newspapers, such as "The Lonely American Just Got a Bit Lonelier" and "Social Isolation Growing in U.S."[9] Another group of sociologists has dug deeper into this new loneliness phenomenon to find that even in marriages people are spending less time together and have fewer shared friends.[10] Psychologists have been just as clear in recent years about their concerns. Jacqueline Olds and Richard Schwartz have argued, for instance, that "people in our society drift away from social connections" because of a fast-paced modern life and the American myth of rugged individualism.[11] According to these researchers, the American people are not much of a people at all. They have become, instead, a nation of isolated individuals.

So troubling has this apparent fragmentation become that an entire cadre of public intellectuals and statesmen has been trying over the past two decades to reverse this trend under the auspices of communitarianism. Guided by the work of Amitai Etzioni, communitarians worry that the separation of individuals in the United States could undermine both its shared values and its traditional culture. As the communitarian movement has conceived the problem, "Neither human existence nor individual liberty can be sustained for long outside the interdependent and overlapping communities to which all of us belong. Nor can any community long survive unless its members dedicate some of their attention, energy, and resources to shared projects."[12] Worried about individuals retreating from community, communitarians work to resituate the individual within the moral, social, and political environment of traditional societal norms. They lament the loss of the social connectedness that once existed in the United States and work to create stronger community ties among individuals. They are attempting, in essence, to reinvigorate democratic engagement by strengthening a shared sense of community. They are trying to keep the American people from fragmenting into ideological enclaves and detached individualism.

While the communitarian corrective is important to note, not everyone seems optimistic about the possibility of bringing the American people back together. This concern about isolated individualism is never more apparent than when researchers turn their attention to American youth. Psychologist Jean Twenge has gone so far as to label today's youth "Generation Me" and has even claimed that the United States is currently facing a narcissistic epidemic in its youth.[13] While not everyone is quite so dramatic, there has been in the past few years no shortage of publications dealing with a generation of young people who seem to do a great deal of navel-gazing. This concern has been particularly salient for corporate America. Since 2007, there has been an explosion of books concerned with how best to motivate and manage selfish youth.[14] That these books routinely refer to young adults entering the workforce in recent years as "trophy kids," the "what's in it for me workforce," and "generation why me" clearly indicates their view of American youth as narcissistic. Young Americans, it seems, are having difficulty not succeeding at everything they do, would prefer that others take care of difficult things, and are primarily concerned with themselves. Company executives and corporate management are struggling to get these selfish, lazy young adults to care more about the organizations in which they work. While motivating them to be better workers may be important for American capitalism, getting them to understand the importance of caring about their fellow citizens is even more central to a healthy American democracy.

Democracy requires that citizens share a sense of community. If the people are to rule, they ought to have a sense of who they are as a people. Such a direct awareness of one another as citizens requires, moreover, a robust civil society—the voluntary civic and social organizations, clubs, and informal networks that exist apart from and in connection to both the state and the market. As Peter Levine has argued, "No democracy—indeed, no reasonably just regime of any type—can manage without private, voluntary, nonprofit associations. In turn, these associations need citizens who have certain relevant skills, habits, and virtues."[15] Echoing Levine's claim, Stephen Macedo and a group of eighteen political scientists recently argued that "at the heart of civic engagement is associational life. Modern mass democracies need associations to organize communities, link neighbors to one another, integrate neighborhoods in cities and towns, and forge bonds between people across geographic distances."[16] What these scholars are pointing out, of course, is something democratic thinkers have known since Aristotle: a democracy requires citizens to know one another. As noted in chapter 3, Aristotle believed that this need to know one's fellow citizens required that democracies remain quite small. In a large, pluralistic society such as the

United States, the best one can hope for is a vibrant civil society of networks of individuals interacting through associational connections.

In recent years, there has been a great deal of concern about the health of civil society in the United States. For the most part, these concerns have coalesced around the concept of social capital. Although social capital has been defined in a number of different ways by various researchers, one recent definition offers a relatively concise overview of the term: "Social capital refers to connections among individuals—social networks and the norms of reciprocity and trustworthiness that arise from them."[17] One of the primary assumptions of social capital is that those who join together with others to solve community problems will increasingly come to trust others. As most notions of democratic engagement acknowledge that all citizens must be willing to make sacrifices for the community, an ability to trust others is imperative for a healthy civil society. Moreover, an ability to trust others leads to reciprocity, which, according to Robert Putnam, is a citizen's faith that when he does something of value for someone today, something of value will be done for him at a later time.[18] While a number of scholars have recognized that there is a dark side to social capital that can lead to the exclusion of some and to the reinforcement of negative group behaviors, most researchers agree that some civic and social associations have the positive benefit of enhancing levels of trust and reciprocity. It is, after all, difficult to imagine people collectively ruling if they do not trust or feel compelled to sacrifice for one another.

While most can agree that the ideas represented within the social capital concept are indeed important for democracy, not everyone agrees on just what has been happening to social capital in the United States over the past several decades. On one side of this debate is a group of scholars who contend there has been a clear and troubling decline in the levels of social capital, especially among American youth. Macedo and his colleagues provide a good summary of this continued belief that associational life in the United States is not what it used to be, as they "conclude (tentatively) that overall levels [of associational life] have declined somewhat and (less tentatively) that the mix and characteristic structures of associational life have changed significantly."[19] The American people are not coming together as often as they used to, nor in the same ways when they do. This is especially true for young Americans. In a 2009 report, one group of researchers noted this negative trend by comparing survey data from young people between the 1970s and the early 2000s. They concluded rather succinctly, "Unfortunately, young adults—especially those who are not college-bound—are less likely today than they were in the 1970s to be connected to a wide range of institutions, including churches, voluntary associations, unions, and political parties."[20] It is apparently, then, an accepted truth among many researchers that American youth are disconnected from one another and the larger communities with which they ought to identify.

While not denying that membership in most civic and social organizations has declined in recent years, on the other side of this debate is a group of researchers who suggest young people are as active in civil society as previous generations, although today's youth prefer newer forms of organizing that do not require as much commitment. As was noted in chapter 4, no one has made this argument as forcefully as sociologist Michael Schudson. In his recent work, Schudson has gone so far as to question the narrow definition of associational life preferred by many social capital scholars. In questioning how they define associational life, Schudson discovered a number of important civic groups and behaviors that he believes do constitute a robust civil society. In his own, somewhat ironic, words, he admits to "sing[ing] the praises of episodic organizations, NIMBY organizations, litigious cranks and twelve-step groups."[21] While he does not want to disparage more traditional forms of associational life, Schudson's point is that joining a social protest or therapeutic group might still produce important civic benefits. If Schudson is correct about the benefits derived from alternative forms of associational life, then young people may be doing just fine. As political scientist Cliff Zukin and his colleagues have noted, young adults are just as likely as older generations, if not more so, to volunteer for nonelectoral groups, participate in a charitable race/walk, and raise money for charity.[22] While they may eschew membership-based organizations and the responsibilities and obligations that accompany them, young people do seem willing to get involved in their own ways.

The dividing line in the debate about young Americans and their sense of shared community lies between those who believe matters are getting seriously grave and those who seem to think there is nothing at all to worry about. American youth are either a selfish lot who care little for others or simply a new generation that joins together in new types of organizations. As the young people in this study have demonstrated in their high school newspaper deliberations, the either-or dichotomy seems oversimplified. These young adults have come to see politics from a more personalized perspective, but they also seem a long way off from being the isolated, indifferent individuals so many have portrayed them as being. They still add up, even if their sum may not look familiar to some.

Personalizing Politics

One of the most profound changes in the American political landscape over the past few decades has been the rise of a more personalized politics, due largely to the changing economic and globalizing forces of postmodernity. Anthony Giddens refers to this new politics as "life politics." His concept "concerns political issues which flow from processes of self-actualization in post-traditional contexts." Given the changing nature of the contemporary world, individuals have been placed in a more direct and personalized political relationship with the world around them. Questions of nuclear power and weapons, for instance, lead today's individual to make personal choices about her energy consumption instead of contacting legislators to voice her concerns or joining a community organization devoted to limiting the building of new nuclear power plants. For Giddens, a life politics is seen as positive since it becomes a politics of choice, a power that "is generative rather than hierarchical."[23] The individual becomes the genesis for the political. This self-actualizing stance makes politics personal, but it also causes the personal to become political.

Ulrich Beck has also suggested that most people today engage in a politics that is much more about life choices than community decisions. Beck argues that the changing social conditions of the last several decades have led to a type of individualism that is extremely ambivalent and no longer rooted in the stability of metanarratives.[24] Lance Bennett describes this politicizing of personal issues and choices as a "lifestyle politics." For Bennett, this personalized politics "makes sense within the personal life considerations of job, recreation, shopping, entertainment, fashion, sports, self-improvement, family, friends, and the community involvements that can be scheduled around these things."[25] According to these scholars, politics has become largely about personal issues surrounding race, gender, sexuality, occupation, and other such characteristics. These highly personal issues are dealt with by collectives only when they benefit the individual, requiring groups be fluid in nature. All of this has created, they conclude, highly individualized political engagements, which may be especially suited to young adults.

Of course, many people would suggest that teenagers are inherently selfish but will eventually grow out of it. Teenagers are surely self-involved, but it would be wrong to view them as narcissistic. Erik Erickson argues that adolescence is the fifth stage of human development wherein the individual struggles with his personal identity and his role in larger social networks.[26] The ego plays a dominant psychological role during this period, so it is natural to expect teenagers to be internally focused. But, as Erickson notes, the adolescent is also concerned with where and how she fits in with others. While high school students are often focused on themselves, psychology suggests that they should be trying to find where they belong in the larger societal scheme. Some teenagers in the 1960s acted selfishly, of course, and some young people in the 1990s were overtly concerned with community problems. But the general tendency among the young journalists studied here was an increasing focus on personal matters.

Over the past forty-five years, there has been a clear shift in what these young people described as salient political issues. A quick survey of the issues concerning the young journalists in the 1960s and 1970s reveals a more community-based understanding—from the effects of poverty on local communities, to the impact of free speech on the American community, to the war in Vietnam.[27] The editorial staff at Wilson High School in Washington, D.C., demonstrated just how community-focused many political issues were for students in the opening years of this study. In a 1966 editorial, the staff discussed a proposed budget plan that listed the funding of a new "Woodrow Wilson field house as number 37 in a list of 37 priorities." While the new building would clearly benefit the students of Wilson High School, the editorial staff question a number of school officials and students who have been pushing for the budget item to be given higher priority: "Certainly, the efforts of these organizations for the sorely needed field house should be appreciated. However, we can not help but feel that these efforts have questionable emphasis. If the Wilson field house is moved up on the list, projects of other schools will be lowered and some other need will be number 37, and thus go without funds."[28] The political concern expressed by these students is not only about the community; they are even aware of the impact on the larger social good. Clearly, they do not want their personal desires to get in the way of what is best for everyone.

More recently, what constitutes an important problem in the view of the young journalists in this study has shifted from the communal to the personal. This change can be noted in the rise of health issues opened up to public discussion in the 1990s, as represented in the following four stories from four different school papers:

> Young adults . . . don't realize there is a much healthier, perhaps equally likeable method of eating. According to the A.D.A.—the American Dietary Association—vegetarians tend to exhibit lower levels of blood pressure, cholesterol, colon, lung, and possibly breast cancer.[29]

Nose jobs are becoming increasingly common, and they are no longer confined to androgynous pop stars. In fact, rhinoplasty is a procedure that has gained popularity among teenage girls. That's where it starts to concern us, the astute, well-informed, cosmopolitan South students.[30]

So what's the big deal; 52 grams of fat. At the prime age of 14 to 18 fat is no concern, that is something to be worried about during a mid-life crisis. Wrong![31]

Anger is a confusing condition. . . . Realizing how to identify anger is just a matter of communicating and reasoning. Violence should be immediately eliminated; no further pain is necessary.[32]

These textual examples highlight a number of salient problems—vegetarian eating, plastic surgery, obesity, and personal violence. Each problem is important, of course, but each also represents the public airing of what was once considered a personal issue. Regardless of whether these students have larger communal and political concerns regarding health issues, their choice to discuss such matters is striking. Indeed, many of the young people in this study have naturally begun to think of the personal as public.

There is perhaps no better way to describe the extent of this change in focus than to compare two years of high school newspaper coverage. Oak Park High School's *Northmen's Log* reveals just how significant the shift toward the personal has been. During the 1994–95 school year, the staff of *Northmen's Log* produced 11 issues and 124 pages. Included among each issue's news reports, entertainment pages, and sports news, there was a two-page special feature that took up almost 20 percent of the newspaper's space. So what did the student journalists at Oak Park High feel the need to feature for their peers? With the exception of the final feature, which offered a historical perspective on Vietnam's impact on the school,[33] all of the features focused on issues that were once more likely to be seen as personal. Five dealt with problems directly related to being a student. The stress related to the holiday season, making decisions about life after high school, and working while in school were the subjects of three out of these five features.[34] The other two offered students advice on how to deal with their stress through time management and exercise.[35] Three additional features presented students with stories about what it was like to live with divorced parents, to be adopted, and to have alcoholic loved ones.[36] Another feature argued for the importance of students learning to embrace their individuality, and it included three personal profiles of students who seemed to have succeeded at becoming unique individuals.[37] Finally, a feature that appeared in January 1995 reported on suicide by focusing on several interviews with students who had either been contemplating taking their lives or been affected by someone who had.[38] Whatever else was on the minds of these students, personal matters were certainly salient.

By contrast, the students writing for *Northmen's Log* twenty-five years earlier presented their peers with very different issues. Within the 104 pages printed in 14 separate issues during the 1969–70 school year, there were very few articles comparable to the features described above. Interspersed among the stories on school issues, the need to lower the voting age, fears related to Vietnam, and AFS students, only seven brief articles seem, at first glance, similar. Five of these pieces dealt directly with drugs, although three of them were reports on drug-related arrests and community concerns about a perceived drug problem.[39] The other two were a story about an alcoholic's talk at a school assembly and a plea from the paper's editorial board to students to avoid taking LSD.[40] Of the last two comparable articles, one chided students for bad manners when engaging in public displays of affection, and the other reported on the growing fear of a national venereal disease epidemic.[41] Absent from *Northmen's Log* in this earlier school year, then, was any story about how to deal with the difficulties of being a student or what it is like to live with difficult situations or diseases. The students at Oak Park High School during the earlier years of this study felt that such personal issues and problems were not meant for a public forum like the high school newspaper.

Of course, discussion of personal issues such as anger, stress, and adoption can be viewed as beneficial to a nation of young people forced to deal with these problems. One might want to treat this openness as a sign that the young journalists in this study refused to exclude salient issues from public discourse. After all, a student reading an article in his school newspaper about the devastating effects of depression may come to realize some of his problems stem from something other than a temporary malaise. One can even imagine the student who reads this story going to a counselor for advice or getting medication. There is a concern, however, that these highly personal issues will divert attention from political problems more deeply rooted in community. Students focusing on why they should stop eating red meat to help control their weight and prevent heart disease are not, ipso facto, focused on their state's tax incentives for large cattle farmers. Nor will they be aware of how politically motivated the creation of the Food and Drug Administration's food pyramid was or how the national government might change it. This last point has more to do with how young people discuss these personal issues than the nature of the issues themselves.

Rhetorical critic Dana Cloud has argued that Americans have moved into a world of individualized politics as a result of a dominant therapeutic discourse. While Cloud agrees with others that the American people have become increasingly self-interested in the past several decades, she contends that the shift is a result of "the therapeutic as a political strategy of contemporary capitalism, by which potential dissent is contained within a discourse of individual and family responsibility." Cloud found, for instance, that a therapeutic discourse emerged around the Persian Gulf War that helped create a sense of support for Americans, and she notes that this discursive support may have detracted from a more critical and engaged dialogue about the war effort. Cloud's concern is that this rhetoric of therapy depoliticizes political problems in the United States (e.g., race, class, gender) by encouraging an "identification with therapeutic values: individualism, familialism, self-help, and self-absorption."[42] If Cloud is right, one might ask whether young people have learned to speak such a rhetoric. Judging by the seven high school newspapers in this study, many students have been learning to speak a therapeutic rhetoric. That is, they deliberate publicly about personal issues through personalized language.

One clear example of this move to a discourse of more personalized responsibility can be seen in young people's concerns about smoking. Discussing the issue of smoking in high school, one angry student at Newton South High School in 1966 complained that the no-smoking rule was not being enforced. In making his argument that the rule should be applied rigorously, he suggested, "Though it was hoped that it might help students quit the habit, the main purpose is to prevent fire hazards. It also is supposed to help keep the school and its grounds neat and smelling clean."[43] While the student understands the personal health issues related to smoking, his main concern is how the issue might negatively impact the entire school community. His anxieties are about preventing fires and keeping the school clean. For this concerned student, then, the health of individual smokers is of secondary importance.

Thirty years later, students' concerns about smoking had completely reversed themselves. In a *Carrickulum* editorial at Pittsburgh's Carrick High School, one student presented an argument against a new state law making it a crime for a minor to be caught in possession of tobacco products. After complaining that the law was unfair and students should be allowed to smoke outside the school, the editorialist suggested how smoking should be dealt with: "Educational classes on the effects of smoking will help guide minors into the right direction. No one wants to die from cancer or get emphysema, so most likely the right choice would be selected. As for the minors that smoke now, they have already shown that they will not stop smoking. The only way they will quit is when they themselves decide to quit."[44] This student's concern is not with the impact of smoking on the school or community. Rather, he asserts that all individuals, given the right information, should be able to make their own decisions, which is their personal right.

Young people today could, of course, discuss the problems of smoking in a number of other ways. They could examine local policies on teenage smoking and determine whether those policies are being enforced. They could explore how the tobacco industry has systematically targeted teenagers through creative marketing strategies and product placement. They could also attempt to understand the recent legal battles over whether tobacco companies can be held accountable by smokers diagnosed with cancer and what the government has done to help or hinder these lawsuits. They could, that is, come to understand smoking as a collective issue. Instead, the students in this study have increasingly discussed it as a personal problem and therefore focused on smoking-related issues by highlighting individual impact, individual blame, and individual choice.

What is true for smoking is also true for drinking. In a 2008 feature story on lowering the drinking age to eighteen years old, one Newton South High School student framed the entire issue as one of personal responsibility. Citing a recent call by 120 college presidents to lower the drinking age, the student offered opposing viewpoints, although the views were clearly lopsided. On the side of keeping the drinking age at twenty-one, the young reporter presents just one person—the school's principal. The only quote attributed to the principal is a simple claim that he is not in favor of lowering the drinking age; he is given no room to elaborate on why he prefers this. The remainder of the article lays out the reasons why the drinking age should be lowered. One argument is that "if 18-year-olds were able to legally drink, they would have the opportunity to drink in public places, which would cause them to drink more responsibly than they would in private." In addition, the student argues that if eighteen-year-olds were able to buy alcohol legally at a liquor store they would no longer feel "the need . . . to consume large amounts of alcohol quickly." Focusing on how individuals would make better personal choices if given the legal option, the article fails, until the very last paragraph, to suggest any concern for larger community issues. Even then, such concern is limited and quickly dismissed. The student acknowledges that "lowering the drinking age would not completely eliminate dangerous drinking, drunk driving, or parties that get out of control, but many believe that it would greatly reduce the incidence of all of these for drinkers." Even here, one must work to see the concern for others that might be implied in mentioning drunk driving or out-of-control parties. In the end, the young woman reminds her readers of the primary thrust of the article when asserting that those who want to lower the drinking age "believe in giving teenagers the chance at a younger age to learn how to be responsible with their alcohol consumption."[45] Lowering the drinking age ultimately becomes a way to teach young people how to make better personal choices.

Three articles on the problem of teen parenting further illustrate such tendencies. Under the heading "Features," the January 15, 2002, issue of *Carrickulum* presented three stories: "A Day in the Life of a Teen Father," "A Day in the Life of a Teen Mother," and "My Parents no Longer Control Me, My Children Do." The first two stories were written by a student-parent and covered the difficulties of a daily routine that tries to balance school, work, and parenting. The third article was attributed to an anonymous author who had her first child during her senior year and had another child after graduating from high school. All three authors offered personal accounts of how having a child while still in high school impacted their lives. While the stories were clearly framed as warnings for other students, none of the articles discussed larger social issues related to teen sex, such as the school's birth control policy or the community's resources for young parents. Instead, each of the young authors lamented making bad choices and wrote with the hope of teaching others to be more personally responsible for their actions. For these young adults, teen pregnancy was an individual problem with individual implications.

As the young people in this study came to see political issues as personal in nature, they also learned to blame individuals for the problems of others. Discussing the dangers of drinking and driving, one Newton South High School student even questioned the actions of Princess Diana that led to her death:

> The driver of the car in which [Princess Diana] drove had been drinking before driving. Instead of staying in one place, she chose to get in the car with a drunk driver. Perhaps if she had questioned her mortality and stayed at dinner for a little bit longer, it may have turned out differently.

Many face similar situations in their lifetime, and surprisingly many people make the risky choice. Drugs and alcohol have become part of many young people's lives, affecting everyone in some way. . . . People must remember, however, that they are not immortal and should act responsibly, not risking their lives for something as simple as a ride home.[46]

Princess Diana's death is seen here as a direct result of her poor personal decision making. The article's author does not question the restaurant's responsibility or how the government might enforce existing laws more stringently to reduce the numbers of drunk driving fatalities. Nor is there any discussion, as there was in the mainstream media, about paparazzi and a person's right to privacy. The author places the full blame on the individual. According to this student, Princess Diana should have thought of larger issues and not acted so carelessly with her own life—and others should do the same.

These young journalists described the solution to many political problems as the ability to make better personal choices. While the impact of drugs on the nation could be discussed in terms of legal issues and socioeconomic concerns, the young people represented in this study were not looking in those directions by the late 1980s. As a result, the solution to the drug problem was not seen as stronger penalties for drug offenders or a better public education system in low-income areas. Instead, individuals were urged to make better decisions: "More adolescents are being faced with the choice of cocaine due to lower prices and easy access. Life provides a variety of choices. One leads himself either to success or failure. One choice gaining rapid recognition is the decision of whether or not to partake in America's number one major social and health problem—the problem of cocaine. When faced with so many choices in life, why make the choice that could ruin a future?"[47] Although this Washington High School student hints at economic issues and frames the problem as a national one, the only solution identified is personal in nature—correctly choosing to not partake in drug use. The way to solve the drug problem in America was to make individuals understand that they were responsible for making better personal choices. Nancy Reagan seems to have understood this, telling young Americans to "just say no." Many young adults growing up in the 1980s may have heard Reagan's antidrug message and internalized it, leading them to exercise better decision making.

The young adults in this study appear to have learned to overlook the communal impact of the issues that concerned them. Nor do they seem to have understood how a community might serve as a more effective resource in helping them solve their problems. Instead, politics has become personal for them. Personal matters have turned into political issues, and society-wide problems are the result of poor individual decision making. Given Cloud's argument about therapeutic discourse and the overwhelming cultural emphasis in recent decades on personal improvement, self-empowerment, and individual responsibility, it is little wonder that these young people have adopted such attitudes, which have influenced their political and civic lives.

Self-Interested Groups

While one need not blame the young people in this study for adopting a personalized attitude toward political problems, such attitudinal shifts do raise concerns about how this personalization might affect their democratic engagement. One of the primary problems with making personal issues political is that it turns the focus on the self. Politics is, however, about communities of people struggling together. Such struggles require people to attend to one another and find ways to work together in the sharing of community resources. Political theorist Danielle Allen has indeed suggested that democracy requires its citizens to attend to one another, respect one another, and willingly make sacrifices together.[48] As was noted above, many political scientists have been worried for some time now about the lack of contact many Americans have with their neighbors—what scholars today refer to as a lack of social capital. As political theorist James Farr has recently noted, democratic political thought about the importance of groups and associations of free citizens has a long history, even among such divergent thinkers as John Dewey and Karl Marx.[49] And America's ability to create and foster such connections has been a matter of concern since the time of Tocqueville.

While I discussed the question of social capital and group organization above, it is worth returning to this issue briefly before looking at the ways in which the young people in this study talked about groups and organizations among themselves. Returning to this topic brings us back, of course, to Robert Putnam's *Bowling Alone*. What is unique about Putnam's book is how well he is able to document the decline in social capital over the past half century in the United States. As the title indicates, Americans have increasingly lost their ties to various social groups—they have begun bowling alone instead of together in leagues. Examining the membership of national charter-based organizations across the twentieth century, Putnam found that average membership declined by almost half between 1960 and 1997. Across that same time period, church attendance declined by approximately 10 percent, and work-related organizations (e.g., American Nurses Association, American Society of Mechanical Engineers, American Bar Association) followed a similar trend.[50] As organization membership decreased, so too did the percentage of Americans who believed that their neighbors were honest and moral. People have lost their connections with others, Putnam argues, as there has been an overall loss in interpersonal trust.

With that loss, the American people have been doing less and less with others. American civic life, then, is characterized by Putnam as being filled with individuals who do not care to join with others and who would not trust them if they did. While Putnam has repeatedly argued that individuals today are less likely to join organizations such as the PTA, Elks Club, or Rotary Club, he has more recently suggested that people's alienation from one another runs much deeper. It even affects the way they spend their leisure time with others "in informal leisure activities—having friends over for dinner, hanging out in bars, gossiping with neighbors, playing cards."[51]

This tendency to do little with one another has been true of today's younger generations. Since the publication of Bowling Alone, a cottage industry of social capital research has appeared in the areas of political science and communication. Most important for this study, much of this work has pointed to the generational differences in the decline of social capital. As Dhavan Shah and his co-authors have argued, the declining trends in social capital "appear to be based as much on generational differences as individual changes—that is, cohort and life-cycle effects—with 'Gen-Xers' being less participatory, trusting, and satisfied than their 'Baby Boomer' parents, who themselves are less connected and involved than members of the preceding 'Civic Generation' were as young people."[52] According to this research, today's young people are less connected to one another than those of any preceding generation. They are not, at least, connected in the ways that are good for democratic engagement.

Of course, given the amount of time American youth now spend on social networking sites and texting one another on their mobile phones, it is obvious that young people are as connected as ever. The question, then, is not merely about the numbers of connections but, perhaps more importantly, about the types of associations. Whether a young person has five hundred "friends" on Facebook or sends, as was recently reported by the Nielsen Company, a startling average of 3,339 texts a month does not mean she is talking to her peers about political problems or building social trust.[53] To get the benefits of social capital, the argument goes, young people must be joining together in groups and organizations, preferably those that require some form of membership. The question to be asked, therefore, is this: Are today's young people less likely to join with one another in groups and organizations? As revealed in the amount of coverage given to such organizations in this study's high school newspapers, the answer for these young journalists is no. The types of groups and the way students talk about them do, however, suggest that the groups they join have changed.

The clubs and organizations discussed in the high school newspapers from the early years of this study are familiar—DECA, Key Club, and so forth. What is important to note about these organizations is not merely that they existed but the purpose they served for young people in the 1960s and 1970s. They had one primary function—to prepare American youth for an industrious future. In 1969, for instance, some students at Pittsburgh's Carrick High School had the opportunity to attend a conference sponsored by the Key Club. The article on the conference asserts that the "purpose of this leadership conference is to provide worthwhile activities to assist youth in leadership development as they prepare to be marketing and distribution leaders of tomorrow."[54] At Phoenix's Washington High School, students participated actively in Future Farmers of America (FFA). In reporting on an upcoming FFA club event, the *Ram Page* announced that "money raised from the show will be used to finance the annual FFA Parents-Son Banquet, and to operate the chapter's nine acre farm. The club also plans to build a plastic greenhouse on campus for tomatoes."[55] Other organizations mentioned include the French Club and FTA. In Portland, a *Grantonian* report on the FTA organization suggested that "one of the highlights of belonging to Future Teachers of America is being able to be a teacher aid" and learning the skills needed for a future in education.[56] What ties these organizations together is that they are top-down in nature. That is, the clubs and groups that students joined in the early years of this study were largely created by adults.

Over time, two important things happened in the organizational lives of the young people studied here: the number of clubs in each school roughly doubled, and the types of clubs students joined took on new purposes. Looking at Carrick High School as an example, a 1972 issue of *Carrickulum* catalogued all of the clubs that were active in the school at the time.[57] The list included twenty-four school groups, which ranged from the Art Club to the Red Cross. According to the Carrick High website, the number of school clubs more than doubled by 2005, despite the fact that the school's population had declined slightly across the same thirty-three year time period. While student groups such as DECA and Student Council remained visible, newer organizations emerged—groups as varied as the Ski Club and a school chapter of the Health Occupations Students of America (HOSA). Simply put, in recent years young people have created and joined any number of organizations. While it is impossible to gain from the newspapers a sense of how many students joined which groups or the number of informal associations that existed within each school, it is clear that the ability of students to organize together has not diminished over time.

However, beyond the growing number of student groups that emerged in the 1990s, there has certainly been a shift in the types of groups that have surfaced. While the groups of the 1960s and 1970s were primarily designed to help students become productive members of society after graduating, the newer organizations support the more immediate interests and needs of the students themselves. Overall, three types of groups have gained popularity, as evidenced in the seven high school newspapers. These are groups that focus on specific student issues, activities, and social diversity.

The group that has been especially popular among the youth studied here over the past two decades is SADD. Created to fight alcohol-related deaths among young adults, SADD was quick to make its way into schools throughout the nation in the late 1980s. Unlike organizations from earlier decades, SADD membership had few requirements, as an article from *Carrickulum* suggested: "Another year has begun for Students Against Driving Drunk, and once again the members of the SADD club have begun to talk to the student body about drinking and driving. October is SADD awareness month, so students are wearing red ribbons to represent this organization."[58] Beyond talking, wearing ribbons, and making pledges, the student members of SADD were required to do little else, and the national organization has been quick to adjust to changing times. As a *Northmen's Log* article demonstrated, both a new name and an inventive approach have helped the organization stay salient in the lives of young adults. The students in the Students Against Destructive Decisions (SADD's new name as of 1997) at Oak Park High School in Kansas City started putting on a yearly Grim Reaper Day in the late 1990s to highlight that deaths due to drunk driving occurred every thirty-two minutes.[59]

Although SADD is a national organization with charter groups in most high schools, today's students have learned how to create issue-oriented clubs themselves. The events of September 11th led to one such example at Grant High School in Portland. Students looking for a way to help those directly impacted by the terrorist attacks decided to come together and pool their resources: "So was born the latest club available to Grant students: Youth Helping in Times of Crisis. . . . The result was a list that included a money drive, a supplies drive, a college scholarship program for students who lost their parents, having elementary school children draw cards to be sent to the injured and mourning, and button sales. Students volunteered to support the various activities by organizing, contacting businesses and elementary schools, and bringing in coin jars."[60] The organization described here is primarily focused on raising money, and the membership requirements are as simple as bringing in jars to hold money. While the group's purpose is commendable (and one should be quick to praise the students for their active response), that it lasted less than a year demonstrates just how fluid such groups and their memberships can be for young adults today.

In addition to issue-oriented groups, activity clubs have gained traction over the past twenty years. Activity clubs (e.g., Chess Club) have long been a part of high school, of course, and they have remained a fixture at many schools. As evidenced in the school newspapers, over the past twenty years there has been an increase in the number of organizations created to promote and support students' interests. In many instances, these groups are focused on athletics and are not sponsored by the schools themselves. At Washington High School, for instance, the students organized a badminton team to compete with other school teams, although the district did not officially sanction the sport.[61] At Carrick High School, the students started a similar club with the following announcement in *Carrickulum*: "If you are looking for a fun and interesting sport to play, play paintball. . . . Paintball meetings are held Tuesdays before students go out to play."[62] In addition to athletic-oriented organizations, students have formed clubs around their artistic interests. The students at Newton South High School organized an informal group of fans that attended the yearly concerts of the rock band Phish. They reported on the concerts for their peers: "The Newton South Phish contingent is very small in number, but high in spirit. We all congregated at the Worcester Centrum for three shows, starting Friday, November 28 and ending Sunday, November 30."[63] At Grant High School, "a group of students who met after school" created Guerrilla Theater to work on improvisational acting, since the school did not provide a class for those interests. The club was happy to report its successes, although it had "changed to focus more on making productions."[64] These interest-oriented activity groups were, by and large, limited to a few students and highly tailored to the changing needs of their members. They also demonstrated that the young people in this study were "bowling together" in interesting new ways.

As the high school newspapers studied here reveal, one final type of organization that has emerged during the past twenty years is built on celebrating difference. Given the rise of multiculturalism following the civil rights movement in the United States, it may not be surprising to find schools promoting diversity. However, that the students have taken to forming their own groups around these diverse identities may be somewhat unexpected. These student organizations cover a wide range of issues. At Wilson High School in Washington, D.C., for instance, gender was the key denominator in "Teen Woman in Action (TWA), a program started by the Young Women's Project, [which] is a club designed to improve the skills of and provide support for women in order to build them into teen leaders."[65]

Another important club demographic is race. At Houston's Lamar High School, students formed a cross-cultural group in the early 1990s. The Lamar Multi-Ethnic Committee's "purpose [was] to promote cross-cultural understanding through the arts and contacts among the different ethnic groups represented at Lamar."[66] And at Portland's Grant High School, one group of students created the Unity Club, which was "made up of people who wanted to share their culture."[67] These rather savvy students introduced their group to the school community by helping sponsor the annual Martin Luther King Jr. assembly in January 2000. Sexual orientation has also emerged as something around which students have formed associations. In the late 1990s, the students at Newton South High School in a progressive suburb of Boston formed the Gay/Straight Alliance to discuss issues impacting the lives of those in the GLBT community.[68] As the organization noted, anyone was welcome to join, and there were no requirements for membership: "The GSA is a school club that invites people of all sexual orientations to join. In an attempt to fight homophobia in our school and community at large, we meet once a week in an atmosphere of acceptance and freedom that isn't often found elsewhere. More importantly, we have fun."[69]

The final demographic around which students organize is religion. In recounting the club history of their school, student reporters for the *Carrickulum* acknowledged, "We cannot forget the groups that help young men and women grow, otherwise known as Phenomenal Females and Boyz to Men. They are popular clubs that some teens find to help them out of trouble and other predicaments."[70] Students at Newton South High School participated in an annual group meeting to celebrate religion: "On September 16, at 7 AM before classes and during J-Block, Christian students at South gathered around the school flagpole. They joined millions of other teenagers across the nation and the world in prayer for their teachers, school officials, families, friends, and government. This was the eighth annual See You at the Pole (SYATP) day, a day of national student prayer."[71]

At Kansas City's Oak Park High School, one group that seemed to be both thriving and controversial was the school's chapter of the nondenominational Christian organization Young Life. In *Northmen's Log*, one student criticized Young Life because "a majority of the students involved attend solely for the social aspect" and not for any religious reasons. In an opposing editorial, a Young Life member praised the organization for helping him become "a follower of Jesus Christ" and defended the "relationally based" group for its "social environment."[72]

In each of these cases, the students in the various demographic groups appear to have come together in order to share feelings that needed to be validated and celebrated. Their clubs were not so much about others as they were about problems associated with a complex and fragmented identity. Understood this way, groups celebrating difference appear to focus on helping students bond together and share experiences directly related to their various subject positions. Such groups are surely important for young people still struggling to find themselves.

Given the array of clubs the young people in this study reported on, today's high school students are clearly able to join together. These newer clubs and organizations are not, however, the same types of entities seen in previous generations. While the earlier organizations were created primarily by teachers and adults, the newer groups are often created by the students themselves to fulfill a highly particular need. The groups found in today's high schools have adopted an inward focus, thereby requiring very little commitment from their members. In the end, these newer organizations seem more therapeutic than political in nature.

Another way to make sense of the difference in organizations of today versus those of the past is through the distinction made by some social capital scholars between bonding and bridging organizations. Bonding organizations, such as country clubs and therapy groups, focus primarily on member benefits; bridging organizations, such as Habitat for Humanity, are directed outward at engaging the larger community. Of course, many organizations are both bonding and bridging organizations. Most churches, for instance, want to both give their members a sense of religious community and do good works in the towns and cities within which they exist. The question, then, is one of degree.

Among the groups and organizations the young people in this study seem to have been increasingly drawn to, the emphasis was apparently on bonding. One recent article from Grant High School serves to make this point. Written in late 2008, it discusses the seven new clubs started during the fall of that school year. After noting that "making a new club is hard" because "teenagers can be extremely fickle," the article describes each of the new organizations: Black Student Union, Hands and Feet, Crew Club, Communist Club, Salsa Club, Manga Makers Club, and Italian Club. Of the seven new clubs, only two can be clearly defined as bridging groups. The first is the religious organization Hands and Feet, which was created to "perform acts of community service while imparting a Christian sense of good work." The second is the Communist Club, with its two goals of "dispelling common anti-Communist myths and serving the community." The other five clubs were all designed to benefit their members. The Black Student Union's goal was to give black students "a network of support" so that they would do better academically. The Salsa Club and the Italian Club were meant to help members learn about salsa dancing and Italian culture, respectively. The Crew Club "focused on crewing," which is "the act of working on a yacht or other similarly sized boat relying on wind power as a source of movement," while the Manga Makers Club was for students interested in creating the Japanese-style graphic novels commonly known as manga.[73] While all five of these bonding groups certainly offered their members benefits, none of them seemed overly concerned with engaging others in the larger community. In fact, each organization was designed to help a specific group of like-minded individuals.

That these students seem to have created more bonding than bridging organizations is not surprising, especially considering how they described the benefits of joining groups in general. For the most part, the students in this study talked about their reasons for joining various organizations in high school by highlighting what they gained from such involvement. In 2007, one graduating student recounted the many organizations he had joined over his four years at Washington High School after a teacher told him in his freshman year to get involved. The overachieving student admitted to feeling that life was hectic at times, but he summed up his reasons for being a very active member in multiple groups thusly: "Teachers are right when they tell you to get involved. . . . Not only does it help your college application, but it really allows you to see yourself at your best and worst."[74] In advising younger students to also become involved, this young writer argues they should do so for personal reasons. Such arguments were common in the final years of this study. One young woman at Newton South High School in Boston wondered,

> Maybe part of the reason why high school offers such a wide range of groups and activities is so we can develop multiple skills. You could be a football star or a piano prodigy, but without exploring other interests and talents, you'd probably miss out on gaining many important skills. There's a reason why colleges like "well-rounded students." There's a lot to gain from being pretty good at a variety of things. As we grow up, we are told to get out there, to try things we've never done before. We can't keep ourselves open to all the possibilities if we are caught up in one talent or activity. There's a lot that life hands us; it's up to us to make the most of it.[75]

For this student, the reason to join groups and organizations is to become a well-rounded individual and get into college—not necessarily to help others or to do good in one's community.

Of course, there is nothing wrong with becoming well rounded, learning new skills, and challenging oneself. These behaviors surely make people better. Schools are, moreover, a perfectly natural place for such challenges to be offered. That these students understand the benefits of joining various groups and want to share that knowledge with their peers is to be commended. But whether such things make a person more democratically engaged is another matter altogether.

Conclusion

The question of just how individualistic young Americans have become over the past several decades is not an easy one to answer, and the conclusions presented in this chapter are not definitive. What is clear is that, for the young people in this study, political issues were increasingly fused with individual issues. What constitutes a political issue today was considered personal forty-five years ago, and a number of political issues that might once have been discussed in terms of their collective implications are now understood as personal failures. Despite this emphasis on the personalization of the political, there is no reason to believe that young people today are sitting at home by themselves watching television and mindlessly chatting with people they will never meet in person. The more contemporary young journalists in this study were still social creatures.

While they were part of larger social networks, these young adults were not, however, as politically active as their predecessors. They tended not to act together to achieve ends for formal, established communities. William Damon has referred to this phenomenon as a dedication gap. Discussing a number of in-depth interviews with American adolescents conducted in 1999, Damon offers the following summation of this gap: "What struck us was not only what these young people said but also what they did not say. They showed little interest in people outside their immediate circles of friends and relatives (other than fictional media characters and entertainment and sports figures); little awareness of current events; and virtually no expressions of social concern, political opinion, civic duty, patriotic emotion, or sense of citizenship in any form."[76] As Damon notes, young adults most certainly do have social ties with others, but their social ties are limited to a small number of personal connections. Like the students Damon spoke with, the students represented in the later years of this study tended not to think of their roles in larger social groups and local communities. They may not, in fact, have even been aware of these larger social networks and their potential roles in them.

Public intellectual Cornel West sees the problem of American youth as one of possessive individualism versus democratic individuality. For West, this notion of democratic individuality can be seen through "the Emersonian tradition [which] emphasizes the vital role of a citizen's individual commitment to democracy and highlights the vast potentials of American democracy." He argues that democracy needs a community of individual citizens who are personally committed to coming together for the greater good. The United States, however, has become rooted in a troubling state of individualism. West contends that this new individualism stems from a number of problems, including the media and "the uninspiring nature of our national political culture [which] has only enhanced the seductiveness of the pursuit of pleasure and of diverting entertainments, and too many of us have turned inward to a disconnected, narrowly circumscribed family and social life."[77]

While West's distinction is useful, another way of understanding the problem is as a difference between democratic individuality and postmodern fragmentation. To argue that the attitudes displayed by the young journalists in this study demonstrate that they have become obsessed with themselves does not give them credit for their attempts at community building. As was shown above, many of these young people did come together in numerous ways. The troubling aspect of the groups they joined is that they were inwardly focused. According to the student journalists and the organizations they described, young adults join groups that ask little of them but offer important therapeutic benefits. In this sense, the young people in this study have become *independent joiners*—young people who link arms for non-group reasons. They have become, to use the now popular buzzword, networked together in relationships that offer immediate self-fulfillment without long-term responsibilities.

The United States has always been rooted in individualism, but it has historically been counterbalanced by connections to larger communities—towns, states, regions, and nation. These communities, as John Freie has argued, are "not formed by people who get together and agree to sign their names to a document to form a community; rather, they are created over time as people form connections with each other, develop trust and respect for each other, and create a sense of common purpose."[78] The most salient problem for many of today's young people may be that they have lost this sense of common purpose. Due to the economic wealth Americans have enjoyed since World War II and the revolutionary changes in communications technologies that have occurred, America's youth now find themselves in a world that no longer accepts metanarratives to build stronger community ties. Instead, the young people in this study have formed more fragmented communities—smaller, more fluid, and more targeted connections. This may be helpful in a multicultural society, but it does not contribute to community cohesion in clear and direct ways.

This "independent joiner" mentality has deep roots, even among those organizations working to increase youth participation. A recent get-out-the-vote campaign run by the Ad Council highlights just how ingrained this mentality has become. The campaign focuses on political apathy and characterizes young people who do not vote as mannequins: "It's an all too familiar story. There is a young man or woman who is very busy all the time. So busy that he or she has no time to volunteer, stay current on the news, or even vote. Our young specimen is so busy that when it comes to participating in the community, this person is essentially a mannequin. And then it happens: Little by little the person actually turns into a mannequin. How can this be?"[79] The campaign's website offers a survey to help the interested young person find out whether he or she is suffering from mannequinism. The questions ask whether the individual is registered to vote, has voted in recent elections, has volunteered or donated money, reads or watches the news, and discusses current events with friends and family. Nowhere does the survey ask whether the individual belongs to civic organizations. The implied assumption is that the answer is already known. The Ad Council, moreover, does not ask for membership or any commitments, offering little more than a network of websites and a weekly mailing list. The campaign seeks to get young people to vote (a praiseworthy cause) but does nothing to actually bring them together.

In the closing lines of the prophetic poem *The Waste Land*, T. S. Eliot wrote in 1922, "These fragments I have shored against my ruins."[80] The sentiment of such a line must surely be familiar to many of today's youth. As part of a fragmented group, these young adults are left to piece together strands of social networks. Scholars and politicians can accuse young people of being narcissistic, or they can view young adults' attempts to build social networks as an implicit longing for community. As the seven high school newspapers analyzed here demonstrate, not all young people are isolated integers unconcerned with their place in the larger society. Many of them are individuals trying to find themselves in a changing world, pulling together as many connections as they can. Indeed, many of the young adults in this study have been doing what they can to stave off the forces that threaten to separate them. But, as seen in this chapter, they seem unsure about how to accomplish that goal.

7

AMERICAN EVOLUTION, DEMOCRATIC ENGAGEMENT,
AND CIVIC EDUCATION

In the summer of 2001, photographer Robin Bowman began a five-year
project traveling around the United States taking pictures of and talking
with young adults. The result of this endeavor was the 2007 award-winning
book *It's Complicated: The American Teenager.* Part of what made her book so
successful was Bowman's approach to her subject: "I was not there to judge
these kids or to rescue them. My intent wasn't even to definitively answer
any question, only to ask them and record their responses. . . . What we see
and hear in this book merely records a moment in time when our paths
crossed." The teenagers' answers to her questions illuminate the pictures
as much as the photographer's eye. These questions cover a wide range of
subjects: "Where do you get most of your information?" "Do you have a
boyfriend/girlfriend?" "What is one of the biggest problems in the world
that you would like to fix?" "Where were you on September 11, 2001?"[1] The
answers, as well as the pictures, are as diverse as the country in which these
young Americans live.

Bowman's photographs and interviews of 419 teenagers from Maine
to California create a picture of American youth that is humbling for anyone writing about young people writ large. The differences between these
young people are palpable. There is the eighteen-year-old Navy seaman
from Easton, Georgia, who would like to go to the Middle East "and shoot
at people," and the sixteen-year-old high school girl from Ithaca, New York,
who "would just love to have peace in the world." There is the eighteen-year-
old from Darien, Connecticut, who feels that her peers discriminated against
her after she became Miss Teen America, and there is the seventeen-year-old
little person from Nashville, Tennessee, who has never been on a date. There
is the seventeen-year-old Church of God preacher in Varney, West Virginia,
and the nineteen-year-old voodoo priest in Houma, New Orleans. There is
the nineteen-year-old African American father of four in Selma, Alabama,
and the nineteen-year-old Caucasian mother of two in Jones, Alabama,

neither of whom graduated from high school. The youth Bowman presents in her book are the youth of a diverse multicultural democracy. They are Christians, Muslims, and Jews. They are heterosexual and homosexual. They are children of privilege and kids literally living on the street. They are athletes and artists, cheerleaders and criminals, gangbangers and good ol' boys. They are, in short, young America. Bowman is aware of this when she acknowledges, "It is undeniable that our children affect and reflect who we are as individuals and as a nation. Perhaps by coming to know our kids, adolescents on the cusp of adulthood, we can become acquainted, or reacquainted, with ourselves."[2] Implicit in this statement is the assumption that we need to be reacquainted with one another and ourselves. This is an assumption I share.

While Bowman's goal was to paint a picture of American teenagers in individual detail at particular moments in time, my goal in this book has been to paint with a wider brush and broader strokes. Furthermore, my aim was to only portray one part, although an important one, of the lives of some American youth—the civic and political aspect. So instead of individual portraits, I have presented a panoramic painting. It has been, moreover, a moving panorama.

This book has been guided by one basic thesis: as the social and cultural norms of the United States have shifted, the ways in which the American people imagine their democracy have also changed. Like Bowman, my point has been to avoid criticizing the more recent generations of young adults in this study for the way they learned to democratically engage the world around them. Having grown up in a different world, can today's young people be blamed for being different than the youth of an earlier time? Would any good come of disparagingly calling today's youth some name akin to "slackers" or "Generation Xers"? My goal has been, instead, to describe the changing ways in which young people deliberate about politics and community over time. The question is not *if* the youth of today view politics differently than youth in the past, but *how* their views are different. Change is both natural and inevitable.

However, while change may be natural, to suggest that the democratic attitudes and behaviors of American youth have evolved is to place the onus of change on things external to young adults. Indeed, another basic assumption in this book is that the world has changed a great deal during the past five decades. As was noted in chapter 1, these transformations have included technological advancements in communications, an explosion in the human population, a continued shift from rural to sub/urban life in the United States, and an increasingly interconnected global economy. Whether seen as progress or not, these changes occurred rapidly and without anyone's clear intent. They altered the world in which we live and in which American youth grow up. This book has explored the changing ways in which successive generations of students at seven different high schools across the United States have come to imagine and write about democratic engagement in their school newspapers. These young journalists' attitudes and assumptions about democracy are revealed by the way they talk about the world around them, and paying attention to the changes in their discussions over half a century helps illuminate the changing democratic norms that are emerging in response to larger social and cultural shifts. Without blaming or praising them for being different, I have shown how the more recent generations of young adults in this study have learned to engage the political and civic world around them in new ways.

Yet not all the change documented in this book may be positive for a federal republic founded upon the tenets of democracy. If one takes democracy at its basic assumption—that the people rule themselves—there are several underlying precepts generally considered necessary for helping the people get themselves together to rule. First, citizens must have some sense of shared identity. Without at least some notion of collective purpose, people cannot be expected to work together in the sharing of resources. Second, they must have an understanding of governmental processes and a knowledge of current affairs.[3] As has been noted by many political observers, ignorance and democracy are anathema to each other. Third, they must have at least a modicum of social and political trust. Trust of one's fellow citizens is imperative given that democratic citizenship requires some sacrifice, and trust of one's government and its officials is central to a representative democracy.[4] Fourth, they need a healthy level of political efficacy, both internal and external.[5] Citizens, that is, must feel they have the power to make a difference in their communities and a belief that their government is responsive to their suggestions. Finally, citizens must have access to a free and open public sphere.[6] Ample opportunity to exchange ideas and debate various issues is an integral aspect of a healthy democracy and helps foster collective identity, cultural knowledge, and social trust. These five precepts do not, of course, cause democratic engagement, but they are certainly constitutive of the greatest possibility for productive political and civic participation.

What follows in this concluding chapter is an overall assessment of the changing ways in which American youth in this study have written about their democratic engagement in relation to the evolving world around them, with an eye toward how these evolutionary adjustments may be enhancing or undermining American democracy. While I continue to resist blaming contemporary young adults for being somehow less than their predecessors or in some way responsible for the world they are growing up in, I do believe the discursive changes described in the preceding chapters reveal a number of important contradictions and complications for a well-functioning representative democracy. After presenting these challenges, I ultimately turn to what might be done to counterbalance the recent changes, focusing primarily on America's public education system.

The Youth Evolution

The four preceding chapters offered four stories about the changing nature of democratic engagement, as elucidated in the writing of young adults at seven different high schools from across the United States over the past half century. As a subsection of American youth, their deliberations about civic and political matters help illustrate how larger social and cultural shifts have influenced the ways in which the newer generations of young journalists learn democratic engagement. Paying attention to what these young adults have had to say for themselves has revealed a good deal.

Chapter 3 looked at where these young people locate politics and found that for the most part these high school students have increasingly focused their political deliberations on the national and, more recently, international stage. They are more interested in talking about the presidential election than they are the mayor's race or even the election of their U.S. representative. They also seem more concerned about AIDS in Africa than the homeless on their own streets. Such outward trends seem natural given the changes in media production and consumption and the increasing globalization of the past half century. That the young people today have a more concrete concern for national and global issues and peoples from all around the world is, moreover, a positive attribute. Such global awareness may surely be an integral step toward a deep cosmopolitanism that, as political philosopher Kwame Anthony Appiah argues, forces all of us to be more aware of our "obligations to strangers."[7]

While it may have been natural for the high school journalists to shift their focus to national and international issues, what has apparently been lost in this move is a clear connection to local politics. These young people do, of course, still live in local neighborhoods and remain very much aware of their towns and cities. However, they do not seem to have much concern for the political struggles and civic concerns of their local communities. More often than not, they seem to care more about feeding starving children in Africa than they do their impoverished neighbors down the street. They are more aware of the president as a national and international leader than they are the city council's influence on their day-to-day lives. While such cosmopolitan concerns are certainly praiseworthy, local civic and political participation may actually be the breeding ground for the social trust and political efficacy necessary for democratic engagement.

In chapter 4, the focus turned to how money and the increasingly consumeristic society in which American youth now live changed the way the student journalists approach democratic engagement. These students have eschewed many traditional forms of democratic engagement, but they have not, as some researchers have argued, focused their energy on political consumerism. The young adults represented in this study do not talk about boycotting harmful corporations or buycotting green companies any more than they discuss attending a political rally or writing their congressperson a letter. Instead, the high school newspapers reveal that many of these young adults talk of donating money and goods to civic institutions and political causes, along with volunteering sporadically, as far more efficacious behaviors. "Donating" and "volunteering" are, in fact, the two words used most often by young people in the seven high school newspapers to describe the ways in which they engage the world around them.

There is, of course, nothing inherently wrong with giving donations and volunteering one's time as forms of political and civic engagement. Donating canned goods to help feed the hungry and occasionally volunteering at the local soup kitchen are both important ways to be involved in one's community. However, these behaviors may not fully develop the robust civic and political attachments that many political scientists and communication scholars believe are necessary for a healthy democratic public sphere. For some, donations and membership-less volunteering may actually be weak substitutes for more important forms of democratic engagement. Donating money to Habitat for Humanity might make a person feel good about himself, but it does not do anything to change the institutional structures and governmental policies that may lead to extreme poverty and homelessness. Similarly, volunteering sporadically at the local women's shelter can surely give an individual a sense of having made a difference, but such behavior may not build the civic trust and political knowledge necessary for changing laws and creating institutions that might make it easier for battered women to escape their abusive relationships. In short, donations and volunteerism may allow an individual to feel as if he has done some good in the world without actually requiring him to do anything that might build and sustain long-term democratic practices. Doing good and acting democratically are not necessarily the same things.

There is a widespread assumption among many researchers, politicians, and community activists that today's young people are both apathetic about civic issues and cynical toward politicians and government. The discussions examined in chapter 5, however, show that some American youth are still very interested in civic and political problems, but they have taken a protectively critical stance toward public officials and institutions. They have learned this protective criticism through their consumption of popular culture. While citizens who are willing to criticize and question their government are beneficial to democracy, criticism without engagement may not be the best dominant attitude for a public to have. To criticize something may be either productive or destructive, and it may lead to further engagement or total detachment. In its productive orientation, criticism is an attempt to carefully consider something and judge it according to some criteria. The goal in productive criticism is ultimately to make something better—the object itself, knowledge in general, or the public at large. As a destructive method, criticism does little more than attempt to tear things down.

Much of what passes for criticism in popular culture today bears little resemblance to a thoughtful interrogation with the critic's object. Instead, most criticism in popular culture is more concerned with passing judgment on something as liked or disliked, enjoyable or boring. As political sociologist Todd Gitlin has pointed out recently, today "a critic is a chooser. Choosing good against bad work, the critic steers away from reefs toward safe harbors."[8] The concern is that the modern critical attitude largely assumes everything is a reef. This negative critical attitude takes a more defensive stance than might be expected of more productive criticism. In terms of democratic engagement, one must question whether such a negative, defensive starting position can be good in the long term. Democracy needs citizens to at least be willing to try to work together. And this surely requires a modicum of trust and hope.

No argument has gained more traction or been more questioned in recent years than the one made by Robert Putnam in *Bowling Alone*. With perhaps the exception of Theda Scokpol, Putnam has done more than anyone to advance the claim that the American people are increasingly detached from one another. As Putnam famously notes, recent generations of Americans have been far less likely to join together in groups ranging from the American Legion to the local bowling league. While not unsympathetic to Putnam's claims, chapter 6 found that young adults are more willing to join together than many might believe—although their joining does seem far less taxing on their time and energy than previous organizations. The young journalists in this study are simply not the atomized individuals so many scholars seem concerned about. Given the number of organizations still flourishing on high school campuses, these contemporary young adults are clearly aware of one another and have a need to share their lives with others.

However, sharing one's life and spending time with others does not necessarily translate into democratic engagement. The groups that today's American youth seem to be forming and joining are far more fluid in membership requirements and much more focused on personal interests than earlier organizations. It seems, then, American youth are not nearly as fragmented as they are often portrayed, but there may still be reason for concern. Joining together with others who share an interest in classic cars or online gaming may be social, but it may not lead to democratic benefits for the community. Of course, not all groups must be civically or politically inclined, but having a robust network of civic and political organizations does seem beneficial. Joining together for purely personal reasons may ultimately yield little of the robust reciprocity and trust created in membership-based groups of the past.

Taking a step back and looking more broadly at the stories told in this book, one can see a number of potentially troubling contradictions. Over the past five decades, the young people in this study have become increasingly cosmopolitan, but they have lost many of their connections with local politics. They have not completely disengaged from their democracy, but they have taken a more distanced and critical position toward civic and political institutions and their representatives. They have not stopped joining together, but their organizing does seem far more personalized and fluid than that of past generations. Here are contradictions aplenty. But what are we to make of them?

In the past half century, the democratic engagement of the American youth represented here has evolved from a traditional form of citizenship to what must be understood as a form of postmodern democratic engagement. The more traditional citizenship practiced by the youth in the early years of this study was more localized, community oriented, group motivated, and trusting of government. More recently, the students have come to think of political and civic engagement in terms that are more global, individualized, and skeptical. Instead of joining together with fellow community members in an organization that lobbies elected representatives to fix local environmental problems, a young adult in the United States today seems more likely to donate money to an environmental organization that gets his attention with a pithy, humorous advertising slogan about global warming. To suggest that the latter action is any less politically and civically motivated than the former is, quite simply, erroneous. Lobbying an elected representative and donating money to an environmental organization are both, in this instance, intended to help the environment. Both actions are clear examples of democratic engagement by a concerned young person. The actual potential outcome of these two actions is a different issue altogether.

The potential for today's American youth to have a powerful impact on their political communities is certainly there. Much of what can be taken from the analysis in this book is encouraging. Nothing may be more positive than the simple fact that so many of the contemporary young adults in this study still engage in democratic deliberations with their peers. Moreover, it should be clear from the many textual examples offered throughout this book that the young people writing in their high school newspapers are not exceptional. The content and style of the numerous arguments they present are not atypical. These American youth are eager to talk about political matters and civic concerns. They may argue about national and international problems with a critical style that uses popular culture as evidence, but they deliberate nonetheless. As research on the importance of public talk and deliberation begins to demonstrate just how important such discourse is as a precursor for further political and civic action, the evidence suggesting that at least some American youth are still very much committed to the basic impulses of democratic deliberation should be heartening to even the most pessimistic scholars.[9]

In addition to their willingness to talk together about political and civic matters, another positive textual finding in this study is the encouraging level of care and concern many of these young adults seem to have for others. Such caring concern may not be strictly necessary for the political struggles inherent in any representative democracy, but surely a willingness to worry about the well-being of others cannot hurt either. As political philosopher Danielle Allen has convincingly argued, democratic politics does require sacrifice—the willingness to accept that one will not always get his or her way and that the arguments of others will sometimes win the day.[10] Democratic sacrifice can only be helped when citizens already care for one another.

At a tangible level, the American youth of today do seem to care deeply for others. From food drives to monetary donations, the young people in this study are very willing to try to help peoples all over the world. Whether in response to domestic terrorism or international natural catastrophe, many young people want to help. It may be true, of course, that it is not difficult to care for others whom one does not know and to send aid to people caught in some catastrophe. Still, these acts of kindness are optimistic signs for a generation of youth too often characterized as cynical and jaded.

Related to their deliberative impulse and their caring concern for others, another encouraging sign is that so many of the young adults studied here still seem to have a good deal of hope that they and their peers can have some positive effect on the world around them. Although they do not demonstrate a belief that their government is particularly responsive to them (i.e., external efficacy), these young people do demonstrate a continued belief in their own internal efficacy—a faith in their ability to influence their communities. That they keep such faith disguised behind their playfully enacted critical attitudes does not negate the importance of their continued expectation that their democratic actions can lead to change. This hope, this belief that things can always be made better, is required by democracy. As political theorist Patrick Deneen has recently put it, "Democracy is not an undertaking for the faint of heart: it calls for limitless reservoirs of hope against the retreat into easy optimism or the temptation to a kind of democratic cynicism or despair."[11] While American youth may tend toward the latter temptation, they have not given in completely to despair. Although they may need some encouragement and, perhaps, better role models, at least some of today's young adults show evidence that America's democratic reservoirs remain replete with hope.

Given the willingness of the young people in this study to deliberate together, care for one another, and hope for better communities, the American democracy does not seem to be as much at risk due to new generations of disaffected youth as others have suggested in recent years. Whatever civic and political problems the United States faces today are not, moreover, the fault of contemporary American youth. Like all generations that have preceded them, plenty of the contemporary young journalists in this study still show ample evidence of a strong inclination toward democratic engagement with their communities. These inclinations certainly need to be encouraged. Due to the contradictions presented above and the changing world young people now inhabit, we might need to rethink the ways we go about offering such encouragement.

The Future

Given what this study has revealed about the evolution of democratic engagement among some of America's more involved and informed youth, there remains the question of what, if anything, should be done about the current trends in political and civic behavior. While the young adults in this study are certainly not to blame for how they have adapted to the changing world around them, these adjustments are not all positive for a representative democracy. Moreover, these youth do not seem aberrant; surely there are more out there like them. What, then, might be done to help young people become more democratically engaged? Short of changing the world they live in, how might young people's natural political and civic evolution be encouraged in such a way as to strengthen the democratic principles of the United States? While American youth today are not a generation of bad citizens, what might be done to help them and the young people that follow them become better citizens for a stronger democracy?

The short answer is a democratic education better suited to the modern world. While some democratic principles are timeless, every democracy imagines itself differently. With the passage of time, a democracy must learn to reimagine itself, lest it become obsolete for its citizenry. As a democracy and its citizens evolve, so too must democratic education. In its current state, the American public education system may not be doing a particularly good job of teaching young adults how to be better democratic citizens. With all that public schools are asked to do today, such a pedagogical shortcoming may not be particularly surprising. As was mentioned in chapter 2, the large comprehensive high schools of today are overburdened with many wide-ranging goals. Adding to these burdens may be unkind to hardworking teachers and administrators, but suggesting that public schools spend more of their time and resources teaching American youth to be strong democratic citizens is not so much an adding on as it is a refocusing. Changing the education system in the United States to make its pedagogical focus more civic-minded will not be an easy task, especially given current trends in educational thinking. But to not make the case for such change would be undemocratic in itself.

In recent years, the main pedagogical emphasis of public schools in the United States has shifted toward teaching young adults the skills and knowledge necessary to enter America's workforce, either directly after high school or indirectly through postsecondary education. This shift in emphasis is not new. As Stanford University education professor Larry Cuban has recently noted, "At two separate points in our history, the ends of the nineteenth and twentieth centuries, American schools have been vocationalized. Among the civic, academic, and moral goals that have historically guided tax-supported public schools, one became primary: preparing students for the ever-changing workplace."[12] Evidence of this vocational trend can easily be seen today in one of the biggest educational reforms in modern political history—former president George W. Bush's No Child Left Behind Act. In support of the act, Bush argued, "The quality of our public schools directly affects us all. . . . Yet too many children in America are segregated by low expectations, illiteracy, and self-doubt. In a constantly changing world that is demanding increasingly complex skills from its workforce, children are literally being left behind."[13] According to Bush, the U.S. public education system was failing to teach young people how to be better workers. This sentiment has been echoed by the likes of Bill Gates, Microsoft chairman and co-founder of the Bill and Melinda Gates Foundation, who offered a similar argument in 2005 when he addressed the National Governors Association. As Gates put it then, America's public schools were obsolete because "even when they're working exactly as designed [they] cannot teach our kids what they need to know today. Training the workforce of tomorrow with the high schools of today is like trying to teach kids about today's computers on a 50-year-old mainframe."[14] Bob Wise, former West Virginia governor and the president of the Alliance for Excellent Education, voices the same concern in his 2008 book *Raising the Grade: How Secondary School Reform Can Save Our Youth and the Nation*. Wise argues rather succinctly, "We are still preparing too many of today's students for yesterday's world of work."[15] According to Bush, Gates, and Wise, the U.S. education system's primary goal should be to advance America's economic well-being by teaching students the new skills required for an ever-changing work environment.

While many of the nation's political and business leaders have been advocating for educational reform to strengthen the economy, academic and civic leaders have been arguing for the public school system's recommitment to civic learning. Teaching workers and educating citizens are two different goals. The belief in education's civic role goes back to even before the American common schools became common. In an oft-quoted quip, Thomas Jefferson argued for public education in 1816 by noting that "if a nation expects to be ignorant and free, in a state of civilization, it expects what never was and never will be."[16] Jefferson's point—that the freedom of self-rule can only occur through education—is in many ways the backbone of the democratic faith in education. This faith can still be seen almost two centuries later. In a general way, the views of Jefferson and other like-minded educational thinkers are evident today in the policies advocated by a number of civic education organizations. For instance, a report issued in 2003 by the Carnegie Corporation of New York and CIRCLE on the civic mission of schools sums up the influence of earlier thinkers when it suggests that "competent and responsible citizens . . . are informed and thoughtful; . . . participate in their communities; . . . act politically; [and] . . . have moral and civic virtues."[17] According to the fifty-seven educational scholars and practitioners who contributed to the report, America's public schools should play a central role in creating such citizens.

But even if the focus of public schools in the United States can be shifted toward more civic educational goals, how should one go about teaching today's youth to be more engaged democratic citizens? How, that is, could one counterbalance the more negative aspects of the trends presented above? The following democratic educational goals are suggestions that attempt to take into account the lessons this study has learned about some of America's youth. These suggestions accept that the American democracy of today does not function in practice the same way it did half a century ago. Both the United States and the American people are markedly different than they used to be. For no one is this truer than today's young people. Trying to teach them democratic lessons for a society and culture that no longer exist is a futile endeavor. Teaching American youth how to be better citizens today requires taking into account the new forms of mass communications, the realities of globalization, and new economic realities. Thus, the rethinking of civic education in the United States benefits from the lessons in this book. Scholars cannot (and need not) reverse the evolutionary changes that democratic thought among young people has undergone in the past half century, but we can work to adjust these natural adaptations in ways that might produce more engaged citizens and a stronger democracy.

Democratic Problem Solving

One of the benefits of locating politics at a primarily national and international level is that it requires individuals to think of the diverse and complex systems of people and issues that make up our world. It shifts one's perspective beyond him- or herself. Such cosmopolitanism is certainly a good thing. One negative side effect of such thinking, however, may be that it abstracts the very real process of democratic decision making. After all, democratic engagement is more than attitudes and values. It is action. It is, moreover, action taken by individuals within democratic communities. As John Dewey argued a century ago, such action requires both face-to-face interaction and an education system that can teach students to learn by doing.[18] As a site of democratic education, learning by doing means learning how to work together with others in order to make decisions. In his book *Democracy as Problem Solving*, sociologist Xavier de Souza Briggs reminds both scholars and practitioners that democracy entails more than deliberating and choosing representatives. As Briggs argues, democratic practice requires the ability "to change the state of the world through collective action, not only to devise and decide but to *do*."[19] However, this democratic doing can only happen when communities have what Briggs and others refer to as civic capacity—the ability of multiple shareholders to work in concert toward solving problems that arise within a community. Such skills must, of course, be taught.

Teaching American youth how to solve problems together with others within their shared communities may take some work, but it is not outside the scope of the U.S. education system. For some, teaching democratic problem-solving skills means simply rethinking how schools can function as communities in which students have an active role and real agency. Such rethinking may require some school administrators and teachers to give up some of their authoritative power, but this does not mean, as some fear, that chaos will ensue. Allowing students to work together with school officials within necessary boundaries to solve school problems and set norms may actually produce students who are more engaged in the overall learning process. Education scholar Thomas Sergiovanni has argued, for instance, that individual classrooms can even be democratic communities where students and the teacher collaborate to set the class agenda and rules. Sergiovanni notes that treating the classroom as a "democratic community is aimed not just at improving student behavior but at creating the kinds of ties that bond students together and students and teachers together and that bind them to shared ideas and ideals."[20] Such bonding and binding create a sense of belonging that can overcome feelings of alienation and increase a sense of self-efficacy and worth. The democratic process in the classroom and schools also teaches students the necessary skills of self-governance for political life outside of school, where problem solving also occurs within social norms and power structures.

Service Learning

A related concern is how to get American youth to engage others in the democratic public sphere in such a way that these interactions strengthen a sense of political trust and efficacy. One way to produce such outcomes may be through the volunteerism associated with service learning programs. As removed volunteers and independent joiners, today's American youth still very much demonstrate their willingness to help others and join together. What is not so clear is whether they see these two behaviors as being at odds with each other. They will volunteer but do not want to join a group to do so. They will join groups but only insofar as those groups offer them something useful or enjoyable. Could they, under the right circumstances, be willing to join together in groups to help others?

Simply encouraging young adults to join more groups may produce no clear democratic benefits and, depending on the homogeneity of the groups, may actually produce negative results. In their recent review of the current research on civic engagement, political scientists Elizabeth Theiss-Morse and John Hibbing have noted that the link between group organizing and political participation may not be as clear as some believe. They argue, in fact, that the connection between increased social networks and a resulting desire to participate in politics is particularly weak among young adults. In addition, Theiss-Morse and Hibbing note that many groups are homogeneous. They tend to be so because "groups attract people who are similar to the existing group members" and "encourage similarity among members by shunning those who break the norms too often and pressuring the repeat offenders to leave the group."[21] Such homogeneity may offer many advantages for group members, but political efficacy, social trust, and tolerance of others do not seem to be among its benefits.

Service learning programs offer an alternative way to get young adults to engage larger public issues through joining together and interacting with diverse others in their democratic communities. By combining community service activities and academic learning, service learning programs encourage students to take the problem-solving skills they learn in the classroom out into an often more heterogeneous and unfamiliar environment. As political scientist Diane Owen has noted in her review of service learning programs, they do seem to lead to increased democratic engagement.[22] A service learning program is, of course, only as good as its design and implementation, but a number of important indicators have emerged in recent years that have been shown to produce positive outcomes. As one group of social scientists has noted, what makes a successful service learning program is that it engages both teachers and students in academic and civic outcomes, lets students work on public policies of their choice, encourages them to reflect on the process, and sets time limits on expected results.[23] Within this framework, service learning programs have the potential to teach students how to be engaged volunteers and collective joiners.

Media Literacy

As evidenced in chapter 5, American youth are deeply immersed in popular culture. This popular culture is, moreover, very much a mediated culture. While young adults clearly seem to be learning a protectively critical attitude from the television shows, music, and magazines they enjoy, they may be less able to comprehend the very nature of the media they use. However, understanding these media is integral to democratic engagement in the United States today. Media literacy, or media education, is the name for a set of practices that attempt to teach people how to better understand the mediums through which so much human communication occurs today. While media literacy is taught for several pedagogical purposes, it is often incorporated into civic and political education programs as a way to give young citizens a critical set of tools through which to engage the political messages and civic communication they encounter by listening to the radio, watching television or a movie, playing a video game, or surfing the Internet. Media literacy specialist Kathleen Tyner summarizes this argument thusly: "If an informed electorate is the cornerstone of a democratic society, and, if the polls that report that most North Americans get their news and information from electronic media are correct, then it is imperative that students must learn to read and write electronic media, as well as print, in order to fully participate in a democratic society."[24] Central to Tyner's argument is that students will become better citizens through learning how to read (or interact with) mediated communication and how to write (or produce) it as well.

Teaching students how to create mediated communication can help them understand how the technology works, how a particular medium helps shape its content, and how, therefore, to more critically engage it. Unlike the negative form of criticism they seem to be learning from popular culture, media literacy can give students a better appreciation for how to evaluate media content. For instance, instead of engaging a political advertisement with a simple like or dislike response, students learn, through the act of creating their own commercial, how to better understand the way the advertisement constructs its message. Through building their own websites, students can also learn more about the persuasive forces of text, images, and videos working within the same medium. By reflecting on these processes, they can also learn to think about how they engage these various media and what they take away from the experience. As one recent edited collection by scholars and practitioners demonstrates, the possibilities for media literacy are wide-ranging and potentially transformational for democracy.[25]

Rhetorical Pedagogy

As evidenced by the high school newspapers that are the primary focus of this book, young adults are still quite interested in political problems and civic issues. Plenty of them are happy to debate such problems and issues with their peers. They are willing to put forth their ideas and opinions in a relatively open public forum, opening themselves up to criticism from those who disagree. They do not, however, always do so in a way that encourages deliberation. Whether writing about presidential politics or global problems, the high school students in this study did not always make reasoned arguments, critically engage the arguments made by others, or use even the most basic persuasive moves. All too often, their arguments collapsed in on themselves. They repeatedly dismissed others' arguments offhand and did more to alienate others than to change their minds.

Perhaps the reason for the poor quality of many of the arguments made in these newspaper articles is that the study of rhetoric no longer plays an important role in the American education system. This has not always been the case. In his study of early American education, Mark Garrett Longaker has shown, for instance, that the study of rhetoric played a central role in the pedagogy of the nation's founding educators. This was, in many ways, a natural educational concern for those building a national republic. Noting the long history of rhetorical studies in all great republics, Longaker states succinctly, "When early American thinkers adopted republicanism, they also stressed education in rhetoric."[26] Early American educators seemed to inherently understand that teaching students how to critically engage the issues of the day and argue with one another about the remedies for political ills was the best way to ensure a healthy, working republic. As the nature and goals of public education have changed in the past two centuries, rhetorical pedagogy seems to have taken a backseat to math, sciences, and trade skills.

The reasons for the demise of rhetorical studies in American high schools are many and outside the scope of this closing chapter. Whatever the reason, the lack of rhetorical skills demonstrated by the students in this study makes clear the need to reintroduce rhetorical pedagogy into the core curriculum of American secondary education. In his recent assessment of this very problem, rhetorical scholar Michael Hogan has noted that in the many attempts to create greater social capital and reinvigorate democratic deliberation there have been few efforts to "emphasize the most fundamental requirement of a sustainable deliberative democracy: citizens with the communicative competencies needed to participate in civic life. If citizens are to get involved, they need to know how to articulate their own views and to listen to others."[27] In making his case for rhetorical pedagogy, Hogan goes on to suggest that teaching students rhetorical theory can help them make better arguments, that teaching them rhetorical criticism can help them better engage the arguments of others, and that teaching them rhetorical history can help them learn the lessons of the past. All three of these aspects of rhetorical pedagogy would go a long way toward improving the deliberations in which young citizens are already engaged and might just improve our democracy writ large.

Conclusion

The U.S. public education system cannot cure all that ails American democracy. However, if this book has done anything, it has shown that things are not nearly as bad as many would make them out to be. The deliberative impulse of American youth surely demonstrates that a large number of young people continue to be interested in community affairs and political issues. Having grown up in a much different world than their parents and grandparents, they may have attitudes about civic and political engagement that do not look familiar to their elders. These attitudes, moreover, may not lead to the types of engagement that many social scientists are used to measuring. That today's youth engage the world around them in different ways than their predecessors does not mean that such behaviors are worse. These differences certainly should not lead one to conclude that modern American youth are to blame for having disparate assumptions about democratic engagement. Given that they are being socialized into a changed world, what else should they have done?

Still, one might be forgiven for trying to imagine the perfect democratic society of fully engaged citizens. Such a society never has and never will exist, but this does not mean that we should not encourage as many of our young citizens to participate as possible. Life is complicated and people are busy. It is wrong to ask people to devote all their time to democratic politics, and it is wrong to force all people to share the democratic concerns that others seem so adamant about. Some people will always choose to opt out of active, engaged democratic citizenship. In a democratic republic predicated on liberty and equality, such people have the right to opt out, at least in nations without compulsory elections or military service. Still, in a democracy the more the merrier. And the messier.

American youth need all the encouragement we can muster to help them join their democracy as politically and civically active citizens. A democracy with too many citizens opting out of participating will eventually cease to be a democracy. At best, such apathy will lead to oligarchy. At worst, it will lead to dictators and totalitarian regimes. As the young people in this book reveal, we are, thankfully, a long way from such democratic atrophy. Many of today's young adults are more than willing to put forth the effort required for democratic engagement. The quality of democratic engagement does, however, also matter. Those of us concerned about the state of American democracy must continue to do all we can to improve the tenor of our public debates and encourage the patience needed to deal with complex political problems. As the world continues to change rapidly, new generations of American youth will continue to evolve to fit this ever new world. It is our job to help them adapt while also giving them the time-tested skills necessary for democratic engagement with one another. There is no need for panic, but a lack of panic need not lead to complacency.

NOTES

CHAPTER I

1. Michael R. Gordon and Thom Shanker, "Plan Would Shift Some American Troops from Iraq to Afghanistan," *New York Times*, September 5, 2008; Lori Montgomery and Paul Kane, "Lawmakers Reach Accord on Huge Financial Rescue; House Vote Is Imminent on $700 Billion Bailout Plan," *Washington Post*, September 28, 2008; Clifford Krauss, "Gas Prices Climb Quickly as Refineries Remain Closed," *New York Times*, September 15, 2008; U.S. Bureau of the Census, *Income, Poverty, and Health Insurance Coverage in the United States: 2007*, prepared by Carmen DeNavas-Walt, Bernadette D. Proctor, and Jessica C. Smith (Washington, D.C.: U.S. Government Printing Office, 2008); United Press International, "Bush Approval Rating 27 Percent, Poll Says," September 30, 2008; NBC News/Wall Street Journal Poll, http://www.pollingreport.com/right.htm.

2. These numbers are according to McDonald's research, as posted on his blog. See Michael P. McDonald, "2008 Unofficial Voter Turnout," *United States Elections Project* (blog), November 9, 2008, http://elections.gmu.edu/preliminary_vote_2008.html.

3. Michael P. McDonald and Samuel L. Popkin, "The Myth of the Vanishing Voter," *American Political Science Review* 95, no. 4 (2001): 963–74.

4. Jeannie M. Nuss, "Student Voting Efforts Applauded," *Boston Globe*, December 3, 2008.

5. Damien Cave, "Generation O Gets Its Hopes Up," *New York Times*, November 9, 2008.

6. Tracy Fitzsimmons, "2008: Year of the Young Voter," *Washington Post*, November 9, 2008.

7. My use of the word "evolving" is meant to denote the way in which citizenship practices change over time due to shifting social and cultural norms. This is supported by the *Oxford English Dictionary*, which defines "evolving" (adj.) as "that is in process of evolution; developing, changing," and "evolution" (n.) as "a process of gradual change occurring in a system, institution, subject, artifact, product, etc., esp. from a simpler to a more complex or advanced state." This is the term that best captures my basic assumption that it is natural for the democratic practices of successive generations of young adults to change with the developing world around them. Simply put, what it means to act like a citizen today is different than it was fifty years ago; it has evolved, and it will continue to do so.

8. Although Mayer would later delete all of his blog entries on two separate occasions, nothing is ever completely erased from the Internet. His early blog entries can still be found through the Internet Archive's Wayback Machine. This particular post, entitled "(Not) Waiting on the World to Change—Entry No. 1," is available at http://replay.waybackmachine.org/2007 0429040124/http://www.johnmayer.com/blog#329.

9. Charles Taylor, "Cultures of Democracy and Citizen Efficacy," *Public Culture* 19, no. 1 (2007): 123.

10. David Held, *Models of Democracy*, 3rd ed. (Stanford: Stanford University Press, 2006), 157.

11. Martin P. Wattenberg, *Where Have All the Voters Gone?* (Cambridge, Mass.: Harvard University Press, 2002), 105–20.

12. Michael X. Delli Carpini, "An Overview of the State of Citizens' Knowledge About Politics," in *Communicating Politics: Engaging the Public in Democratic Life*, ed. Mitchell S. McKinney, Lynda Lee Kaid, and Dianne G. Bystrom (New York: Peter Lang, 2005), 35.

13. Henry Milner, *Civic Literacy: How Informed Citizens Make Democracy Work* (Hanover, N.H.: University Press of New England, 2002), 3.

14. Peter Levine, *The Future of Democracy: Developing the Next Generation of American Citizens* (Medford, Mass.: Tufts University Press, 2007), 17, 20.

15. Robert D. Putnam, *Bowling Alone: The Collapse and Renewal of American Community* (New York: Simon and Schuster, 2000).

16. Stephen Macedo et al., *Democracy at Risk: How Political Choices Undermine Citizen Participation, and What We Can Do About It* (Washington, D.C.: Brookings Institution Press, 2005), 1.

17. Sidney Verba, Kay Lehman Schlozman, and Henry E. Brady, *Voice and Equality: Civic Volunteerism in American Politics* (Cambridge, Mass.: Harvard University Press, 1995), 38.

18. Cliff Zukin et al., *A New Engagement? Political Participation, Civic Life, and the Changing American Citizen* (New York: Oxford University Press, 2006), 7.

19. Wattenberg, *Where Have All the Voters Gone?*

20. Macedo et al., *Democracy at Risk*, 25.

21. Levine, *Future of Democracy*, 70–73. Throughout this book, I oscillate between the feminine and masculine pronouns in order to avoid gender bias.

22. Putnam, *Bowling Alone*, 252.

23. Macedo et al., *Democracy at Risk*, 28–34.

24. Zukin et al., *A New Engagement?* 100–101.

25. Putnam, *Bowling Alone*, 25–26, quote on 184.

26. Theda Skocpol, *Diminished Democracy: From Membership to Management in American Civic Life* (Norman: University of Oklahoma Press, 2004).

27. Michael Schudson, "The Varieties of Civic Experience," *Citizenship Studies* 10 (November 2006): 591–606.

28. Zukin et al., *A New Engagement?* 72–73.

29. Neil Howe and William Strauss, *Millenials Rising: The Next Great Generation* (New York: Vintage, 2000).

30. Russell J. Dalton, *The Good Citizen: How a Younger Generation Is Reshaping American Politics* (Washington, D.C.: CQ Press, 2008), 29.

31. See Zukin et al., *A New Engagement?* 177–80.

32. *How Young People View Their Lives, Futures, and Politics: A Portrait of "Generation Next"* (Washington, D.C.: The Pew Research Center for the People and the Press, 2007).

33. Alexis de Tocqueville, *Democracy in America*, trans. Harvey Mansfield and Delba Winthrop (Chicago: University of Chicago Press, 2000), 27–28.

34. Richard G. Niemi and Mary A. Hepburn, "The Rebirth of Political Socialization," *Perspectives on Political Science* 24, no. 1 (1995): 7.

35. William Damon, "To Not Fade Away: Restoring Civil Identity Among the Young," in *Making Good Citizens: Education and Civil Society*, ed. Diane Ravitch and Joseph P. Viteritti (New Haven: Yale University Press, 2001), 127.

36. M. Kent Jennings and Laura Stoker, "Social Trust and Civic Engagement Across Time and Generations," *Acta Politica* 39, no. 4 (2004): 369.

37. Marc Hooghe and Britt Wilkenfeld, "The Stability of Political Attitudes and Behaviors Across Adolescence and Early Adulthood: A Comparison of Survey Data on Adolescents and Young Adults in Eight Countries," *Journal of Youth and Adolescence* 37 (February 2008): 155–67.

38. Levine, *Future of Democracy*, 72.

39. See, for example, Michael X. Delli Carpini, *Stability and Change in American Politics: The Coming of Age of the Generation of the 1960s* (New York: New York University Press, 1986), and Stephen E. Bennett and Stephen C. Craig, eds., *After the Boom: The Politics of Generation X* (Lanham, Md.: Rowman and Littlefield, 1997).

40. Levine, *Future of Democracy*, 70.

41. Zukin et al., *A New Engagement?* 11.

42. William A. Corsaro, *The Sociology of Childhood*, 2nd ed. (Thousand Oaks, Calif.: Pine Forge Press, 2005).

43. J. P. Shalloo, review of *The Lost Generation*, by Maxine Davis, *The ANNALS of the American Academy of Political and Social Science* 186 (July 1936): 238–39.

44. Michael Schudson, *The Good Citizen: A History of American Civic Life* (Cambridge, Mass.: Harvard University Press, 1998), 294.

45. Tracy L. M. Kennedy et al., *Networked Families* (Washington, D.C.: Pew Internet and American Life Project, 2008).

46. James Petras and Henry Veltmeyer, "Globalization Unmasked: The Dynamics and Contradictions of Global Capitalism," in *Globalization and Change: The Transformation of Global Capitalism*, ed. Berch Berberoglu (Lanham, Md.: Lexington Books, 2005), 49.

47. Marcelo M. Suárez-Orozco and Desirée Baolian Qin-Hilliard, "Globalization: Culture and Education in the New Millennium," in *Globalization: Culture and Education in the New Millennium*, ed. Marcelo M. Suárez-Orozco and Desirée Baolian Qin-Hilliard (Berkeley: University of California Press, 2004), 2.

48. David C. Soule, "Historical Framework: Cities and Their Regions, Suburbanization, and Federal Policies," in *Urban Sprawl: A Comprehensive Guide*, ed. D. C. Soule (Westport, Conn.: Greenwood Press, 2006), 17.

49. Kevin M. Kruse and Thomas J. Sugrue, "Introduction: The New Suburban History," in *The New Suburban History*, ed. Kevin M. Kruse and Thomas J. Sugrue (Chicago: University of Chicago Press, 2006), 1.

50. George Kozmetsky and Piyu Yue, *The Economic Transformation of the United States, 1950–2000: Focusing on the Technological Revolution, the Service Sector Expansion, and the Cultural, Ideological, and Demographic Changes* (West Lafayette: Purdue University Press, 2005), 7–8.

51. Nicole Stoops, *Educational Attainment in the United States: 2003*, Current Population Report P20-550 (Washington, D.C.: U.S. Census Bureau, 2004), http://www.census.gov/prod/2004pubs/p20-550.pdf.

52. Jacob S. Hacker, *The Great Risk Shift: The Assault on American Jobs, Families, Health Care, and Retirement and How You Can Fight Back* (New York: Oxford University Press, 2006), 12–15, quote on 12.

53. Richard Sennett, *The Culture of the New Capitalism* (New Haven: Yale University Press, 2006).

54. See, for instance, Charles T. Clotfelter, *After Brown: The Rise and Retreat of School Desegregation* (Princeton: Princeton University Press, 2004).

CHAPTER 2

1. To get a sense of just how prevalent movies and television shows have been in the United States, see Roy Fisher, Ann Harris, and Christine Jarvis, *Education in Popular Culture: Telling Tales on Teachers and Learners* (New York: Routledge, 2008).

2. Department of Education, "Nonpublic Education: A Vital Part of U.S. K–12 Education," June 2008, http://www.ed.gov/nclb/choice/schools/onpefacts.pdf.

3. Walter C. Parker, *Teaching Democracy: Unity and Diversity in Public Life* (New York: Teachers College Press, 2003).

4. Edwin T. Merritt et al., *Magnet and Specialized Schools of the Future* (Lanham, Md.: Scarecrow Education, 2005).

5. Bill Gates, prepared remarks for the National Governors Association/Achieve Summit, February 26, 2005, http://www.nga.org/cda/files/es05gates.pdf.

6. Bob Wise, *Raising the Grade: How Secondary School Reform Can Save Our Youth and Nation* (San Francisco: Jossey-Bass, 2008).

7. Parker, *Teaching Democracy.*

8. Diane Ravitch, "Education and Democracy," in *Making Good Citizens: Education and Civil Society*, ed. Diane Ravitch and Joseph P. Viteritti (New Haven: Yale University Press, 2001), esp. 16–17.

9. John Dewey, *Democracy and Education: An Introduction to the Philosophy of Education* (New York: Macmillan, 1916), 94–116.

10. Robert M. Hutchins, *The University of Utopia* (Chicago: University of Chicago Press, 1953), 3.

11. E. D. Hirsch, *Cultural Literacy: What Every American Needs to Know* (Boston: Houghton Mifflin, 1987).

12. Dewey, *Democracy and Education*, 22.

13. David Tyack, introduction to *School: The Story of American Public Education*, ed. Sarah Mondale and Sarah B. Patton (Boston: Beacon Press, 2001), 4.

14. Ravitch, "Education and Democracy," 18.

15. James D. Anderson, introduction to "1950–1980: Separate and Unequal," in Mondale and Patton, *School*, 126.

16. Diane Ravitch, introduction to "1900–1950: As American as Public School," in Mondale and Patton, *School*, 63–64.

17. Deirdre A. Gaquin and Katherine A. DeBrandt, eds., *Education Statistics of the United States*, 3rd ed. (Lanham, Md.: Bernan, 2001), 94–102.

18. Brown v. Board of Education, 347 U.S. 483 (1954).

19. Danielle S. Allen, *Talking to Strangers: Anxieties of Citizenship Since* Brown v. Board of Education (Chicago: University of Chicago Press, 2004), 4–7.

20. It should be noted that prior to 1972 no distinctions in nonwhite racial categories were made in the gathering of educational statistics. Gaquin and DeBrandt, *Education Statistics*, 94–102.

21. According to one recent Department of Education report, the national status dropout rates for sixteen- to twenty-four-year-olds decreased from 14.6 percent in 1972 to 8.7 percent in 2007. See Emily Forrest Cataldi, Jennifer Laird, and Angelina KewalRamani, *High School Dropout and Completion Rates in the United States: 2007*, NCES 2009-064 (Washington, D.C.: U.S. Department of Education, 2009), http://nces.ed.gov/pubs2009/2009064.pdf.

22. Floyd M. Hammack, introduction to *The Comprehensive High School Today*, ed. Floyd M. Hammack (New York: Teachers College Press, 2004), 1.

23. James B. Conant, *The American High School Today: A First Report to Interested Citizens* (New York: McGraw-Hill, 1959), 7.

24. Floyd M. Hammack, "What Should Be Common and What Should Not?" in Hammack, *The Comprehensive High School Today*, 12.

25. Ibid., 11–12.

26. Arthur G. Powell, Eleanor Farrar, and David K. Cohen, *The Shopping Mall High School: Winners and Losers in the Education Marketplace* (Boston: Houghton Mifflin, 1985).

27. *Oxford English Dictionary*, s.v. "teenager."

28. Jean-Jacques Rousseau, *Emile, or On Education*, trans. and ed. Christopher Kelly and Allan Bloom (Lebanon, N.H.: Dartmouth College Press, 2010), 361.

29. G. Stanley Hall, *Adolescence: Its Psychology and Its Relations to Physiology, Anthropology, Sociology, Sex, Crime, Religion, and Education*, vol. 1 (New York: D. Appleton, 1904), xv.

30. Jon Savage, *Teenage: The Creation of Youth Culture* (New York: Viking, 2007), 66.

31. Thomas Hine, *The Rise and Fall of the American Teenager* (New York: Avon Books, 1999), 4, 11.

32. Grace Palladino, *Teenagers: An American History* (New York: HarperCollins, 1996), 5, 7.

33. Savage, *Teenage*, 448.

34. Sharon L. Nichols and Thomas L. Good, *America's Teenagers—Myths and Realities: Media Images, Schooling, and the Social Costs of Careless Indifference* (Mahwah, N.J.: Lawrence Erlbaum, 2004), 9.

35. Peter Marin, "The Open Truth and Fiery Vehemence of Youth," in *High School*, ed. Ronald Gross and Paul Osterman (New York: Simon and Schuster, 1971), 27.

36. Erik H. Erikson, *Identity: Youth and Crisis* (New York: W. W. Norton, 1968), 129.

37. Pamela Perry, *Shades of White: White Kids and Racial Identities in High School* (Durham: Duke University Press, 2002), 10.

38. See C. J. Pascoe, *Dude, You're a Fag: Masculinity and Sexuality in High School* (Berkeley: University of California Press, 2007); Perry, *Shades of White*; and Beverly Daniel Tatum, *"Why Are All the Black Kids Sitting Together in the Cafeteria?" and Other Conversations About Race* (New York: Basic Books, 1997).

39. Penelope Eckert, *Jocks and Burnouts: Social Categories and Identity in the High School* (New York: Teachers College Press, 1989), 179.

40. Douglas E. Foley, *Learning Capitalist Culture: Deep in the Heart of Tejas* (Philadelphia: University of Pennsylvania Press, 1994), esp. 135–40.

41. Murray Milner Jr., *Freaks, Geeks, and Cool Kids: American Teenagers, Schools, and the Culture of Consumption* (New York: Routledge, 2004).

42. For one recent summary of the argument for understanding news media as mediated deliberation, see John Gastil, *Political Communication and Deliberation* (Los Angeles: Sage, 2008), 43–76.

43. Freedom Forum, *Death by Cheeseburger: High School Journalism in the 1990s and Beyond* (Arlington, Va.: Freedom Forum, 1994).

44. See Gene Gilmore, ed., *High School Journalism Today* (Danville, Ill.: Interstate, 1967); Edmund C. Arnold and Hillier Krieghbaum, *Handbook of Student Journalism: A Guide for Staff and Advisors* (New York: New York University Press, 1976); Tom E. Rolnicki, C. Dow Tate, and Sherri Taylor, *Scholastic Journalism*, 10th ed. (Ames: Iowa State University Press, 2001); and Jim Streisel, *High School Journalism: A Practical Guide* (Jefferson, N.C.: McFarland, 2007).

45. Kenneth Dautrich, David A. Yalof, and Mark Hugo López, *The Future of the First Amendment: The Digital Media, Civic Education, and Free Expression Rights in America's High Schools* (Lanham, Md.: Rowman and Littlefield, 2008), 68.

46. Freedom Forum, *Death by Cheeseburger*, 16, 22.

47. Tinker v. Des Moines Independent Community School District, 393 U.S. 503 (1969).

48. Hazelwood School District v. Kuhlmeier, 484 U.S. 260 (1988).

49. Lillian L. Kopenhaver and J. William Click, "High School Newspaper Still Censored Thirty Years After Tinker," *J&MC Quarterly* 78, no. 2 (2001): 327–39; Sara-Ellen Amster, *Seeds of Cynicism: The Undermining of Journalistic Education* (Lanham, Md.: University Press of America, 2006).

50. Thomas V. Dickson, "Self-Censorship and Freedom of the Public High School Press," *Journalism Educator* 49, no. 3 (1994): 56–63.

51. Jack Dvorak, *High School Electronic Journalism Survey* (Washington, D.C.: Radio and Television News Directors Foundation, 2002).

52. Jack Dvorak and Changhee Choi, "High School Journalism, Academic Performance Correlate," *Newspaper Research Journal* 30, no. 3 (2009): 75–89; *High School Journalism Confronts Critical Deadline* (Blue Springs, Mo.: Journalism Education Association Commission on the Role of Journalism in Secondary Education, 1987).

53. Dvorak and Choi, "High School Journalism," 80.

54. *High School Journalism Matters: NAA Foundation's 2008 Research Study Shows a Positive Link Between High School Journalism and Academic Achievement* (Arlington, Va.: Newspaper Association of America Foundation, 2008), http://www.naafoundation.org/docs/Foundation/Research/journalism-matters_full.pdf.

55. *High School Journalism Confronts Critical Deadline*.

56. See U.S. Census Bureau, "United States and Puerto Rico—Metropolitan Area," http://factfinder.census.gov/servlet/GCTTable?_bm=y&-geo_id=01000US&-_box_head_nbr=GCT-PH1-R&-ds_name=DEC_2000_SF1_U&-format=US-10S.

57. "Enrollment Hits 2450," *Northmen's Log*, September 19, 1969.

58. *School Desegregation in the St. Louis and Kansas City Areas* (Washington, D.C.: Missouri Advisory Committee to the U.S. Commission on Civil Rights, 1981).

59. All demographic data on the seven schools from 1991 to the present comes from the Common Core of Data, a program of the National Center for Education Statistics. It is available online at http://nces.ed.gov./ccd/.

60. "Black History—U.S. History," *Denebola*, November 13, 1968.

61. "Racial Tension Mounts in Newton Schools," *Denebola*, November 10, 1970.

62. "Blacks Hold Assembly Protest," *Beacon*, February 6, 1970.

63. "A Discussion of Wilson," *Beacon*, December 23, 1970.

64. See William Henry Kellar, *Make Haste Slowly: Moderates, Conservatives, and School Desegregation in Houston* (College Station: Texas A&M University Press, 1999).

65. See Guadalupe San Miguel Jr., *Brown, Not White: School Integration and the Chicano Movement in Houston* (College Station: Texas A&M University Press, 2001).

66. "Class Officers Elected," *Lancer*, April 25, 1974. In later years, the newspaper was titled the *Lamar Lancer*.

67. Joe W. Trotter and Jared N. Day, *Race and Renaissance: African Americans in Pittsburgh Since World War II* (Pittsburgh: University of Pittsburgh Press, 2010), 216.

68. Ethan Johnson and Felecia Williams, "Desegregation and Multiculturalism in the Portland Public Schools," *Oregon Historical Quarterly* 111, no. 1 (2010): 6–37.

69. John Dewey, *The Public and Its Problems* (Athens, Ohio: Swallow Press/Ohio University Press, 1954), 154.

CHAPTER 3

1. For midterm election data on eighteen- to twenty-nine-year-olds, see Mark Hugo Lopez, Karlo Barrios Marcelo, and Emily Hoban Kirby, *Youth Voter Turnout Increases in 2006* (College Park, Md.: CIRCLE, 2007).

2. For presidential election data on eighteen- to twenty-nine-year-olds, see Emily Hoban Kirby and Kei Kawashima-Ginsberg, *The Youth Vote in 2008* (College Park, Md.: CIRCLE, 2009).

3. Plato, *The Laws of Plato*, trans. Thomas L. Pingle (Chicago: University of Chicago Press, 1988).

4. Aristotle, *The Politics*, trans. T. A. Sinclair (New York: Penguin, 1991), 403, 405.

5. Benedict Anderson, *Imagined Communities*, rev. ed. (London: Verso, 1991), 36.

6. Alexander Hamilton, James Madison, and John Jay, *The Federalist Papers*, ed. Robert Scigliano (New York: Modern Library, 2000), 59.

7. John Dewey, *The Public and Its Problems* (Athens, Ohio: Swallow Press/Ohio University Press, 1954), 114.

8. Robert Dahl, "The City in the Future of Democracy," *American Political Science Review* 61, no. 4 (1967): 965.

9. Kevin O'Leary, *Saving Democracy: A Plan for Real Representation in America* (Stanford: Stanford University Press, 2006).

10. Anthony Downs, *An Economic Theory of Democracy* (New York: Harper, 1957).

11. Craig J. Calhoun, *Social Theory and the Politics of Identity* (Oxford: Blackwell, 1994), 20.

12. Amy Gutmann, introduction to *Multiculturalism: Examining the Politics of Recognition*, ed. Amy Gutmann (Princeton: Princeton University Press, 1994), 10.

13. Kwame Anthony Appiah, *The Ethics of Identity* (Princeton: Princeton University Press, 2005), 65.

14. Erving Goffman, *The Presentation of Self in Everyday Life* (New York: Anchor Books, 1959).

15. Kenneth Burke, *A Rhetoric of Motives* (Berkeley: University of California Press, 1969), 20.

16. For a fuller discussion of this, see ibid., esp. 55–59.

17. Kenneth Burke, *A Grammar of Motives* (Berkeley: University of California Press, 1969), 336.

18. Dana Anderson, *Identity's Strategy: Rhetorical Selves in Conversion* (Columbia: University of South Carolina Press, 2007), 35–57.

19. Barry Brummett, *Reading Rhetorical Theory* (New York: Harcourt Brace, 2000), 743.

20. "New Driving Requirements," *Denebola*, September 20, 1967.

21. "Youth Government," *Beacon*, May 30, 1972.

22. "Central Crack-Down Decreases Gatherings," *Ram Page*, September 20, 1968.

23. "Pride, Inc. Encourages Dignity in Washington's Negro Areas," *Beacon*, May 24, 1968.

24. "Hippies Gather at Tempe for Love-In," *Ram Page*, May 12, 1967.

25. "Mayor's Conference," *Carrickulum*, December 19, 1969.

26. "McCall, Duncan Speak to Students on Issues," *Grantonian*, November 4, 1966.

27. "Spain Works for Solon; Thinks D.C. 'Wondrous,'" *Ram Page*, October 15, 1965.

28. "Delegate Election Nears; Candidates Pledge Change," *Beacon*, March 5, 1971.

29. "Fauntroy Wins, Image Changes," *Beacon*, April 7, 1971.

30. "Bush, Allen to Speak at Graduation Programs," *Lancer*, May 23, 1968.

31. "Political Awareness Survey Finds South Clueless," *Denebola*, February 14, 1986.

32. "Danforth Addresses Oakies: Declaims Campus Violence," *Northmen's Log*, September 18, 1970; "Parents Speak on Levy Issue," *Northmen's Log*, May 14, 1971.

33. "Carnival Attracts Northmen," *Northmen's Log*, May 14, 1971.

34. "Black Mayor a First in Kansas City," *Northmen's Log*, April 19, 1991; "Trash Dumped in Northland? Landfill Creates Environmental, Economic Concerns," *Northmen's Log*, December 21, 1990.

35. "Students Aid Drinan in Primary Win," *Denebola*, September 29, 1970; "Citizens Discuss NCDF Project; Debate Building Code Problem," *Denebola*, October 27, 1970.

36. "Silber Clarifies His Position" and "Weld Stresses His Priorities," *Denebola*, October 31, 1990; "Weld Squeaks by in Complex Election," *Denebola*, November 22, 1990; "State House Budget Cuts May Mean Less Aid to Cities and Towns," *Denebola*, June 6, 1991.

37. "Scholars' Class Tours Pittsburgh," *Carrickulum*, October 28, 1988.

38. "Reporters Find Portland Does Have 'Places to Go and People to See,'" *Grantonian*, March 1, 1979.

39. "Municipal Elections Deserve Attention," *Denebola*, October 21, 2009.

40. Patrick Henry, "Dangerous Ambiguities," June 5, 1788, http://www.constitution.org/rc/rat_va_04.htm#henry-01.

41. George Washington, "Farewell Address," 1796, http://avalon.law.yale.edu/18th_century/washing.asp.

42. Anderson, *Imagined Communities*, 47.

43. "We Must Prevent Future Watergates," *Denebola*, March 13, 1974.

44. "Irangate Overpublicized," *Grantonian*, March 20, 1987.

45. "Impeachment Too Drastic a Punishment for Clinton," *Denebola*, September 29, 1998.

46. "Why Reagan?" and "Why Mondale?" *Beacon*, October 1984.

47. "Debates Continue, yet Less Is Said," "Grabbing the Female Vote," and "Palin; Missing Facts, Experience," *Grantonian*, October 30, 2008.

48. "Twelve Facts About Bottled Water," *Grantonian*, October 30, 2008.

49. "Political Races Grow," *Carrickulum*, April 28, 1988.

50. "Stand and Be Counted," *Denebola*, September 24, 2008.

51. "Point Counter Point," *Northmen's Log*, October 28, 2005.

52. "Right-Wing Limbaugh Takes America by Storm," *Grantonian*, June 11, 1993.

53. "Shows We'd Like to See," *Rampage*, January 12, 1996.

54. "The Senator Trent Lott Controversy," *Carrickulum*, February 14, 2003.

55. "Christopher Reeve: A Hero in the Real World," *Denebola*, October 2004.

56. "It's Handguns that Kill People," *Beacon*, May 1982.

57. "Sex Education," *Northmen's Log*, January 16, 1987.

58. "Lack of Confidence May Lead to Gender Bias," *Denebola*, March 17, 1995.

59. "The Tragedy of the Space Shuttle *Columbia*," *Carrickulum*, February 14, 2003.

60. "Oklahoma Tragedy Hits Close to Home," *Northmen's Log*, May 12, 1995.

61. "In Memoriam: Space Shuttle Heroes," *Lancer*, February 1986.

62. "Freedom Demonstrations Unreal," *Ram Page*, October 19, 1966.

63. "Vietnam Demonstrators Spark Cries of Anarchy, Cowardice, Barbarism," *Beacon*, November 19, 1965.

64. "Student Opinions Vary; Draft Girls—Dodge Army; Vietnam Policy Polled," *Denebola*, March 24, 1966.

65. "Red Cross Sponsor Viet Nam Project," *Lancer*, October 20, 1966.

66. "Draft Survey Reveals Beliefs," *Grantonian*, February 14, 1969.

67. John P. Robinson and Mark R. Levy, eds., *The Main Source: Learning from Television News* (Beverly Hills: Sage, 1986).

68. Anderson, *Imagined Communities*, 43.

69. See, for instance, the not uncontroversial argument made by Michael Hardt and Antonio Negri in *Empire* (Cambridge, Mass.: Harvard University Press, 2001).

70. Tony Clarke, "Global Corporate Rule: Unmasking the Political Agenda of Transnational Corporations in APEC and the Processes of Globalization," available at http://www.islandnet.com/plethora/mai/agenda.html. The Polaris Institute (www.polarisinstitute.org) was launched in 1997 in response to what its founders perceived as the growing control of corporations on governmental policies in Canada and elsewhere. One of its main goals is helping foster active citizenship.

71. Fredric Jameson, *Postmodernism, or The Cultural Logic of Late Capitalism* (Durham: Duke University Press, 1991), xviii–xix.

72. Karl Marx and Friedrich Engels, *The Marx-Engels Reader*, ed. Robert C. Tucker (New York: W. W. Norton, 1978), 475.

73. Immanuel Kant, "Perpetual Peace: A Philosophical Sketch," in *Kant: Political Writings*, ed. H. S. Reiss (Cambridge: Cambridge University Press, 1970), 93–130.

74. Adam Smith, *Wealth of Nations* (Amherst, N.Y.: Prometheus Books, 1991).

75. Adair Turner, *Just Capital: The Liberal Economy* (New York: Macmillan, 2002), 317.

76. John Hoffman, *Citizenship Beyond the State* (Thousand Oaks, Calif.: Sage, 2004), 115.

77. John Tomlinson, *Globalization and Culture* (Chicago: Chicago University Press, 1999), 4.

78. "AFS Students Arrive," *Grantonian*, September 12, 1968.

79. "Assembly Presents Four AFS Students," *Northmen's Log*, September 27, 1968.

80. "Apartheid: The Issue," *Beacon*, December 1985 (emphasis in original).

81. "Adventure to Africa Helps Student See World Different," *Northmen's Log*, November 8, 1985.

82. "Make an Impact Through Amnesty International," *Grantonian*, October 22, 1998.

83. "Tsunami: In Asia," *Lamar Life*, April 2005.

84. "WHS Contributes to Haitian Relief," *Rampage*, February 19, 2010.

85. "Haiti Survivors Receive Help," *Northmen's Log*, February 19, 2010.

86. Letter to the editor, *Beacon*, January 1992.

87. "How Big of a Problem Is Global Warming?" *Carrickulum*, February 20, 2002.

88. "Putin's 'Reforms' Dangerous," *Denebola*, September 30, 2004.

89. "Starvation in Some Places, Obesity in Others," *Rampage*, December 19, 2002.

90. "Save the Whales, Kill Your TV, Hug a Tree," *Grantonian*, December 17, 1998.

91. "A Struggle for Acceptance," *Denebola*, November 25, 2009.

92. "Uganda Bill Bans Homosexuality," *Denebola*, December 23, 2009.

93. "America Out of El Salvador," *Beacon*, May 1982.

94. "Is World Peace Really Worth Fighting For?" *Rampage*, January 16, 1992.

95. "Imagining the Unimaginable," *Northmen's Log*, April 11, 2003.

96. "American Patriotism Flying High," *Grantonian*, September 28, 2001.

97. David Held, "Democracy and Globalization," in *Re-imagining Political Community: Studies in Cosmopolitan Democracy*, ed. Daniele Archibugi, David Held, and Martin Kohler (Cambridge: Polity Press, 1998), 13; Appiah, *Ethics of Identity*; Kwame Anthony Appiah, *Cosmopolitanism: Ethics in a World of Strangers* (New York: W. W. Norton, 2006).

98. Kant, "Perpetual Peace," 107–8.

CHAPTER 4

1. Karlyn Kohrs Campbell and Kathleen Hall Jamieson, *Presidents Creating the Presidency: Deeds Done in Words* (Chicago: University of Chicago Press, 2008), 231–34.

2. Vanessa B. Beasley, *You, the People: American National Identity in Presidential Rhetoric* (College Station: Texas A&M University Press, 2004), 154.

3. Alexis de Tocqueville, *Democracy in America*, trans. Harvey Mansfield and Delba Winthrop (Chicago: University of Chicago Press, 2000).

4. Fredric Jameson, *Postmodernism, or The Cultural Logic of Late Capitalism* (Durham: Duke University Press, 1991), xx, 265–78.

5. Zygmunt Bauman, *Liquid Modernity* (Cambridge: Polity Press, 2000), 76. See also Zygmunt Bauman, *Life in Fragments* (Cambridge: Polity Press, 1996).

6. Lizabeth Cohen, *A Consumer's Republic: The Politics of Mass Consumption in Postwar America* (New York: Alfred A. Knopf, 2003), 8.

7. Ibid., 112–14.

8. Ibid., 9.

9. Benjamin R. Barber, *Consumed: How Markets Corrupt Children, Infantilize Adults, and Swallow Citizens Whole* (New York: W. W. Norton, 2007), 36.

10. Ibid., 82–84.

11. Ibid., 126.

12. Michael Schudson argues, for instance, that "nearly all of us . . . are and necessarily must be consumers as well as citizens. There are important distinctions between ordinary consumer behavior and ordinary civic behavior, but they are not invidious distinctions." See Michael Schudson, "Citizens, Consumers, and the Good Society," *The ANNALS of the American Academy of Political and Social Science* 611 (2007): 238.

13. Lawrence B. Glickman, *Buying Power: A History of Consumer Activism in America* (Chicago: University of Chicago Press, 2009), 26, quote on 306.

14. Juliet B. Schor, *Born to Buy: The Commercialized Child and the New Consumer Culture* (New York: Scribner, 2004), 14–16.

15. Ibid., 9.

16. Sandra L. Cavert, "Children as Consumers: Advertising and Marketing," *Future of Children* 18, no. 1 (2008): 205–34.

17. Schor, *Born to Buy*, 23.

18. Jean Twenge has noted that "in 1967, when the Boomers were in college, 45% of freshmen said it was important to be well-off financially. By 2004, 74% embraced this life goal." See Jean M. Twenge, *Generation Me: Why Today's Young Americans Are More Confident, Assertive, Entitled—and More Miserable than Ever Before* (New York: Free Press, 2006), 99.

19. "WHS Students Support 'Save Camelback' Fund," *Ram Page*, December 3, 1965.

20. "'Marshmallow Winter' Title of Xmas Formal," *Ram Page*, December 3, 1965.

21. "Cans Collected," *Rampage*, December 19, 2002.

22. Thorstein B. Veblen, *The Theory of the Leisure Class* (New York: Dover, 1994).

23. Benjamin Franklin, *The Autobiography of Benjamin Franklin* (New York: W. W. Norton, 1985).

24. "Current Girls' Fashions Ridiculous," *Ram Page*, January 31, 1966.

25. "Vests, Umbrellas Big with 'Traditional Look,'" *Lancer*, November 9, 1967.

26. "Past and Present Fashion Parallel Seen in 'Do Your Thing' Clothing Approach," *Grantonian*, February 12, 1971.

27. "Wild Stripes Lead Latest 'Twiggy' Fad," *Northmen's Log*, September 22, 1967.

28. Mike Featherstone, *Consumer Culture and Postmodernism* (Thousand Oaks, Calif.: Sage, 1991), 87.

29. While I do not closely examine how marketers have taken up branding as a way to sell an image rather than a product, it is worth noting that branding may be an integral part of the change described below. For further analysis of this trend, see Naomi Klein, *No Logo* (New York: Picador, 2000). Particularly connected to the current argument is Klein's assertion that

"the astronomical growth in the wealth and cultural influence of multinational corporations over the last fifteen years can arguably be traced back to a single, seemingly innocuous idea developed by management theorists in the mid-1980s: that successful corporations must primarily produce brands, as opposed to products" (3).

30. "Promising Designers Emerge from Satiny," *Beacon*, October 1984.
31. "Fashion Show Comes to Grant June 11," *Grantonian*, June 10, 1999.
32. "Student Reviews Fashion Trends Throughout the School," *Carrickulum*, February 5, 1997.
33. "Brrrr. . . . It's Cold Out Here! Warm Up in Style," *Rampage*, January 18, 2002.
34. "Looking at Head-to-Toe Fashions," *Rampage*, December 19, 2002.
35. "His Own Style," *Lamar Life*, Winter 2004.
36. "Spring into Fashion," *Lamar Life*, Spring 2004.
37. "Summer Fashion," *Lamar Life*, Summer 2005.
38. Michael Schudson, *The Good Citizen: A History of American Civic Life* (Cambridge, Mass.: Harvard University Press, 1998), 182.
39. "No Parking Stickers Required in Future?" *Northmen's Log*, September 22, 1967.
40. "Towing: Is Your Car Safe?" *Lamar Life*, April 2005.
41. "No Coffee, Soda Pop for Lunch," *Grantonian*, December 9, 1966.
42. "Petition Drafted to Improve School Lunch," *Denebola*, September 2010.
43. "Youth Tackles Politics," *Northmen's Log*, September 27, 1968.
44. "Go Ahead, Vote!" *Beacon*, October 1980.
45. See, for instance, "Apathy of Americans Leaves Them Clueless," *Denebola*, October 30, 1998.
46. "Use the Power That's Rightly Yours, Vote in '92," *Grantonian*, October 16, 1992.
47. "A View from the Top," *Denebola*, October 25, 1996.
48. "School Encourages Voter Registration," *Northmen's Log*, October 10, 2008.
49. Wendy M. Rahn and John Transue, "Social Trust and Value Change: The Decline of Social Capital in American Youth, 1976-1995," *Political Psychology* 19, no. 3 (1998): 545-65.
50. Marsha Richins and Scott Dawson, "A Consumer Values Orientation for Materialism and Its Measurement: Scale Development and Validation," *Journal of Consumer Research* 19, no. 3 (1992): 303-16.
51. Rahn and Transue, "Social Trust," 550.
52. Dhavan V. Shah et al., "Political Consumerism: How Communication and Consumption Orientations Drive 'Lifestyle Politics,'" *The ANNALS of the American Academy of Political and Social Science* 611 (2007): 219.
53. "Charging Head First into Debt," *Carrickulum*, December 11, 2001.
54. Neil Howe, William Strauss, and R. J. Matson, *Millennials Rising: The Next Great Generation* (New York: Vintage, 2000).
55. "Warning: Trends Poison South," *Denebola*, March 24, 2005.
56. "Advertisers Target Profitable Teen Market," *Denebola*, March 24, 2005.
57. "10 Trends You Love to Follow," *Denebola*, March 24, 2005.
58. "Teen Spending Excessive Despite Recession," *Denebola*, February 10, 2010.
59. "V. P. Pacifies," *Denebola*, March 13, 1967.
60. "Teen Group Sings at Prom," *Ram Page*, May 12, 1967.
61. Amy L. Best, *Prom Night: Youth, Schools, and Popular Culture* (New York: Routledge, 2000).
62. "Dance Moves Without Benefit," *Northmen's Log*, May 5, 2006.
63. W. Lance Bennett, "Branded Political Communication: Lifestyle Politics, Logo Campaigns, and the Rise of Global Citizenship," in *Politics, Products, and Markets: Exploring Political Consumerism Past and Present*, ed. Michele Micheletti, Andreas Follesdal, and Dietlind Stolle (New Brunswick: Transaction, 2004), 103.
64. W. Lance Bennett, "Lifestyle Politics and Citizen Consumers: Identity, Communication, and Political Action in Late Modern Society," in *Media and the Restyling of Politics*, ed. John Corner and Dick Pels (Thousand Oaks, Calif.: Sage, 2003), 137-50.

65. Michele Micheletti, *Political Virtue and Shopping: Individuals, Consumerism, and Collective Action* (New York: Palgrave Macmillan, 2003), xiv.

66. Cohen, *Consumer's Republic.*

67. Anthony Giddens, *Modernity and Self-Identity: Self and Society in the Late Modern Age* (Stanford: Stanford University Press, 1991).

68. Margaret Scammell, "The Internet and Civic Engagement: The Age of the Citizen Consumer," *Political Communication* 17, no. 4 (2000): 351–55.

69. Michele Micheletti, Andreas Follesdal, and Dietlind Stolle, introduction to *Politics, Products, and Markets*, x.

70. Dietlind Stolle, Marc Hooghe, and Michele Micheletti, "Politics in the Supermarket: Political Consumerism as a Form of Political Participation," *International Political Science Review* 26, no. 3 (2005): 245–69.

71. "Small Mac?" *Denebola*, October 31, 2003; "Materialism Embedded in Student Clothing," *Denebola*, February 7, 2004.

72. "Local Low Cost Theaters Fit Any Student's Budget," *Grantonian*, September 26, 2003; "Businesses Won't Cash in on BND," *Grantonian*, November 21, 2003; "Sweatshops Dehumanize Employees," *Grantonian*, February 27, 2004.

73. "Goal Attained as Drive Ends," *Grantonian*, October 15, 1965.

74. "SC Workday Nets $138: Kuch, Hall Top Earners," *Ram Page*, October 29, 1965.

75. "Pepsters Sell Rah-Rah Paraphernalia," *Beacon*, October 15, 1965.

76. "United Way Succeeds Again," *Northmen's Log*, October 27, 2000.

77. "Grant Fundraiser Concert Tonight," *Grantonian*, March 14, 2003.

78. "Prom: Just a Magnificent Obsession," *Rampage*, May 1, 1998.

79. "WHS Family Unites for Terror Victims: School Fundraisers Net over $3,000," *Rampage*, October 5, 2001.

80. "Getting Involved: Ways the Average Oakie Can Do Their Part," *Northmen's Log*, October 5, 2001.

81. "Tsunami: In Asia," *Lamar Life*, April 2005.

82. "Haitian Relief Efforts Fading at South," *Denebola*, March 2010.

83. "Seniors Experience Giving at Local Homeless Shelter" and "Students Scramble for Summer Volunteering, Camps," *Rampage*, May 12, 2000.

84. "More than Just Once a Year," *Northmen's Log*, November 30, 2001.

85. "Giving a Helping Hand to Those Less Fortunate," *Carrickulum*, December 15, 1997.

86. "Volunteering Builds Character, Resume," *Grantonian*, October 18, 2002.

87. "Community Service," *Denebola*, October 5, 1997.

88. Sidney Verba, Kay Lehman Schlozman, and Henry E. Brady, *Voice and Equality: Civic Volunteerism in American Life* (Cambridge, Mass.: Harvard University Press, 1995).

89. Dale Blyth, Rebecca Saito, and Thomas Beikas, "A Quantitative Study of the Impact of Service-Learning Programs," in *Service-Learning: Applications from the Research*, ed. A. S. Waterman (Mahwah, N.J.: Erlbaum, 1997), 39–56.

90. Linda J. Sax and Alexander W. Astin, "The Benefits of Service: Evidence from Undergraduates," *Educational Record* 78, nos. 3–4 (1997): 25–32.

91. Theda Skocpol, *Diminished Democracy: From Membership to Management in American Civic Life* (Norman: University of Oklahoma Press, 2003), 127.

92. "Poverty Runs Rampant Throughout Developing World," *Northmen's Log*, October 27, 2007.

93. Giddens, *Modernity and Self-Identity.*

94. Richard Sennett, *The Culture of the New Capitalism* (New Haven: Yale University Press, 2006), 133, 169–70.

95. Ibid., 171.

96. Alan Aldridge, *Consumption* (Cambridge: Polity Press, 2003), 14.

97. "How to Help," Dana-Farber Cancer Institute, http://www.dfci.harvard.edu/how/.

98. American Red Cross, http://www.redcross.org/.

CHAPTER 5

1. Josh Tyrangiel, "Bono: The World's Biggest Rock Star Is Also Africa's Biggest Advocate," *Time*, March 4, 2002.

2. Harold D. Lasswell, *Politics: Who Gets What, When, How* (New York: Meridian, 1958).

3. For an account of Frost's talk in the fall of 1962, see George Monteiro, "Robert Frost's Liberal Imagination," *Iowa Review* 28 (Winter 1998): 104–27.

4. John Street, "The Celebrity Politician: Political Style and Popular Culture," in *Media and the Restyling of Politics*, ed. John Corner and Dick Pels (Thousand Oaks, Calif.: Sage, 2003), 85–86.

5. "Clinton Writes to 'West Wing' Character," *USA Today*, February 27, 2004.

6. Kenneth Burke, *Philosophy of Literary Form*, 3rd ed. (Berkeley: University of California Press, 1974), 293–304.

7. Barry Brummett, "Electric Literature as Equipment for Living: Haunted House Films," *Critical Studies in Mass Communication* 2, no. 3 (1985): 247–61.

8. Trevor Parry-Giles and Shawn J. Parry-Giles, *The Prime-Time Presidency: "The West Wing" and U.S. Nationalism* (Urbana: University of Illinois Press, 2006).

9. John Storey, *Inventing Popular Culture: From Folklore to Globalization* (Malden, Mass.: Blackwell, 2003), 15.

10. Ibid., 45.

11. John Seabrook, *Nobrow: The Culture of Marketing, the Marketing of Culture* (New York: Vintage, 2001).

12. Susan Sontag, *Against Interpretation* (New York: Dell, 1966).

13. John Storey, *Cultural Theory and Popular Culture* (London: Pearson, 2001), 147.

14. Zygmunt Bauman, *Postmodernity and Its Discontents* (New York: New York University Press, 1997), 100.

15. For two recent exemplary texts in this area, see Jonathon S. Epstein, ed., *Youth Culture: Identity in a Postmodern World* (Malden, Mass.: Blackwell, 1998), and Andy Bennett and Keith Kahn-Harris, eds., *After Subculture: Critical Studies in Contemporary Youth Culture* (New York: Palgrave Macmillan, 2004).

16. See Henry Giroux, *Disturbing Pleasures: Learning Popular Culture* (New York: Routledge, 1994).

17. "Sonny, Cher at WHS," *Ram Page*, October 15, 1965.

18. "Lovin' Spoonful Concert Coming," *Lancer*, November 17, 1966.

19. "Gary Bennett 'Come(s) Alive' on WIIC," *Carrickulum*, December 22, 1967.

20. "Joplin Joins Mounting Victims of Drug World," *Ram Page*, October 23, 1970.

21. "Neil Diamond Gets Standing Ovation," *Ram Page*, December 22, 1970.

22. "Erich Segal's 'Love Story' Makes Strongest Willed Person to Weep," *Ram Page*, January 15, 1971.

23. "'Ryan's Daughter' Now Playing at Palms Theatre; Movie Controversial," *Ram Page*, March 5, 1971.

24. "'The Exorcist' Holds No Threats of Demons," *Ram Page*, March 15, 1974.

25. "God Creates Again," *Ram Page*, October 1, 1980.

26. "Exercise Your Right to Vote," *Ram Page*, October 1, 1980.

27. "Billy Joel Didn't Start the Fire, but He Sure Did Rekindle It," *Rampage*, December 21, 1990.

28. "Cupid's Arrows Hits the Movies," *Rampage*, February 8, 1991.

29. "'Little Things' and Marty Stuart," "Who Says Country Isn't Cool?," "*Lambs, Enemy*: Two of This Year's Best," and "Unlocking *The Doors*," *Rampage*, March 8, 1991.

30. "Motown's Temptations Find 'Groove' 'Creating Soul' for Pleasure, Profits," *Beacon*, December 1966.

31. "Gordon Parks Reviews His Life in Movie," *Beacon*, October 1969.

32. "DOONESBURY Draws Vast, Devoted Following," *Beacon*, June 1971.

33. "Woody Allen in 'Bananas,'" *Beacon*, June 4, 1971.

34. "Critic's Corner," *Beacon*, March 1, 1974.

35. "New Book About 'Beatles' Is Best Seller," *Carrickulum*, November 1972.

36. "Teen Health Clinic Belies Stereotypes" and "Most Fall Sports End with Winning Season," *Grantonian*, November 20, 1992.

37. "A & P Anticipate End of Anchovy Eaters," *Grantonian*, November 20, 1992.

38. "Students on Way to Film 'Stardom'" and "Utah Saints Creates Techno-Dance Music of Future," *Grantonian*, November 20, 1992.

39. "'Malcolm X' and Act III Raise Interest of Students," *Grantonian*, November 20, 1992.

40. "1992 Has Marked End of the Magic," *Grantonian*, November 20, 1992.

41. Christopher Georges, "The Boring Twenties; Grow Up, Crybabies, You're America's Luckiest Generation," *Washington Post*, September 12, 1993.

42. David Paul Kuhn, "The Young March Toward Cynicism," Real Clear Politics, October 12, 2010, http://www.realclearpolitics.com/articles/2010/10/12/the_young_march_toward_cyni cism_jon_stewart_steven_colbert_rally_to_restore_sanity_107532.html.

43. Raymond Williams, *Keywords* (New York: Oxford University Press, 1983), 84–85.

44. "*Zachariah* First Electric Western," *Grantonian*, February 26, 1971.

45. "*Tommy*: A Movie?" *Beacon*, June 10, 1975.

46. "'Halloween II' Disappointing Minus Director Carpenter," *Grantonian*, November 12, 1981.

47. "'Terms' Is Worth Seeing," *Northmen's Log*, January 20, 1984.

48. "Choice Pics," *Denebola*, January 23, 1985.

49. "*Rocky IV*'s Appeal," *Ram Page*, December 20, 1985.

50. "Movie Review: *Pearl Harbor*," *Northmen's Log*, May 25, 2001.

51. "Movie Review: *The Dish*," *Lamar Lancer*, October 2000.

52. "DiCaprio's Latest: No Day at 'The Beach,'" *Grantonian*, March 16, 2000.

53. "Mandy Moore's Bubblegum Pop Leaves a Bad Taste," *Grantonian*, January 20, 2000.

54. "Smith Loses His Touch with 'Lost,'" *Northmen's Log*, April 29, 2005.

55. "311 Sinks to New Low with Whiny 'Soundsystem,'" *Grantonian*, November 18, 1999.

56. John M. Sloop, "The Emperor's New Makeup: Cool Cynicism and Popular Music Criticism," *Popular Music and Society* 23, no. 1 (1999): 52.

57. "Music Reviews," *Lamar Life*, April 2005.

58. "Night Lights Shine Bright," *Northmen's Log*, October 15, 2004.

59. "*Valentine's Day* Releases Love," *Rampage*, March 10, 2010.

60. "*Private Parts*: Not So Private After All," *Northmen's Log*, March 21, 1997.

61. "Classic TV: *Beavis and Butthead*," *Carrickulum*, April 11, 2002.

62. Steven Best and Douglas Kellner, "Beavis and Butt-Head: No Future for Postmodern Youth," in Epstein, *Youth Culture*, 83.

63. "'80s Resurgence Overshadows Other Fads," *Grantonian*, October 27, 2000.

64. "Celebrities Set Bad Example," *Northmen's Log*, March 16, 2006.

65. "Cyberspace Is All Atwitter About Twitter Craze," *Rampage*, May 21, 2009.

66. "Palin Don't Preach," *Denebola*, September 24, 2008.

67. Jon Simons, "Popular Culture and Mediated Politics: Intellectuals, Elites, and Democracy," in Corner and Pels, *Media and the Restyling of Politics*, 171–89.

68. Liesbet van Zoonen, *Entertaining the Citizen: When Politics and Popular Culture Converge* (Lanham, Md.: Rowman and Littlefield, 2005).

69. John Street, *Politics and Popular Culture* (Cambridge: Polity Press, 1997), 45–46.

70. Darrell M. West and John Orman, *Celebrity Politics* (Upper Saddle River, N.J.: Pearson, 2003), 9.

71. John Fiske, *Media Matters: Race and Gender in U.S. Politics* (Minneapolis: University of Minnesota Press, 1996).

72. David L. Swanson, "The Homologous Evolution of Political Communication and Civic Engagement: Good News, Bad News, and No News," *Political Communication* 17, no. 4 (2000): 411.

73. Robert Hariman, *Political Style: The Artistry of Power* (Chicago: University of Chicago Press, 1995), 9.

74. Barry Brummett, "Communities, Identities, and Politics: What Rhetoric Is Becoming in the Twenty-First Century," in *New Approaches to Rhetoric*, ed. Patricia A. Sullivan and Steven R. Goldzwig (Thousand Oaks, Calif.: Sage, 2004), 295–96.

75. Barry Richards, "The Emotional Deficit in Political Communication," *Political Communication* 21, no. 3 (2004): 339–52.

76. "Newspaper Industry Honored in October," *Lancer*, October 6, 1966.

77. "Students Gain Journalistic Experience from WTOP," *Beacon*, November 30, 1970.

78. "The Media Influences Americans," *Northmen's Log*, May 14, 1982.

79. See Timothy Cook, *Governing with the News* (Chicago: University of Chicago Press, 1998).

80. See Maxwell McCombs and George Estrada, "The News Media and the Pictures in Our Heads," in *Do the Media Govern? Politicians, Voters, and Reporters in America*, ed. Shanto Iyengar and Richard Reeves (Thousand Oaks, Calif.: Sage, 1997), 237–47.

81. See Stephen D. Reese, "Framing Public Life," in *Framing Public Life: Perspectives on Media and Our Understanding of the Social World*, ed. Stephen D. Reese, Oscar Gandy, and August Grant (Mahwah, N.J.: Lawrence Erlbaum, 2001), 7–32.

82. Michael Schudson, *Discovering the News* (New York: Basic Books, 1978).

83. "Is It News, or Just a Case of Déjà Vu?" *Rampage*, May 2, 1997.

84. "Journalism: Forum for Political Debate," *Denebola*, March 10, 1997.

85. "Biased Media Coverage Obvious," *Grantonian*, January 17, 2003.

86. "Mass Media: Mass Information, Mass Manipulation," *Northmen's Log*, March 21, 1997.

87. "Media Loses Focus in Election Coverage," *Denebola*, October 29, 2008.

88. "The President's Place," *Beacon*, April 1982.

89. "Bush's 'Family Values' Unreal," *Grantonian*, September 25, 1992.

90. "Forget the Candidates; Let's Vote for Mickey," *Rampage*, November 1, 1996.

91. "Politicians Are Immature," *Denebola*, October 30, 1998.

92. "Nightmare on 36th Street," *Grantonian*, February 21, 2003.

93. Salvador Dalí, *The Collected Writings of Salvador Dalí*, trans. Haim Finkelstein (Cambridge: Cambridge University Press, 1998), 267.

94. Marcel Jean, *The History of Surrealist Painting* (New York: Grove Press, 1960), 207.

95. "We Must Prevent Future Watergates," *Denebola*, March 13, 1974.

96. "Clinton Says 'There Are No Overnight Miracles' for America's Economy," *Grantonian*, November 20, 1992.

97. "Campaign 2000; God, Please Help Us," *Rampage*, November 9, 2000.

98. "MTV Adds Some Pop to Politics," *Denebola*, October 29, 2004.

99. "Students Remain Uniformed: Adolescents Direct Focus on Pop Culture," *Northmen's Log*, October 24, 2008.

100. "Send the Media to Rehab," *Denebola*, October 25, 2007.

101. Joseph N. Cappella and Kathleen Hall Jamieson, *Spiral of Cynicism: The Press and the Public Good* (New York: Oxford University Press, 1997).

102. Timothy E. Cook, *Governing with the News: The News Media as a Political Institution* (Chicago: University of Chicago Press, 1998), 118.

103. Michael Olander, *Media Use Among Young People* (College Park, Md.: CIRCLE, 2003).

104. Larry Neumeister, "When It Comes to Slang, Just Remember to Stay 'Cool,'" *Chicago Sun-Times*, February 11, 2006.

105. Malcolm Gladwell, "The Coolhunt," *New Yorker*, March 17, 1997.

CHAPTER 6

1. For an example of this argument, see Vanessa B. Beasley, *You, the People: American National Identity in Presidential Rhetoric* (College Station: Texas A&M University Press, 2004).

2. Alexis de Tocqueville, *Democracy in America*, trans. Harvey Mansfield and Delba Winthrop (Chicago: University of Chicago Press, 2004), 381, 663.

3. Jean Baudrillard, *America*, trans. Chris Turner (New York: Verso, 1989), 15.

4. Bernard-Henri Lévy, "In the Footsteps of Tocqueville," *Atlantic Monthly*, July/August 2005.

5. David Reisman, *The Lonely Crowd: A Study of the Changing American Character*, rev. ed. (New Haven: Yale University Press, 2001).

6. Richard Sennett, *The Fall of Public Man* (New York: W. W. Norton, 1992).

7. Robert Bellah et al., *Habits of the Heart: Individualism and Commitment in American Life* (1985; Berkeley: University of California Press, 1996), 50, xi.

8. Miller McPherson, Lynn Smith-Lovin, and Matthew E. Brashears, "Social Isolation in America: Changes in Core Discussion Networks over Two Decades," *American Sociological Review* 71, no. 3 (2006): 371.

9. Henry Fountain, "The Lonely American Just Got a Bit Lonelier," *New York Times*, July 2, 2006; Shankar Vedantam, "Social Isolation Growing in U.S.," *Washington Post*, June 23, 2006.

10. Paul R. Amato et al., *Alone Together: How Marriage in America Is Changing* (Cambridge, Mass.: Harvard University Press, 2009).

11. Jacqueline Olds and Richard S. Schwartz, *The Lonely American: Drifting Apart in the Twenty-First Century* (Boston: Beacon Press, 2009), 11.

12. Amitai Etzioni, *New Communitarian Thinking: Persons, Virtues, Institutions, and Communities* (Charlottesville: University Press of Virginia, 1995).

13. Jean M. Twenge, *Generation Me: Why Today's Young Americans Are More Confident, Assertive, Entitled—and More Miserable than Ever Before* (New York: Free Press, 2007); Jean M. Twenge and W. Keith Campbell, *The Narcissism Epidemic: Living in the Age of Entitlement* (New York: Free Press, 2009).

14. Cam Marston, *Motivating the "What's in It for Me?" Workforce: Manage Across the Generational Divide and Increase Profits* (Hoboken, N.J.: Wiley, 2007); Ron Alsop, *The Trophy Kids Grow Up: How the Millennial Generation Is Shaking Up the Workplace* (San Francisco: Jossey-Bass, 2008); Buddy Hobart and Herb Sendek, *Gen Y Now: How Generation Y Changes Your Workplace and Why It Requires a New Leadership Style* (Pittsburgh: Select Press, 2009); Nicole A. Lipkin and April J. Perrymore, *Y in the Workplace: Managing the "Me First" Generation* (Franklin Lakes, N.J.: Career Press, 2009); Bruce Tulgan, *Not Everyone Gets a Trophy: How to Manage Generation Y* (San Francisco: Jossey-Bass, 2009).

15. Peter Levine, *The Future of Democracy: Developing the Next Generation of American Citizens* (Medford, Mass.: Tufts University Press, 2007), 17.

16. Stephen Macedo et al., *Democracy at Risk: How Political Choices Undermine Citizen Participation, and What We Can Do About It* (Washington, D.C.: Brookings Institution Press, 2005), 117.

17. Robert D. Putnam, *Bowling Alone* (New York: Simon and Schuster, 2000), 9.

18. Robert D. Putnam, "The Prosperous Community: Social Capital and Public Life," *American Prospect* 13 (Spring 1993): 35–42.

19. Macedo et al., *Democracy at Risk*, 50.

20. Constance Flanagan, Peter Levine, and Richard Settersten, *Civic Engagement and the Changing Transition to Adulthood* (Medford, Mass.: CIRCLE, Tufts University, 2009), 8.

21. Michael Schudson, "The Varieties of Civic Experience," *Citizenship Studies* 10 (November 2006): 596.

22. Cliff Zukin et al., *A New Engagement? Political Participation, Civic Life, and the Changing American Citizen* (New York: Oxford University Press, 2006), 72–75.

23. Anthony Giddens, *Modernity and Self-Identity: Self and Society in the Late Modern Age* (Stanford: Stanford University Press, 1991), 214.

24. Ulrich Beck, *The Reinvention of Politics: Rethinking Modernity in the Global Social Order* (Cambridge: Polity Press, 1996).

25. W. Lance Bennett, "Branded Political Communication: Lifestyle Politics, Logo Campaigns, and the Rise of Global Citizenship," in *Politics, Products, and Markets: Exploring Political Consumerism Past and Present*, ed. Michele Micheletti, Andreas Follesdal, and Dietlind Stolle (New Brunswick: Transaction, 2004), 103.

26. Erik H. Erickson, *Identity: Youth and Crisis* (New York: W. W. Norton, 1994).

27. "Walk for Development in Houston," *Lancer*, May 7, 1971; "Freedom Challenge," *Carriculum*, Winter 1968; "Rams Favor War Escalation," *Ram Page*, November 10, 1967.

28. "Back the Budget," *Beacon*, May 27, 1966.

29. "Vegetarianism: Promoting an Alternative Diet," *Beacon*, May 20, 1993.

30. "South Nose Plastic Surgery," *Denebola*, September 29, 1998.

31. "Work Needed on Eating Habits," *Northmen's Log*, November 13, 1998.

32. "Anger, a Natural Feeling; How Should You Deal with It?" *Rampage*, November 9, 1993.

33. "New Information Leaves Vietnam in Question," *Northmen's Log*, May 12, 1995.

34. "The Christmas Crunch," *Northmen's Log*, December 22, 1994; "Keeping Options Open," *Northmen's Log*, March 10, 1995; "Learning to Relate," *Northmen's Log*, April 21, 1995.

35. "Time Management," *Northmen's Log*, September 23, 1994; "Exercise: Energetic Oakies Quest for Better Health," *Northmen's Log*, February 16, 1995.

36. "Divorce: Teenagers Cope with Separation of Parents as New Problems Arise," *Northmen's Log*, November 4, 1994; "Adoption: The Holidays Are a Time of Curiosity for Adopted Oakies as They Wonder About Their Biological Families," *Northmen's Log*, December 2, 1994; "Living with Alcoholics," *Northmen's Log*, March 31, 1995.

37. "Individuality," *Northmen's Log*, October 14, 1995.

38. "Suicide," *Northmen's Log*, January 27, 1995.

39. "Drugs Primary Reason for Arrests in K.C.," *Northmen's Log*, November 7, 1969; "Drug Probe in Clay County, 20 Area Students Involved," *Northmen's Log*, March 6, 1970; "Area Adults Voice Opinions on Drug Problem," *Northmen's Log*, March 20, 1970.

40. "Former Alcoholic Talks to Interested Students," *Northmen's Log*, January 23, 1970; "LSD Results in 'Bad Scene,'" *Northmen's Log*, October 3, 1969.

41. "PDA Exhibits Bad Manners," *Northmen's Log*, October 29, 1969; "VD Means Trouble for Some Students," *Northmen's Log*, November 21, 1969.

42. Dana L. Cloud, *Control and Consolation in American Culture and Politics: Rhetorics of Therapy* (Thousand Oaks, Calif.: Sage, 1998), xiii, 2.

43. "Smoke Smoldering South's Students Smoker's Haven," *Denebola*, March 24, 1966.

44. "Circumstances Should Sustain Smoking for Students," *Carrickulum*, November 3, 1997.

45. "A Lower Drinking Age: Dangerous Risk or Safe Alternative?" *Denebola*, September 24, 2008.

46. "Unnecessary Risks Sometimes Lead to Tragic Consequences," *Denebola*, November 20, 1997.

47. "Cocaine: A Decision of Life and Death," *Ram Page*, October 19, 1988.

48. Danielle S. Allen, *Talking to Strangers: Anxieties of Citizenship Since* Brown v. Board of Education (Chicago: University of Chicago Press, 2004).

49. James Farr, "Social Capital: A Conceptual History," *Political Theory* 31, no. 10 (2003): 1–28.

50. Putnam, *Bowling Alone*, 48–92.

51. Robert D. Putnam, "Community-Based Social Capital and Educational Performance," in *Making Good Citizens: Education and Civil Society*, ed. Diane Ravitch and Joseph P. Viteritti (New Haven: Yale University Press, 2001), 61.

52. Dhavan V. Shah, Nojin Kwak, and R. Lance Holbert, "'Connecting' and 'Disconnecting' with Civic Life: Patterns of Internet Use and the Production of Social Capital," *Political Communication* 18, no. 2 (2001): 143.

53. Sarah Perez, "Teens Still Love Texting, but Mobile App Use Is Growing," *New York Times*, October 15, 2010.

54. "Carrick Deca Competes," *Carrickulum*, Winter 1969.

55. "FFA to Crown Sweetheart at Horse Show," *Ram Page*, November 10, 1967.

56. "Future Teachers Plan Excursion to Stayton—'as FTA Highlight,'" *Grantonian*, February 13, 1970.

57. "Get Involved—Sandwich a Club In," *Beacon*, October 6, 1972.

58. "SADD Takes Action Against Drinking," *Carrickulum*, November 1, 1996.

59. "SADD Cancels Drinking Awareness Event," *Northmen's Log*, April 29, 2005.

60. "Club Rises from Tragedy," *Grantonian*, September 28, 2001.

61. "Badminton Keeps Eye on Birdie," *Rampage*, October 6, 2000.

62. "Ready, Aim, Fire (Splat!)," *Carrickulum*, December 11, 1998.

63. "Phish Jams with Faithful Fans at Concert Series," *Denebola*, December 23, 1997.

64. "What Is Guerrilla Theater?" *Grantonian*, December 17, 1998.

65. "Wilson Women's Group Working to Improve Wilson's Appearance and Attitude," *Beacon*, January 31, 2005.

66. "We Are the World," *Lamar Lancer*, April 1991.

67. "MLK Assembly Carries Inspiration for the Future, Introduces the Unity Club," *Grantonian*, January 20, 2000.

68. "*Good Morning America* Visits Gay/Straight Alliance," *Denebola*, October 28, 1993.

69. "GSA Marches Unite Nation in Cause," *Denebola*, June 11, 1998.

70. "Happy Go Lucky Club to Alien Talk; Clubs over Time," *Carrickulum*, Spring 2000.

71. "Students Come Together to Pray," *Denebola*, September 29, 1998.

72. "Point Counter Point: Young Life," *Northmen's Log*, February 10, 2006.

73. "New Clubs Abundant at Grant," *Grantonian*, December 2, 2008.

74. "Reflecting upon Life During School, Become Involved," *Rampage*, May 25, 2007.

75. "Students Should Focus Their Efforts on Trying a Variety of Fields," *Denebola*, October 2009.

76. William Damon, "To Not Fade Away: Restoring Civil Identity Among the Young," in Ravitch and Viteritti, *Making Good Citizens*, 124.

77. Cornel West, *Democracy Matters: Winning the Fight Against Imperialism* (New York: Penguin, 2004), 86, 65.

78. John F. Freie, *Counterfeit Community: The Exploitation of Our Longings for Connectedness* (Lanham, Md.: Rowman and Littlefield, 1998), 21.

79. "Mannequinism: An In-Depth Report," http://www.fightmannequinism.org/indepthreport/index.asp.

80. T. S. Eliot, *The Waste Land and Other Poems* (San Diego: Harcourt, 1934), 46.

CHAPTER 7

1. Robin Bowman, *It's Complicated: The American Teenager* (New York: Umbrage Editions, 2007), 10.

2. Ibid., 11.

3. Michael X. Delli Carpini and Scott Keeter, *What Americans Know About Politics and Why It Matters* (New Haven: Yale University Press, 1997).

4. Danielle S. Allen, *Talking to Strangers: Anxieties of Citizenship Since Brown v. Board of Education* (Chicago: University of Chicago Press, 2004).

5. Sidney Verba, Kay Lehman Schlozman, and Henry E. Brady, *Voice and Equality: Civic Voluntarism in American Politics* (Cambridge, Mass.: Harvard University Press, 1995), 343–54.

6. Lawrence R. Jacobs, Fay Lomax Cook, and Michael X. Delli Carpini, *Talking Together: Public Deliberation and Political Participation in America* (Chicago: University of Chicago Press, 2009), 161–62.

7. Kwame Anthony Appiah, *Cosmopolitanism: Ethics in a World of Strangers* (New York: W. W. Norton, 2006), 158.

8. Todd Gitlin, *Media Unlimited: How the Torrent of Images and Sounds Overwhelms Our Lives* (New York: Metropolitan Books, 2001), 135.

9. For evidence of this research, see Jacobs, Cook, and Delli Carpini, *Talking Together*, and Katherine Cramer Walsh, *Talking About Race: Community Dialogues and the Politics of Difference* (Chicago: University of Chicago Press, 2007).

10. Allen, *Talking to Strangers*, 25–36.

11. Patrick J. Deneen, *Democratic Faith* (Princeton: Princeton University Press, 2005), 12.

12. Larry Cuban, introduction to "1980–2000: The Bottom Line," in *School: The Story of American Public Education*, ed. Sarah Mondale and Sarah B. Patton (Boston: Beacon Press, 2001), 174.

13. George W. Bush, foreword to the proposal for No Child Left Behind, usinfo.org/enus/education/overview/docs/proposal.pdf.

14. Bill Gates, prepared remarks for the National Governors Association/Achieve Summit, February 26, 2005, http://www.nga.org/cda/files/eso5gates.pdf.

15. Bob Wise, *Raising the Grade: How Secondary School Reform Can Save Our Youth and the Nation* (San Francisco: Jossey-Bass, 2008), xvi.

16. Thomas Jefferson, letter to Colonel Charles Yancey, January 6, 1816.

17. Carnegie Corporation of New York and CIRCLE, *The Civic Mission of Schools* (New York: Carnegie Corporation of New York; Medford, Mass.: CIRCLE, Tufts University, 2003), 10.

18. While these themes can be found throughout much of Dewey's work, he makes perhaps his strongest case for face-to-face communication as central to democracy in the closing chapter of *The Public and Its Problems* (Athens, Ohio: Swallow Press/Ohio University Press, 1954).

19. Xavier de Souza Briggs, *Democracy as Problem Solving: Civic Capacity in Communities Across the Globe* (Cambridge, Mass.: MIT Press, 2008), 8.

20. Thomas J. Sergiovanni, *Building Community in Schools* (San Francisco: Jossey-Bass, 1994), 120–21.

21. Elizabeth Theiss-Morse and John R. Hibbing, "Citizenship and Civic Engagement," *Annual Review of Political Science* 8 (2005): 234.

22. Diane Owen, "Service Learning and Political Socialization," *PS: Political Science and Politics* 33 (September 2000): 638–40.

23. Stephen Macedo et al., *Democracy at Risk: How Political Choices Undermine Citizen Participation and What We Can Do About It* (Washington, D.C.: Brookings Institution Press, 2005), 126.

24. Kathleen Tyner, *Literacy in a Digital World: Teaching and Learning in the Age of Information* (Mahwah, N.J.: Lawrence Erlbaum, 1998), 162.

25. Kathleen Tyner, ed., *Media Literacy: New Agendas in Communication* (New York: Routledge, 2010).

26. Mark Garrett Longaker, *Rhetoric and the Republic: Politics, Civic Discourse, and Education in Early America* (Tuscaloosa: University of Alabama, 2007), 37.

27. J. Michael Hogan, "Rhetorical Pedagogy and Democratic Citizenship: Reviving the Traditions of Civic Engagement and Public Deliberation," in *Rhetoric and Democracy: Pedagogical and Political Practices*, ed. Todd F. McDorman and David M. Timmerman (East Lansing: Michigan State University Press, 2008), 76.

INDEX